The *Best* of
COUNTRY COOKING
1998

Editor: Julie Schnittka
Art Director: Ellen Lloyd
Food Editor: Coleen Martin
Assistant Editor: Jean Steiner
Food Photography Artists: Stephanie Marchese, Vicky Marie Moseley
Photography: Scott Anderson, Glenn Thiesenhusen, Mike Huibregste
Photo Studio Coordinator: Anne Schimmel
Publisher: Roy Reiman

©1998, Reiman Publications, L.P.
5400 S. 60th St., Greendale WI 53129
International Standard Book Number: 0-89821-235-9
International Standard Serial Number: 1097-8321
All rights reserved.
Printed in U.S.A.

For additional copies of this book or information on other books, write:
Taste of Home Books, P.O. Box 990, Greendale WI 53129.
Credit card orders call toll-free: 1-800/558-1013.

PICTURED ON THE COVER. Clockwise from the bottom: Meat Loaf Potato Surprise (p. 7), Three-Pepper Pasta Salad (p. 58) and Italian Snack Bread (p. 86).

PICTURED ABOVE. Clockwise from top right: Peanut Butter Chocolate Cake (p. 103), Pumpkin-Pecan Cake (p. 103), Cranberry-Orange Pound Cake (p. 104) and Carrot Layer Cake (p. 104).

It's the *Best*—Guaranteed!

IF you're like most cooks today, you can't afford kitchen "flops". With time so tight, *thinking* your family *might* like a new recipe isn't enough…you have to be *certain* they *will*.

Well, now that you have *The Best of Country Cooking 1998* in your hands, start serving! This giant collection's 347 down-home recipes—a new one for almost every day of the year—include the very best ones from recent issues of *Country Woman*, *Country*, *Country EXTRA*, *Reminisce* and *Reminisce EXTRA* magazines plus other proven favorites. All are hearty, wholesome and satisfying—guaranteed.

You see, these recipes weren't "developed" in some high-tech industrial "kitchen". Instead, they're from the personal recipe files of hundreds of home cooks across North America. Each has been sampled and approved by the toughest critic around—a hungry family just like yours!

But that's not all. Before being selected, *every* recipe in this book was thoroughly tested—many of them twice—by us as well. So you can be doubly confident it's a "keeper" that doesn't require a tryout first.

Go ahead *today* and take your pick of this beautiful book's 66 Main Dishes—Chicken with Potato Stuffing (a favorite around Carla Kreider's Quarryville, Pennsylvania table), Shepherd's Pie (top-tasting farm-style fare from Diane Gillingham of Carman, Manitoba) and 64 others.

There's also a Chili & Soups chapter full of kettle creations like Beans and Barley Chili from Gail Applegate, Myrtle Beach, South Carolina. And turn to Breads & Rolls for a bounty of oven-fresh goodies such as Apricot Cheese Danish (a make-ahead breakfast treat for Florence Schafer's family in Jackson, Minnesota).

Chocolate Truffle Cookies—in the Sweet Treats chapter—earned Sharon Miller of Thousand Oaks, California a prize at the county fair…while Peppermint Ice Cream Cake from Gloria Kaufmann of Orrville, Ohio is a cool and creamy finale for any meal.

As you page through *The Best of Country Cooking 1998*, watch for this special symbol. It signifies a "best of the best" recipe—a winner of a coast-to-coast cooking contest one of our magazines sponsored.

That's just a *small* sample of what's inside this tried-and-true taste treasury that in addition contains a mouth-watering medley of hearty salads, show-stealing side dishes and country-style canned goods besides.

You'll enjoy some extra-special features, too, most other cookbooks overlook:

Meals in Minutes—six complete meals (18 recipes in all) that go from start to finish in *30 minutes or less!*

Cooking for Two—a separate chapter with 44 recipes all properly proportioned to serve two people.

Taste of the Past—Six memorable meals made up of old-fashioned dishes seasoned with warm memories.

Want more? *The Best of Country Cooking 1998* offers individual sections on cooking quick-and-easy fare, canning, baking bread and building a "Pretzel Log Cabin". Finally, throughout this colorful compendium are lots of ingenious kitchen tips from everyday cooks plus dozens of "restricted diet" recipes marked with this check ✓ that use less sugar, salt and/or fat (most detail *Diabetic Exchanges*).

See why we call this book "The Best"? Now, just wait until you and your family *taste* why!

CONTENTS

Main Dishes...6

Chili & Soups...40

Garden-Fresh Salads...56

Vegetables &
Side Dishes...66

Breads & Rolls...76

Sweet Treats...98

Condiments &
Canned Goods...128

Meals in Minutes...136

Our Most
Memorable Meals...148

Cooking for Two...160

Index begins on page 180

THE DICTIONARY may define meat and potatoes as "basic".
But there's nothing ordinary about these innovative main dishes.
Plain and simple, they're all hearty good eating with a
deliciously unexpected dash of pizzazz.

PERFECTLY PAIRED. Clockwise from top: Herbed Cornish Pasties (p. 7), Chicken Potato Bake (p. 8), Meat Loaf Potato Surprise (p. 7) and Beef Stew with Potato Dumplings (p. 8).

Main Dishes

HERBED CORNISH PASTIES

Maribeth Edwards, Follansbee, West Virginia

(Pictured at left)

These hand-held golden packets are packed with the irresistible combination of beef and potatoes.

> 2 cups all-purpose flour
> 1 teaspoon salt
> 1/2 teaspoon dried basil
> 1/2 teaspoon dried thyme
> 1/2 cup shortening
> 1/4 cup butter *or* margarine
> 5 to 6 tablespoons ice water

FILLING:

> 1 pound boneless beef chuck, cut into
>   1/2-inch cubes
> 2 tablespoons vegetable oil, *divided*
> 1 teaspoon salt
> 1/8 teaspoon pepper
> 2 tablespoons all-purpose flour
> 1 cup water
> 2 medium potatoes, peeled and diced
> 1/2 cup diced carrot
> 1/2 cup diced onion
> 1 egg, lightly beaten

In a bowl, combine flour, salt, basil and thyme; cut in shortening and butter until crumbly. Add water, 1 tablespoon at a time, tossing lightly with a fork until mixture forms a ball. Cover and chill for at least 30 minutes. Meanwhile, brown beef in a skillet in 1 tablespoon oil; sprinkle with salt and pepper. Remove with a slotted spoon; set aside. Add remaining oil to skillet; gradually stir in flour until smooth. Cook and stir over medium heat for about 2-3 minutes or until lightly browned. Gradually add water; whisk until smooth. Return beef to skillet. Reduce heat; cover and simmer for 20 minutes. Add potatoes, carrot and onion. Cover and simmer for 25 minutes or until tender. Remove from the heat; cool. Divide pastry into four equal portions. On a lightly floured surface, roll out one portion into a 9-in. circle. Mound 3/4 cup filling on half of circle. Moisten edges with water; fold dough over filling and press edges with a fork to seal. Place on an ungreased baking sheet.

Repeat with remaining pastry and filling. Cut three slits in top of each; brush with egg. Bake at 400° for 25-30 minutes or until golden brown. **Yield:** 4 servings.

MEAT LOAF POTATO SURPRISE

Lois Edwards, Citrus Heights, California

(Pictured at left and on cover)

Although I'm retired after years of teaching school, my days continue to be full. So easy dishes like this are a blessing to me.

> 1 cup soft bread crumbs
> 1/2 cup beef broth
> 1 egg, beaten
> 4 teaspoons dried minced onion
> 1 teaspoon salt
> 1/4 teaspoon Italian seasoning
> 1/4 teaspoon pepper
> 1-1/2 pounds ground beef
> 4 cups frozen shredded hash browns,
>   thawed
> 1/3 cup grated Parmesan cheese
> 1/4 cup minced fresh parsley
> 1 teaspoon onion salt

SAUCE:

> 1 can (8 ounces) tomato sauce
> 1/4 cup beef broth
> 2 teaspoons prepared mustard

Additional Parmesan cheese, optional

In a bowl, combine crumbs, broth, egg and seasonings; let stand for 2 minutes. Add the beef and mix well. On a piece of waxed paper, pat meat mixture into a 10-in. square. Combine hash browns, cheese, parsley and onion salt; spoon over meat. Roll up, jelly-roll style, removing waxed paper as you roll. Pinch edges and ends to seal; place with seam side down in an ungreased shallow baking pan. Bake at 375° for 40 minutes. Combine the first three sauce ingredients; spoon over loaf. Return to the oven for 10 minutes. Sprinkle with Parmesan if desired. **Yield:** 8 servings.

Meat-and-Potato Combo Proves Plain Delicious

IF YOU want to fill your house with the most wonderful aroma, Shawn Asiala of Boca Raton, Florida, suggests you make Beef Stew with Potato Dumplings.

"Everyone who tries it loves this flavorful stew and asks me to share the recipe," says Shawn.

"This stew is simple to prepare, even well in advance. You can make a double or triple batch, freeze part and thaw it on the day you want to serve it," Shawn suggests. "Leftovers are tasty anytime, too—just pop them into the microwave and onto the table."

BEEF STEW WITH POTATO DUMPLINGS

(Pictured on page 6)

1/4 cup all-purpose flour
3/4 teaspoon salt
1/2 teaspoon pepper
2 pounds beef stew meat, cubed
2 medium onions, chopped
2 tablespoons vegetable oil
2 cans (10-1/2 ounces *each*) condensed beef broth, undiluted
3/4 cup water
1 tablespoon red wine vinegar
6 medium carrots, cut into 2-inch chunks
2 bay leaves
1 teaspoon dried thyme
1/4 teaspoon garlic powder
DUMPLINGS:
1 egg
3/4 cup seasoned dry bread crumbs
1 tablespoon all-purpose flour
1 tablespoon minced fresh parsley
1 tablespoon minced onion
1/2 teaspoon dried thyme
1/2 teaspoon salt
1/2 teaspoon pepper
2-1/2 cups finely shredded raw potatoes
Additional all-purpose flour

In a plastic bag, combine flour, salt and pepper. Add meat; toss to coat. In a 4-qt. Dutch oven, cook meat and onions in oil until the meat is browned and onions are tender. Stir in broth, water, vinegar, carrots and seasonings; bring to a boil. Reduce heat; cover and simmer for 1-1/2 hours or until meat is almost tender. Remove bay leaves. In a bowl, beat egg; add the crumbs, flour, parsley, onion and seasonings. Stir in potatoes; mix well. With floured hands, shape into 1-1/2-in. balls. Dust with flour. Bring stew to a boil; drop dumplings onto stew. Cover and simmer for 30 minutes (do not lift cover). Serve immediately. **Yield:** 6 servings.

CHICKEN POTATO BAKE

Myrtle Nelson, Wetaskiwin, Alberta

(Pictured on page 6)

When I came up with this recipe, I was looking for something that didn't require last-minute fuss.

1 cup dry bread crumbs
1/2 cup all-purpose flour
2 teaspoons salt
2 teaspoons paprika
1 teaspoon seasoned salt
1 teaspoon sugar
1 teaspoon onion powder
1 teaspoon rubbed sage
1 teaspoon dried oregano
1/2 teaspoon pepper
1/2 teaspoon celery seed
1/2 teaspoon dried parsley flakes
1/4 teaspoon garlic powder
3-1/2 to 4 pounds chicken pieces, skin removed
3 tablespoons vegetable oil
POTATOES:
1 teaspoon vegetable oil
1 teaspoon seasoned salt
1 teaspoon dried parsley flakes
1/2 teaspoon paprika
1/8 teaspoon garlic powder
1/8 teaspoon pepper
4 medium red potatoes, cut into 1-inch cubes

In a shallow bowl, combine the first 13 ingredients. Dip chicken in oil; coat with crumb mixture. Place on a greased 15-in. x 10-in. x 1-in. baking pan. For potatoes, combine oil, salt, parsley, paprika, garlic powder and pepper in a bowl. Add potatoes; stir until coated. Place around chicken. Bake, uncovered, at 350° for 1 hour or until potatoes are tender and chicken juices run clear. **Yield:** 4 servings.

HAM SLICE WITH PEACHES

Erika Klop, Agassiz, British Columbia

A ham slice is a convenient way to get dinner on the table in a hurry. Here peaches add a sweet touch.

    1 can (16 ounces) sliced peaches
    1 ham slice (about 1-1/2 pounds)
    1 tablespoon butter *or* margarine
    1 tablespoon sugar
    2 teaspoons cornstarch
    1/8 teaspoon nutmeg
    1/2 cup orange juice
    1 tablespoon lemon juice
Hot cooked rice

Drain peaches, reserving 1/2 cup syrup; set aside. In a large skillet, brown ham slice on both sides in butter over medium heat. Remove ham to a platter and keep warm, reserving drippings in skillet. In a small bowl, mix sugar, cornstarch and nutmeg. Add orange juice, lemon juice and reserved peach syrup; stir until smooth. Add to drippings in skillet. Cook until thick, stirring constantly. Stir in peaches and heat through. Add ham slice and heat for 2-3 minutes. Cut into serving-size pieces. Serve over rice. **Yield:** 4-6 servings.

CORNED BEEF AND CABBAGE

Connie Lou Blommers, Pella, Iowa

Even though I'm not Irish, St. Patrick's Day—with traditional food like this—is my favorite time of year!

    1/4 cup packed brown sugar
    2 teaspoons finely grated orange peel
    2 teaspoons yellow mustard
    1/4 teaspoon ground cloves
    1 corned beef brisket (2 to 3 pounds)
    2 medium onions, sliced
    2 quarts water
    1 cup apple juice
    8 carrots, cut into 3-inch pieces
    1 small head cabbage

In a small bowl, combine the first four ingredients; set aside. In a Dutch oven, place corned beef and seasoning packet. Add onions, water and apple juice; bring to a boil. Reduce heat; cover and simmer for 2 to 2-1/2 hours or until meat is tender. Remove brisket from cooking liquid and place in a greased roasting pan. Rub sugar mixture over warm meat. Bake at 350° for 15 minutes. Meanwhile, add carrots to cooking liquid. Cover and simmer for 10 minutes. Cut cabbage into eight wedges, leaving a portion of the core on each wedge; add to carrots. Cover and simmer for 15-20 minutes

or until vegetables are tender. Thinly slice meat; serve with vegetables. **Yield:** 8 servings.

BEEF AND CHEDDAR QUICHE

Jeanne Lee, Terrace Park, Ohio

(Pictured below)

This recipe is easy to prepare, so it's perfect for a busy schedule.

    3/4 pound ground beef
    1 unbaked pastry shell (9 inches)
    3 eggs, beaten
    1/2 cup mayonnaise
    1/2 cup milk
    1/2 cup chopped onion
    4 teaspoons cornstarch
    1 teaspoon salt
    1/2 teaspoon pepper
    2 cups (8 ounces) shredded cheddar
      cheese, *divided*

In a skillet, cook the beef until browned. Meanwhile, line unpricked pastry shell with a double thickness of heavy-duty foil. Bake at 450° for 5 minutes. Remove foil; bake for 5 minutes more. Set aside. Drain beef; place in a large bowl. Add the eggs, mayonnaise, milk, onion, cornstarch, salt, pepper and 1 cup cheese. Pour into crust. Bake at 350° for 35-40 minutes or until a knife inserted near the center comes out clean. If necessary, cover the edges of crust with foil to prevent overbrowning. Sprinkle with remaining cheese. Let stand 5-10 minutes before cutting. **Yield:** 6-8 servings.

equals 3 very lean meat, 1-1/2 vegetable; also, 137 calories, 314 mg sodium, 82 mg cholesterol, 9 gm carbohydrate, 22 gm protein, 1 gm fat.

PORK ROAST

Denise Collins, Chillicothe, Ohio

We used to raise our own hogs. This recipe was given to me by a fellow farmer who also had pork on the dinner table a couple of times a week.

- 1 envelope onion soup mix
- 2 garlic cloves, minced
- 1 tablespoon dried rosemary, crushed
- 1/2 teaspoon salt
- 1/2 teaspoon pepper
- 1/4 teaspoon ground cloves
- 3 cups water, *divided*
- 1 pork loin roast with bone (4 to 5 pounds)
- 24 small red potatoes, halved (2 to 3 pounds)
- 1-1/2 cups sliced onions

In a bowl, combine the first six ingredients. Stir in 1/2 cup water; let stand for 3 minutes. Place roast, fat side up, on a greased rack in a roasting pan. Pour remaining water into the pan. Combine potatoes and onions; spoon around the roast. Brush vegetables and roast with seasoning mixture. Bake, uncovered, at 325° for 2-1/2 to 3 hours or until a meat thermometer reads 160°-170° and potatoes are tender. Baste and stir potatoes occasionally. Tent with foil if browning too fast. Thicken juices for gravy if desired. Let stand 10 minutes before slicing. **Yield:** 8-10 servings.

BAKED WALLEYE

Joyce Szymanski, Monroe, Michigan

(Pictured above)

We live very close to Lake Erie, which is nicknamed the "Walleye Capital of the World". I'm always looking for new recipes for this fish...I came up with this one on my own.

✓ This tasty dish uses less sugar, salt and fat. Recipe includes *Diabetic Exchanges*.

- 3/4 cup chopped onion
- 3/4 cup chopped green pepper
- 3/4 cup chopped celery
- 1 tablespoon dried parsley flakes
- 1/2 teaspoon garlic powder
- 1/2 teaspoon pepper
- 1/2 teaspoon seasoned salt
- 1 cup V-8 juice
- 1 pound walleye fillets

In a saucepan, combine the first eight ingredients; bring to a boil. Reduce heat; simmer, uncovered, until vegetables are crisp-tender, stirring occasionally, about 5 minutes. Place fish in a greased 13-in. x 9-in. x 2-in. baking pan. Pour vegetable mixture over the fish. Cover and bake at 350° for 30 minutes or until fish flakes easily with a fork. **Yield:** 4 servings. **Diabetic Exchanges:** One serving (prepared with low-sodium V-8)

CITRUS GLAZED CHICKEN

Mary Hogarth, Lynden, Ontario

I don't make very many main dishes with fruit in them, but my two children and I love this recipe. The chicken's very tender, and the sauce is absolutely wonderful.

- 1 tablespoon lemon juice
- 1 tablespoon orange juice
- 1/2 teaspoon grated lemon peel
- 1/2 teaspoon grated orange peel
- 4 boneless skinless chicken breast halves
- 1 tablespoon vegetable oil
- 1 garlic clove, minced

2 green onions, thinly sliced
1/4 teaspoon ground ginger
1 tablespoon butter *or* margarine
1 tablespoon all-purpose flour
1/2 teaspoon salt
3/4 cup milk
1 tablespoon chopped fresh parsley

In a shallow bowl, combine the first four ingredients. Pound the chicken to 1/4-in. thickness; dip into citrus mixture. In a large skillet over medium heat, brown the chicken in oil for about 2 minutes per side. Remove chicken. In the same skillet, cook garlic, onions and ginger in butter for 1 minute. Add flour and salt; cook and stir for 1 minute. Gradually stir in milk; bring to a boil. Cook and stir for 2 minutes. Return chicken to pan; sprinkle with parsley. Simmer for 8-10 minutes or until chicken juices run clear, turning occasionally. **Yield:** 4 servings.

SHAMROCK STEW

Robin Perry, Seneca, Pennsylvania

(Pictured at right)

You don't have to be Irish to enjoy this savory stew. Homemade dumplings make it extra special.

✓ This tasty dish uses less sugar, salt and fat. Recipe includes *Diabetic Exchanges*.

1/4 cup all-purpose flour
3/4 teaspoon salt, optional
1/4 teaspoon pepper
1-1/2 to 2 pounds round steak, cut into 1-inch cubes
1 tablespoon vegetable oil
1 can (8 ounces) tomato sauce
2 cups water
1 large onion, sliced
1 teaspoon dried marjoram
1 bay leaf
1 pound carrots, cut into 1-inch pieces
1 package (10 ounces) frozen peas
DUMPLINGS:
1 cup all-purpose flour
1 teaspoon baking powder
1/4 cup milk
1 egg, beaten
1 tablespoon vegetable oil
1 tablespoon chopped fresh parsley, optional

In a medium bowl, combine flour, salt if desired and pepper; set aside 2 tablespoons. Add meat to bowl and toss to coat. In a 6-qt. Dutch oven over medium heat, brown the meat in oil. Stir in toma-

to sauce, water and reserved flour mixture. Add onion, marjoram and bay leaf; bring to a boil. Reduce heat; cover and simmer for 2 hours, stirring occasionally. Add carrots; cover and simmer for 45 minutes. Stir in peas. Cover and simmer for 15 minutes or until the vegetables are tender. Remove bay leaf. For dumplings, combine flour and baking powder. Stir in milk, egg, oil and parsley if desired. Drop by tablespoonfuls onto simmering stew. Cover and cook for 12-14 minutes or until done. Do not lift the cover. Serve immediately. **Yield:** 8 servings. **Diabetic Exchanges:** One 1-cup serving (prepared with skim milk and without added salt) equals 3 lean meat, 2 vegetable, 1-1/2 starch; also, 333 calories, 325 mg sodium, 95 mg cholesterol, 36 gm carbohydrate, 31 gm protein, 9 gm fat.

POTATO LASAGNA

Mara Beaumont, South Milwaukee, Wisconsin

(Pictured below)

At our house, this is a regular—it's as much fun to fix as it is to eat! (Sometimes, we even make extras of the potatoes to serve as appetizers.) Since it's so thick, it's great for potlucks as well.

 2 tablespoons vegetable *or* olive oil
 2 garlic cloves, minced
 1/2 teaspoon salt
 1/2 teaspoon pepper
 7 medium potatoes, sliced 1/4 inch thick
 1 pound bulk Italian sausage
 1 large onion, chopped
 2 packages (10 ounces *each*) frozen chopped spinach, thawed and drained
 1 cup ricotta cheese
 1/4 cup Italian-seasoned dry bread crumbs
Dash cayenne pepper
Additional salt and pepper to taste
 2 cups (8 ounces) shredded mozzarella cheese
 1/2 cup chicken broth
 2 tablespoons grated Parmesan cheese

In a large bowl, combine oil, garlic, salt and pepper. Add potatoes and toss to coat; spread evenly in an ungreased 15-in. x 10-in. x 1-in. baking pan. Cover tightly with foil. Bake at 425° for 35-40 minutes or until tender. Cool at least 15 minutes. Meanwhile, in a large skillet, brown sausage and onion; drain. Combine spinach, ricotta, crumbs, cayenne, salt and pepper; mix well. Arrange a third of the potatoes evenly in a greased 13-in. x 9-in. x 2-in. baking dish. Layer with half of the spinach mixture, half of the sausage and half of the mozzarella. Repeat with a third of the potatoes and the remaining spinach mixture, sausage and mozzarella. Pour broth over all. Top with remaining potatoes; sprinkle with Parmesan. Bake, uncovered, at 350° for 30-35 minutes. Let stand 5 minutes before serving. **Yield:** 8-10 servings.

TACO SKILLET SUPPER

Edna Havens, Wann, Oklahoma

Using ground turkey breast in place of traditional ground beef makes this meal a little lighter.

✓ This tasty dish uses less sugar, salt and fat. Recipe includes *Diabetic Exchanges*.

 4 cups thinly sliced peeled potatoes
 1 small onion, chopped, *divided*
 1 teaspoon low-sodium chicken bouillon granules
 1 cup hot water
 1 pound ground turkey breast
 1 envelope low-sodium taco seasoning mix
 1/4 cup skim milk
1-1/4 cups salsa, *divided*
 1/2 cup quick-cooking oats
Egg substitute equivalent to 1 egg

Coat a 2-qt. baking dish with nonstick cooking spray; add potatoes and 1 tablespoon onion. Dissolve bouillon in water; pour 1/2 cup over potatoes. Combine turkey, taco seasoning, milk, 1/4 cup salsa, oats, egg substitute and remaining onion; mix well. Spread over potatoes. Combine remaining salsa and chicken broth; pour over the turkey mixture. Bake, uncovered, at 350° for 1 hour or until the potatoes are tender. **Yield:** 8 servings. **Diabetic Exchanges:** One serving equals 2 very lean meat, 1-1/2 starch; also, 193 calories, 683 mg sodium, 18 mg cholesterol, 25 gm carbohydrate, 18 gm protein, 2 gm fat.

░░░░░░░░░░░░░
LOW-FAT BEEF STEW

Marian Stallknecht, Lawrenceville, Georgia

Now even folks on restricted diets can indulge in a hearty helping of stew!

✓ This tasty dish uses less sugar, salt and fat. Recipe includes *Diabetic Exchanges*.

  1 pound round steak, trimmed and cubed
  1 teaspoon vegetable oil
  1 can (14-1/2 ounces) no-salt-added diced
    tomatoes, undrained
  1 cup water
  1 teaspoon sugar
1/2 teaspoon Worcestershire sauce
1/2 teaspoon dried thyme
1/4 teaspoon pepper
  1 bay leaf
  4 medium carrots, cut into 3-inch chunks
  4 medium potatoes, peeled and halved
  1 cup frozen peas

In a 4-qt. Dutch oven, brown beef in oil. Add the next seven ingredients; cook over medium heat for 10 minutes. Add carrots and potatoes; cover and simmer until the vegetables are tender, about 30 minutes. Remove bay leaf. Stir in peas; heat through. **Yield:** 8 servings. **Diabetic Exchanges:** One 1-cup serving equals 1-1/2 lean meat, 1 starch, 1 vegetable; also, 159 calories, 70 mg sodium, 38 mg cholesterol, 20 gm carbohydrate, 16 gm protein, 5 gm fat.

░░░░░░░░░░░░░
MUSHROOM BACON BURGERS

Gail Kuntz, Dillon, Montana

(Pictured above)

During summer, I use the barbecue grill often. Food just tastes better, and cleanup is much easier. This recipe is a delicious way to dress up plain hamburgers.

  1 pound ground beef
  1 can (4 ounces) mushroom stems and
    pieces, drained
  4 bacon strips, cooked and crumbled
  2 tablespoons diced green onions
  1 teaspoon Worcestershire sauce
  1 teaspoon soy sauce
1/2 teaspoon salt
  4 to 5 hamburger buns
Tomato slices, optional

In a bowl, combine the first seven ingredients; mix well. Shape into four to five patties. Grill over medium-hot heat or fry in a skillet for 10-12 minutes or until no longer pink, turning once. Serve on buns with tomato if desired. **Yield:** 4-5 servings.

CHICKEN WITH POTATO STUFFING

Carla Kreider, Quarryville, Pennsylvania

(Pictured below)

This is a great Sunday meal or "company dish"—as long as you're prepared with second helpings! The aroma of this chicken roasting makes folks ask, "When will dinner be ready?".

> 6 medium red potatoes, cut into 1-inch cubes
> 1 pound Italian sausage
> 1 cup finely chopped onion
> 1 tablespoon butter *or* margarine
> 4 teaspoons dried parsley flakes, *divided*
> 1 teaspoon salt
> 3/4 teaspoon dried rosemary, crushed
> 2-3/4 teaspoons dried thyme, *divided*
> 1/2 teaspoon pepper
> 1 roasting chicken (7 to 7-1/2 pounds)
> 1 tablespoon vegetable oil
> 1 cup water

Cook potatoes in boiling salted water until almost tender; drain and set aside. Cook sausage in boiling water for 10 minutes; drain. Halve each sausage lengthwise, then cut into 1/2-in. pieces. In a large skillet over medium heat, cook potatoes, sausage and onion in butter until sausage is browned and onion is tender. Add 2 teaspoons parsley, salt, rosemary, 3/4 teaspoon thyme and pepper. Stuff chicken. Place remaining stuffing in a greased 1-1/2-qt. baking dish; cover and refrigerate. Place chicken in a roasting pan; brush with oil and sprinkle with remaining parsley and thyme. Add water to pan. Bake, uncovered, at 350° for 1-1/2 hours. Place baking dish of stuffing in oven. Bake chicken and stuffing for 45 minutes or until a meat thermometer reads 180°. Thicken pan drippings for gravy if desired. **Yield:** 8 servings.

CONEY DOGS

Donna Sternthal, Sharpsville, Pennsylvania

The whole gang will munch up these "top dogs" in a jiffy. Mom and I make them as a fun and festive main course for get-togethers. Leftovers are no problem—there never are any!

> 2 pounds ground beef
> 3 small onions, chopped
> 3 cups water
> 1 can (12 ounces) tomato paste
> 5 teaspoons chili powder
> 2 teaspoons rubbed sage

2 teaspoons salt
1 teaspoon pepper
1/2 teaspoon garlic salt
1/2 teaspoon dried oregano
1/4 teaspoon cayenne pepper
24 hot dogs, cooked
24 hot dog buns
Shredded cheddar cheese, optional

In a large skillet, cook beef and onions until beef is browned and onions are tender; drain. Stir in water, tomato paste and seasonings. Cover and simmer for 30 minutes, stirring occasionally. Serve over hot dogs; sprinkle with cheese if desired. **Yield:** 24 servings.

BAKED LEMON CHICKEN

Aida Babbel, Bowen Island, British Columbia

I found this recipe many years ago when my children were toddlers. I've changed it a little over the years to make it my own. Everyone in my family just loves it!

✓ This tasty dish uses less sugar, salt and fat. Recipe includes *Diabetic Exchanges.*

3 tablespoons all-purpose flour
1/4 teaspoon pepper
4 boneless skinless chicken breast halves
(1-1/2 pounds)
2 tablespoons vegetable oil
1 medium onion, chopped
1 tablespoon butter *or* margarine
1 cup chicken broth
3 tablespoons lemon juice
2 teaspoons dried basil
1/2 teaspoon dried thyme
4 lemon slices
2 tablespoons minced fresh parsley
Hot cooked rice, optional

In a shallow bowl, combine flour and pepper; dredge the chicken. Set remaining flour mixture aside. In a skillet, brown chicken in oil; transfer to an ungreased 9-in. square baking dish. In a saucepan, saute onion in butter. Add reserved flour mixture; stir to form a thick paste. Gradually add broth, lemon juice, basil and thyme; mix well. Bring to a boil; cook and stir for 2 minutes or until thickened and bubbly. Pour over the chicken. Top each half with a lemon slice. Sprinkle with parsley. Cover and bake at 350° for 25-30 minutes or until the juices run clear. Serve over rice if desired. **Yield:** 4 servings. **Diabetic Exchanges:** One serving (prepared with margarine and low-sodium broth and served without rice) equals 4 lean meat, 1 vegetable, 1/2 starch; also, 287 calories, 104 mg sodium, 73 mg cholesterol, 12 gm carbohydrate, 29 gm protein, 13 gm fat.

SEAFOOD RICE CASSEROLE

Pat Wieghorst, Phillipsburg, New Jersey

(Pictured above)

My family loves rice and clams, so I decided to combine them in this recipe. It was a hit! This dish is very filling and satisfying. Cooking and creating new recipes are two of my favorite pastimes.

✓ This tasty dish uses less sugar, salt and fat. Recipe includes *Diabetic Exchanges.*

3 cups cooked long grain rice
1/3 cup chopped onion
2 tablespoons chopped green chilies
1 can (6-1/2 ounces) chopped clams, undrained
1 can (5 ounces) evaporated milk
1/4 cup seasoned bread crumbs
1/2 cup shredded cheddar cheese

In a 1-1/2-qt. baking dish coated with nonstick cooking spray, combine rice, onion and chilies. In a bowl, combine clams and milk; pour over rice mixture. Sprinkle with crumbs and cheese. Bake, uncovered, at 350° for 45 minutes. **Yield:** 4 main-dish or 8 side-dish servings. **Diabetic Exchanges:** One 1/2-cup serving (prepared with evaporated skim milk) equals 2 starch, 1 lean meat; also, 195 calories, 207 mg sodium, 24 mg cholesterol, 29 gm carbohydrate, 12 gm protein, 3 gm fat.

CHICKEN AVOCADO MELT

Pat Cade, Canyon Lake, Texas

(Pictured below)

Avocados are used in many Southwestern recipes, so I feel this represents my region well. It's very easy to make and tastes so good. Family and friends love it.

    4 boneless skinless chicken breast halves
1/3 cup cornstarch
    1 teaspoon ground cumin
    1 teaspoon garlic powder
    1 teaspoon salt
1/8 teaspoon cayenne pepper
    1 egg
    2 tablespoons water
1/2 cup cornmeal
1/4 cup vegetable oil
    1 medium avocado, thinly sliced
    2 cups (8 ounces) shredded Monterey Jack
       cheese
Sour cream, salsa and sliced green onions,
    optional

Pound chicken to 1/4-in. thickness; set aside. In a shallow bowl, combine cornstarch, cumin, garlic powder, salt and cayenne. In another bowl, beat egg and water. Dip chicken into egg, then into the cornstarch mixture; coat with cornmeal. In a large skillet, brown chicken in oil until golden brown on both sides. Place in a greased 13-in. x 9-in. x 2-in. baking dish; arrange avocado evenly on top. Bake, uncovered, at 350° for 10-15 minutes or until juices run clear. Sprinkle with cheese. Serve with sour cream, salsa and green onions if desired. **Yield:** 4 servings.

BEEF AND POTATO BOATS

Linda Wheeler, Harrisburg, Pennsylvania

Back when I was teaching elementary school (I'm now a busy stay-at-home mom), my class would put together a Mother's Day cookbook. Many of the dishes are still my favorites—this one included.

    4 large baking potatoes (8 to 10 ounces
       each)
    2 tablespoons butter *or* margarine
1-1/4 teaspoons salt, *divided*
Dash pepper
1/4 to 1/3 cup milk
    1 pound ground beef
    1 small onion, chopped
    6 bacon strips, cooked and crumbled
1/2 cup sour cream
1/4 cup shredded cheddar cheese

Wash potato skins and prick with a fork. Bake at 400° for 60-70 minutes or until tender. Allow potatoes to cool to the touch. Slice a small portion off the top of each potato. Carefully scoop out the pulp, leaving a 1/4-in. shell. In a bowl, mash the pulp with butter, 1/2 teaspoon salt, pepper and milk; set aside. In a saucepan over medium heat, brown the beef and onion; drain. Cool 10 minutes. Add bacon, sour cream and remaining salt. Spoon into potato shells. Top each with a fourth of the mashed potato mixture; sprinkle with cheese. Place potatoes on an ungreased baking sheet. Bake at 400° for 20-25 minutes or until heated through. **Yield:** 4 servings.

UPPER PENINSULA PASTIES

Carole Lynn Derifield, Valdez, Alaska

I grew up in Michigan's Upper Peninsula, where many people are of English ancestry and pasties—traditional meat pies often eaten by hand—are popular.

    2 cups shortening
    2 cups boiling water
5-1/2 to 6 cups all-purpose flour
    2 teaspoons salt

FILLING:

        12 large red potatoes (about 6
            pounds), peeled
        4 medium rutabagas (about 3
            pounds), peeled
        2 medium onions, chopped
        2 pounds ground beef
        1 pound ground pork
        1 tablespoon salt
        2 teaspoons pepper
        2 teaspoons garlic powder
        1/4 cup butter *or* margarine
Half-and-half cream, optional

In a large bowl, stir shortening and water until
shortening is melted. Gradually stir in flour and
salt until a very soft dough is formed; cover and refrigerate for 1-1/2 hours. Quarter and thinly slice
potatoes and rutabagas; place in a large bowl with
onions, beef, pork and seasonings. Divide dough
into 12 equal portions. On a floured surface, roll
out one portion at a time into a 10-in. circle.
Mound about 2 cups filling on half of each circle;
dot with 1 teaspoon butter. Moisten edges with water; fold dough over filling and press edges with a
fork to seal. Place on ungreased baking sheets. Cut
several slits in top of pasties. Brush with cream if
desired. Bake at 350° for 1 hour or until golden
brown. Cool on wire racks. Serve hot or cold.
Store in the refrigerator. **Yield:** 12 servings.

SAUSAGE 'N' NOODLE DINNER

Phyllis Dennewitz, Frankfort, Ohio

(Pictured above)

*I adapted this dish from a recipe my German grand-
mother gave me. It reminds me of my heritage whenever I make it.*

        1 pound bulk pork sausage
        1 medium head cabbage (about 1-1/2
            pounds), thinly sliced
        1 large onion, thinly sliced
        1 large carrot, shredded
        2 teaspoons chicken bouillon granules
    1/4 cup boiling water
        2 cups (16 ounces) sour cream
    3/4 teaspoon salt
    1/2 teaspoon pepper
        8 ounces noodles, cooked and drained
Fresh parsley, optional

In a large skillet, brown and crumble the sausage;
drain. Add cabbage, onion and carrot; mix well.
Dissolve the bouillon in water; pour over vegetables. Cover and cook over medium-high heat
until the vegetables are tender, about 10-15 minutes. Reduce heat; stir in sour cream, salt and pepper. Heat through. Transfer to a serving bowl;
add hot noodles and toss. Garnish with parsley if
desired. **Yield:** 4-6 servings.

Quick & Easy Meat 'n' Potatoes

FOR country appetites, there's nothing like a hearty meat-and-potatoes meal that's been cooked to perfection for hours. But when you're in a hungry hurry, turn to these pages.

🔲🔲🔲🔲🔲🔲🔲🔲🔲

COUNTRY-STYLE SCRAMBLED EGGS

Joyce Platfoot, Wapakoneta, Ohio

Bacon, green pepper and spuds spruce up ordinary scrambled eggs.

       8 bacon strips, diced
       2 cups diced red potatoes
   1/2 cup chopped onion
   1/2 cup chopped green pepper
       8 eggs
   1/4 cup milk
       1 teaspoon salt
   1/4 teaspoon pepper
       1 cup (4 ounces) shredded cheddar
          cheese

In a skillet, cook bacon until crisp; remove with a slotted spoon. In the drippings, cook and stir potatoes over medium heat for 12 minutes or until tender. Add onion and green pepper; cook and stir for 3-4 minutes or until crisp-tender; drain. Stir in bacon. Beat eggs, milk, salt and pepper; pour into skillet. Cook and stir gently until the eggs are set. Sprinkle with cheese and let stand until melted. **Yield:** 4 servings.

🔲🔲🔲🔲🔲🔲🔲🔲🔲

QUICK BEEF STEW

Laura McCormick, Lebanon Missouri

This recipe deliciously proves savory stews don't have to simmer for hours.

       5 medium red potatoes, diced
       2 cups water

       2 pounds ground beef
       1 medium onion, chopped
       1 package (16 ounces) frozen mixed
          vegetables
       1 can (14-1/2 ounces) diced tomatoes,
          undrained
       1 can (10 ounces) diced tomatoes with
          green chilies, undrained
       1 can (8 ounces) tomato sauce
   1/2 teaspoon chili powder
   1/2 teaspoon salt
   1/4 teaspoon garlic powder

Place the potatoes and water in a microwave-safe dish; microwave on high until almost tender, about 12-14 minutes. Set aside (do not drain). In a 3-qt. microwave-safe dish, cook beef and onion on medium until beef is browned, about 14 minutes; drain. Add potatoes and remaining ingredients. Cover and microwave on medium for 20 minutes or until potatoes are tender and vegetables are heated through. **Yield:** 12 servings.

🔲🔲🔲🔲🔲🔲🔲🔲🔲

HEARTY HASH

Kathy Winzer, Coulee Dam, Washington

You can prepare this filling family favorite start to finish in under 30 minutes!

   1/4 cup butter or margarine
       4 cups diced cooked roast beef
       6 cups diced peeled potatoes
   3/4 cup chopped onion
   1-1/2 cups beef broth
       1 teaspoon salt
   1/4 teaspoon pepper

In an electric skillet, melt butter. Add the beef, potatoes, onion, broth, salt and pepper. Cover and simmer, stirring occasionally, until potatoes are tender, about 25 minutes. Thicken if desired. **Yield:** 6-8 servings.

German Pizza

Marsha Benda, Round Rock, Texas

Hash browns make a delectable "crust" in this breakfast-style pizza.

        1/4 cup butter *or* margarine
          3 cups frozen shredded hash browns
        1/8 teaspoon salt
    Pinch pepper
          4 eggs, lightly beaten
        1/2 pound fully cooked ham, julienned
        1/2 cup shredded cheddar cheese

In a medium nonstick skillet over low heat, melt butter. Add potatoes, salt and pepper; cover and cook for 15 minutes, stirring occasionally. Pour eggs over the potatoes; sprinkle with ham. Cover and cook for 10-12 minutes or until the eggs are set. Sprinkle with cheese; cook, uncovered, until melted. Cut into wedges. **Yield:** 6 servings.

Penny Casserole

Janet Ware Novotny, Grand Island, Nebraska

(Pictured at right)

You save both time and money with this flavorful economical casserole.

    1-1/4 pounds red potatoes, cubed
         10 hot dogs (1 pound), sliced
          2 tablespoons diced onion
          1 cup frozen peas, thawed
          1 can (10-3/4 ounces) condensed cream
            of mushroom soup, undiluted
          3 tablespoons butter *or* margarine, melted
          1 tablespoon prepared mustard
        1/8 teaspoon pepper

In a saucepan, cook the potatoes in boiling salted water until tender; drain. In a greased 2-1/2-qt. baking dish, combine the potatoes, hot dogs, onion and peas. Combine soup, butter, mustard and pepper; gently stir into potato

mixture. Bake, uncovered, at 350° for 25 minutes or until heated through. **Yield:** 6-8 servings.

Sausage 'n' Sweet Potatoes

Joan Hoch, Boyertown, Pennsylvania

With just four ingredients and short preparation time, dinner will be ready in about half an hour.

          2 cans (15 ounces *each*) sweet potatoes,
            drained
          5 medium apples, peeled and quartered
          2 tablespoons brown sugar
          1 pound smoked sausage, sliced 1 inch
            thick

In a 2-1/2-qt. greased baking dish, layer sweet potatoes and apples. Sprinkle with sugar. Top with sausage. Cover and bake at 375° for 30 minutes or until the apples are tender. **Yield:** 6-8 servings.

RUTABAGA PIE

Patricia Kron, Oak Creek, Wisconsin

(Pictured above)

This is a variation of a recipe my mom used to make. I changed a few things so it's easier to prepare. It's a main dish my whole family enjoys.

    3 cups diced peeled rutabagas
    2 cups diced peeled potatoes
    1 pound ground beef
    1/2 cup chopped onion
    1/2 cup sliced celery
    1/4 cup steak sauce
    1 teaspoon salt
    1/4 teaspoon pepper
Pastry for double-crust pie (9 inches)

In a large saucepan, cook rutabagas and potatoes in boiling salted water just until tender; drain and set aside. In a skillet over medium heat, cook beef, onion and celery until meat is browned and vegetables are tender; drain. Add rutabagas, potatoes, steak sauce, salt and pepper. Line a 9-in. pie pan with bottom pastry. Fill with rutabaga mixture. Top with remaining pastry; flute edges and cut slits in top. Bake at 425° for 10 minutes. Reduce heat to 350°; bake 35- 40 minutes longer or until crust is golden. **Yield:** 6-8 servings.

CHICKEN CREOLE

Dolly Hall, Wheelwright, Kentucky

I like food with a little zip to it, and this recipe fills the bill. It's especially good served over rice.

✓ This tasty dish uses less sugar, salt and fat. Recipe includes *Diabetic Exchanges.*

    4 boneless skinless chicken breast halves
        (1-1/2 pounds), cut into 1-inch cubes
    1 teaspoon salt, *divided*, optional
    1/4 teaspoon pepper
    1 tablespoon vegetable oil
    1 cup finely chopped onion
    1/2 cup finely sliced celery
    1/2 cup diced green pepper
    2 garlic cloves, minced
    1 can (14-1/2 ounces) diced tomatoes,
        undrained
    1/2 cup water
1-1/2 teaspoons paprika
Dash cayenne pepper
    1 bay leaf
    2 teaspoons cornstarch
    1 tablespoon cold water

Combine chicken, 1/2 teaspoon salt if desired and pepper; toss lightly. In a large skillet over medium heat, brown chicken in oil; remove and set aside. In the same skillet, saute the onion, celery, green pepper and garlic until tender. Stir in tomatoes, water, paprika, remaining salt if desired, cayenne pepper and bay leaf; bring to a boil. Reduce heat; cover and simmer for 10 minutes. Add chicken. Blend cornstarch and cold water; stir into chicken mixture and bring to a boil. Simmer, uncovered, for 10-15 minutes or until chicken is tender. Remove bay leaf before serving. **Yield:** 4 servings. **Diabetic Exchanges:** One 1-1/4-cup serving (prepared without added salt) equals 3 lean meat, 2-1/2 vegetable; also, 223 calories, 410 mg sodium, 73 mg cholesterol, 12 gm carbohydrate, 29 gm protein, 7 gm fat.

ITALIAN STUFFED TOMATOES

Michele Shank, Gettysburg, Pennsylvania

Served with crusty French bread, this makes a great summer meal. My husband and our two daughters ask me to fix it for them frequently.

    8 medium tomatoes
    1/2 pound bulk Italian sausage
    3/4 cup chopped onion
    2 garlic cloves, minced

1 cup chopped zucchini
2 tablespoons minced fresh basil *or* 2 teaspoons dried basil
1 tablespoon minced fresh oregano *or* 1 teaspoon dried oregano
1 tablespoon red wine vinegar
1/2 teaspoon salt
1/4 teaspoon pepper
1-1/2 cups cooked long grain rice
3/4 cup shredded provolone *or* mozzarella cheese
6 tablespoons shredded Parmesan cheese, *divided*
3 tablespoons chopped fresh parsley

Cut a thin slice off the top of each tomato. Leaving a 1/2-in.-thick shell, scoop out the pulp; chop pulp and set aside. Invert the tomatoes onto paper towels to drain. Meanwhile, cook sausage, onion and garlic in a skillet until sausage is browned; drain. Add tomato pulp, zucchini, basil, oregano, vinegar, salt and pepper. Simmer, uncovered, for 10 minutes. Remove from the heat. Stir in rice, provolone, 3 tablespoons Parmesan and parsley; spoon about 2/3 cup into each tomato. Place in an ungreased 13-in. x 9-in. x 2-in. baking dish. Sprinkle remaining Parmesan on top. Cover and bake at 350° for 20 minutes. Uncover and bake 15 minutes more or until the tomatoes are heated through. **Yield:** 8 servings.

CHILI CHOPS

Thelma Lee Peedin, Newport News, Virginia

(Pictured below)

These chops make a delicious meal. They're a definite favorite at our house. I like to serve them over rice along with fresh-from-the-oven corn bread.

6 pork chops (1/2 inch thick)
2 tablespoons vegetable oil
1/2 teaspoon salt
1/8 teaspoon pepper
1 can (10-3/4 ounces) condensed tomato soup, undiluted
1 can (15-1/2 ounces) kidney beans, undrained
1/2 cup sliced onion
1 tablespoon chili powder
1/2 teaspoon garlic powder
6 green pepper rings

In a large ovenproof skillet, brown chops in oil; drain. Remove the chops; sprinkle with salt and pepper. Combine soup, beans, onion, chili powder and garlic powder in the same skillet. Arrange chops over the soup mixture. Cover and bake at 325° for 35 minutes or until the chops are tender. Top each with a green pepper ring. Bake, uncovered, 10 minutes more. **Yield:** 6 servings.

VEGETABLE MEATBALL STEW

Elaine Grose, Elmira, New York

(Pictured below)

People who try this comment on how much they love the sweet potatoes. But they can never quite seem to pinpoint my "secret ingredient"—the parsnips!

    4 cups water
    2 medium potatoes, cut into 1-inch cubes
    2 medium carrots, cut into 3/4-inch slices
    1 large onion, cut into eighths
    2 tablespoons beef bouillon granules
    1 bay leaf
    1 teaspoon dried thyme
    1 teaspoon dried basil
  1/2 teaspoon salt
  1/2 teaspoon pepper
    1 pound ground round *or* chuck
  1/2 cup seasoned dry bread crumbs
    1 egg, beaten
    1 teaspoon Worcestershire sauce
    2 medium sweet potatoes, peeled and cut into 1-inch cubes
    2 medium parsnips, peeled and cut into 3/4-inch slices
    1 cup frozen peas
  1/3 cup all-purpose flour
  1/2 cup cold water
  1/4 teaspoon browning sauce, optional

In a large Dutch oven or soup kettle, bring water to a boil. Add potatoes, carrots, onion and seasonings; return to a boil. Reduce heat; cover and simmer for 10 minutes. Meanwhile, combine beef, bread crumbs, egg and Worcestershire sauce. Shape into 1-in. balls; add to Dutch oven along with sweet potatoes and parsnips. Bring to a boil. Reduce heat; cover and simmer for 15 minutes or until vegetables are tender. Discard bay leaf. Stir in peas. Combine flour and cold water; stir into stew along with browning sauce if desired. Bring to a boil; cook and stir for 2 minutes or until thickened. **Yield:** 6 servings.

ITALIAN BEEF ROLL-UPS

Joanne Gruff, James Creek, Pennsylvania

I was asked to make this dish but I didn't have a recipe, so I invented my own. It must have turned out pretty good, because I was asked to share my recipe.

    2 pounds ground chuck
    2 eggs, lightly beaten
    1 cup Italian-seasoned bread crumbs
  1/2 cup milk
    5 teaspoons dried minced onion
1-1/2 teaspoons salt
  1/4 teaspoon pepper
    3 to 3-1/2 pounds round steak (1/4 inch thick) *or* minute steaks
    2 tablespoons vegetable oil
    4 cups spaghetti sauce, *divided*
Hot cooked spaghetti *or* other pasta, optional

In a large bowl, combine ground chuck, eggs, crumbs, milk, onion, salt and pepper; mix thoroughly. Shape into twelve 3-in. rolls. Cut steak into twelve 6-1/2-in. x 3-1/2-in. pieces. Wrap each roll in a piece of steak; secure with toothpicks. In a skillet over medium heat, brown roll-ups in oil. Spread 2 cups of spaghetti sauce in a 13-in. x 9-in. x 2-in. baking dish. Place roll-ups over sauce; cover with remaining sauce. Cover and bake at

350° for 50-55 minutes or until steak is tender. Remove toothpicks. Serve over pasta if desired. **Yield:** 12 servings.

NEW ENGLAND FISH BAKE

Norma DesRoches, Warwick, Rhode Island

(Pictured above)

I've lived in Rhode Island for over 35 years and love the fresh seafood dishes served here. This is a favorite of mine. My mother-in-law gave me the recipe.

4 medium potatoes, peeled
1 teaspoon all-purpose flour
1 small onion, sliced into rings
1/2 teaspoon salt
1/4 teaspoon pepper
3/4 cup milk, *divided*
1-1/2 pounds cod fillets *or* freshwater fish
   (trout, catfish or pike)
3 tablespoons grated Parmesan cheese,
   optional
2 tablespoons minced fresh parsley *or* 2
   teaspoons dried parsley flakes
1/4 teaspoon paprika

Place potatoes in a saucepan and cover with water; bring to a boil. Cook until almost tender; drain. Slice 1/8 in. thick; place in a greased shallow 2-qt. baking dish. Sprinkle with flour. Top with onion; sprinkle with salt and pepper. Pour half of the milk over potatoes. Place fish on top; pour remaining milk over fish. Sprinkle with Parmesan cheese if desired. Cover and bake at 375° for 20-30 minutes or until fish flakes easily with a fork. Sprinkle with parsley and paprika. **Yield:** 3-4 servings.

2 teaspoons dried tarragon
2 teaspoons dried basil
1 teaspoon dried chives
1 teaspoon ground sage
1 teaspoon pepper
1 boneless pork loin roast (3-1/2 to 4 pounds)

In a large oven cooking bag or resealable plastic bag, combine the first eight ingredients. Add roast; seal and turn to coat. Place bag in a shallow roasting pan. Refrigerate overnight, turning bag several times. If using the cooking bag, make several 1/2-in. slits in top of bag. If not, remove roast from plastic bag and place in the roasting pan; pour marinade over roast. Cover the pan (leave uncovered if using cooking bag) and bake at 325° for 2 to 2-1/2 hours or until a thermometer reads 160°. Let stand 15 minutes before slicing. **Yield:** 6-8 servings.

CHICKEN STEW

Linda Emery, Tuckerman, Arkansas

Rely on this slow-cooker stew on busy weekends when you'd rather not be in the kitchen. Chicken, vegetables and seasonings give this good-for-you stew great flavor.

✓ This tasty dish uses less sugar, salt and fat. Recipe includes *Diabetic Exchanges*.

2 pounds boneless skinless chicken breasts, cut into 1-inch cubes
2 cans (14-1/2 ounces *each*) fat-free chicken broth
3 cups cubed peeled potatoes
1 cup chopped onion
1 cup sliced celery
1 cup thinly sliced carrots
1 teaspoon paprika
1/2 teaspoon pepper
1/2 teaspoon rubbed sage
1/2 teaspoon dried thyme
1 can (6 ounces) no-salt-added tomato paste
1/4 cup cold water
3 tablespoons cornstarch

In a slow cooker, combine the first 11 ingredients; cover and cook on high for 4 hours. Mix water and cornstarch until smooth; stir into stew. Cook, covered, 30 minutes more or until the vegetables are tender. **Yield:** 10 servings. **Diabetic Exchanges:** One 1-cup serving equals 3 very lean meat, 2 vegetable, 1/2 starch; also, 193 calories, 236 mg sodium, 59 mg cholesterol, 16 gm carbohydrate, 24 gm protein, 3 gm fat.

HERBED PORK ROAST

Elizabeth Area, Stillwater, Oklahoma

(Pictured above)

I received this recipe when we moved to Oklahoma. A going-away party was held for us, and the guests were asked to bring their favorite recipe as a remembrance. Every time I make it, a flood of wonderful memories fills my heart.

1 cup soy sauce
2 tablespoons lemon juice
2 garlic cloves, minced

TOMATO-FRENCH BREAD LASAGNA

Patricia Collins, Imbler, Oregon

(Pictured below)

Usually, I make this as a side dish to go with veal cutlets or a roast. You could also serve it as a main dish along with a salad and hot garlic bread if you like.

 1 pound ground beef
1/3 cup chopped onion
1/3 cup chopped celery
 2 garlic cloves, minced
 14 slices French bread (1/2 inch thick)
 4 large tomatoes, sliced 1/2 inch thick
 1 teaspoon dried basil
 1 teaspoon dried parsley flakes
 1 teaspoon dried oregano
 1 teaspoon dried rosemary, crushed
 1 teaspoon garlic powder
3/4 teaspoon salt
1/2 teaspoon pepper

 2 teaspoons olive *or* vegetable oil, *divided*
 3 tablespoons butter *or* margarine
 3 tablespoons all-purpose flour
1-1/2 cups milk
1/3 cup grated Parmesan cheese
 2 cups (8 ounces) shredded mozzarella cheese

In a skillet, brown beef, onion, celery and garlic; drain and set aside. Toast bread; line the bottom of an ungreased 13-in. x 9-in. x 2-in. baking dish with 10 slices. Top with half of the meat mixture and half of the tomatoes. Combine seasonings; sprinkle half over tomatoes. Drizzle with 1 teaspoon oil. Crumble remaining bread over top. Repeat layers of meat, tomatoes, seasonings and oil. In a saucepan over medium heat, melt the butter; stir in flour until smooth. Gradually stir in milk; bring to a boil. Cook and stir until thickened and bubbly, about 2 minutes. Remove from the heat; stir in Parmesan. Pour over casserole. Top with mozzarella. Bake, uncovered, at 350° for 40-45 minutes or until bubbly and cheese is golden brown. **Yield:** 8-10 servings.

per. Add water just to cover; bring to a boil. Place cabbage on top of vegetables. Reduce heat; cover and simmer for 1 hour or until the vegetables are tender. Drain. Cut cabbage into wedges; remove core. Serve meat and vegetables with horseradish if desired. **Yield:** 8 servings.

ORANGE-GLAZED CHICKEN WITH RICE

Irlene Schauer, Rochester, Minnesota

I've enjoyed cooking ever since I was a child. I can remember standing on a stool and watching Mother make bread on the old Hoosier cupboard. I prepared meals for 23 years at a retirement home and made this recipe often.

    1/2 cup currant jelly
    1/2 cup cold water, *divided*
    1/4 cup orange juice concentrate
      2 tablespoons cornstarch
      1 teaspoon dry mustard
Dash hot pepper sauce
    1/2 cup all-purpose flour
    1/4 teaspoon salt
      1 broiler-fryer chicken (3-1/2 to 4
        pounds), cut up
      2 tablespoons vegetable oil
RICE:
      1 cup diced celery
    1/4 cup chopped onion
      2 tablespoons butter *or* margarine
1-1/3 cups water
1-1/3 cups uncooked instant rice
      2 tablespoons orange juice concentrate
    1/2 teaspoon salt

In a saucepan, combine jelly, 1/4 cup water and concentrate. Cook and stir on low until jelly is melted. Combine cornstarch and remaining water; gradually stir into jelly mixture along with mustard and hot pepper sauce. Bring to a boil, stirring constantly. Cook about 2 minutes more; remove from heat and set aside. Combine flour and salt; dredge chicken. In a skillet over medium heat, brown chicken in oil. Place in a greased 13-in. x 9-in. x 2-in. baking dish. Pour sauce over chicken. Cover and bake at 350° for 20 minutes. Baste with sauce. Bake, uncovered, 45 minutes longer or until juices run clear. Meanwhile, in a saucepan, saute celery and onion in butter until crisp-tender. Add water; bring to a boil. Stir in rice, concentrate and salt. Cover and remove from the heat; let stand 5-7 minutes or until wa-

SUNDAY BOILED DINNER

Arlene Oliver, Bothell, Washington

(Pictured above)

Generally, I start this dinner early in the morning or right before church. It originated with my Pennsylvania Dutch mother and grandmother. When I first served it to my husband, he enjoyed the hearty root vegetables so much that he asked me to make the dish more frequently, even during the summertime.

      1 smoked boneless ham *or* pork
        shoulder (about 2 pounds)
      1 medium onion, quartered
      2 pounds carrots, halved
      2 pounds red potatoes, quartered
      2 pounds rutabagas, peeled and cut into
        1-1/2-inch cubes
      1 teaspoon salt
    1/2 teaspoon pepper
      1 medium cabbage, halved
Prepared horseradish, optional

In a large Dutch oven or soup kettle, place ham, onion, carrots, potatoes, rutabagas, salt and pep-

Main Dishes

ter is absorbed. Serve chicken over rice. **Yield:** 4-6 servings.

OLD-FASHIONED TOMATO GRAVY

Laurie Fisher, Greeley, Colorado

My mother-in-law gave me this recipe. It's her very favorite breakfast. My husband, our two sons and I also enjoy it for a light supper. Especially on a cold day, it's great with warm peach cobbler or bread pudding.

    1/2 pound sliced bacon, diced
    1 small onion, chopped
    2 tablespoons all-purpose flour
    1/8 teaspoon salt
    Pinch pepper
    1 can (14-1/2 ounces) diced tomatoes,
      undrained
    3 cups tomato juice
    6 to 8 hot biscuits, split

In a skillet, cook bacon until crisp. Remove to paper towels to drain; discard all but 2 tablespoons drippings. Cook onion in drippings until tender. Stir in flour, salt and pepper; cook and stir over low heat until mixture is golden brown. Gradually add tomatoes and tomato juice; stir well. Bring to a boil over medium heat. Cook and stir for 2 minutes. Reduce heat; simmer, uncovered, for 10-15 minutes or until thickened, stirring occasionally. Stir in bacon. Serve over biscuits. **Yield:** 6-8 servings.

CLASSIC SWISS STEAK

Lorraine Dyda, Rancho Palos Verdes, California

(Pictured at right)

When I prepare this dish for my husband and me, I always serve rolls or bread to dip in the sauce. We enjoy it to the last drop! For a large group, the recipe can be doubled and served in a casserole.

    2 large carrots, sliced
    2 tablespoons vegetable oil, *divided*
    1 pound boneless round steak *or* sirloin
      steak
    1 can (14-1/2 ounces) diced tomatoes,
      undrained
    1 can (8 ounces) tomato sauce
    1 teaspoon sugar

    1/2 teaspoon dried oregano
    1/2 cup chopped onion
    1/2 cup chopped celery
    1 can (4 ounces) sliced mushrooms,
      drained
    Cooked egg noodles

In a large skillet, saute carrots in 1 tablespoon oil until crisp-tender; remove and set aside. Cut meat into four pieces. Add meat and remaining oil to skillet; cook over medium-high heat until browned on both sides. Add tomatoes, tomato sauce, sugar and oregano; cover and simmer for 1 hour. Add the onion, celery, mushrooms and carrots; cover and simmer for 45 minutes or until the meat and vegetables are tender. Thicken if desired. Serve over noodles. **Yield:** 4 servings.

COUNTRY FRIED CHICKEN

Rebecaka Miller, Rocky Mountain, Virginia

(Pictured below)

This is one of our favorite recipes to take along on a picnic. We like to eat the chicken cold, along with a salad and watermelon. It's a real treat!

      1 cup all-purpose flour
      2 teaspoons garlic salt
      2 teaspoons pepper
      1 teaspoon paprika
  1/2 teaspoon poultry seasoning
  1/2 cup milk
      1 egg, beaten
      1 broiler-fryer chicken (3 to 3-1/2 pounds)
Vegetable oil

In a large bowl or resealable plastic bag, combine the first five ingredients. In a bowl, combine milk and egg. Cut chicken into pieces (remove skin if desired). Toss chicken in the flour mixture. Dip into egg mixture, then return to flour mixture. Heat about 1 in. of oil in a large skillet. Fry chicken in batches until golden brown on all sides. Return all chicken to pan; reduce heat to medium and cook until juices run clear, about 30 minutes. **Yield:** 4 servings.

ASPARAGUS TOMATO QUICHE

Dorothy Hussey, Bishop, California

Here's a recipe that features those savory stalks of the first delicious crop of asparagus. It might look difficult, but it's actually simple to make.

      1 unbaked pastry shell (10 inches)
    10 fresh asparagus spears
      4 eggs
      3 tablespoons all-purpose flour
1-1/2 cups half-and-half cream
      1 teaspoon salt
      1 teaspoon paprika
  1/2 teaspoon ground mustard
      2 cups (8 ounces) shredded Swiss cheese
      1 medium tomato, cut into 6 slices

Line unpricked pie shell with a double thickness of heavy-duty foil. Bake at 450° for 5 minutes. Remove foil; return to the oven for 5 minutes. Remove from the oven; reduce heat to 350°. Cut

six asparagus spears 4 in. long for garnish; set aside. Cut remaining asparagus into 1-in. pieces; place in bottom of pie shell. In a bowl, beat eggs and flour. Add cream, salt, paprika and mustard; beat until smooth. Stir in cheese. Pour over asparagus. Bake for 30 minutes. Arrange asparagus spears, spoke fashion, on top. Bake for 10-15 minutes or until a knife inserted near the center comes out clean. Place tomatoes in between asparagus spears. **Yield:** 6 servings.

WILD RICE AND HAM CASSEROLE

Stacey Diehl, Lecanto, Florida

My grandmother gave me this recipe. The blend of flavors is fantastic. It's so simple to make and can easily be doubled for a large gathering.

  1 package (6-1/4 ounces) quick-cooking long grain and wild rice mix
  1 package (10 ounces) frozen cut broccoli, thawed and drained
  2 cups cubed fully cooked ham
  1 can (10-3/4 ounces) condensed cream of mushroom soup, undiluted
  1 cup mayonnaise
  2 teaspoons prepared mustard
  1 cup (4 ounces) shredded cheddar cheese

Prepare the rice according to package directions. Spoon into an ungreased 2-1/2-qt. baking dish. Top with broccoli and ham. Combine soup, mayonnaise and mustard. Spread over rice mixture and mix gently. Cover and bake at 350° for 45 minutes or until bubbly. Sprinkle with cheese. Let stand 5 minutes before serving. **Yield:** 6 servings.

PORK AND SWEET POTATOES

Jean Christie, Penticton, British Columbia

(Pictured above right)

My family enjoys sweet potatoes. A friend gave me this recipe a few years ago, and I've made it often. It's a perfect fall meal.

✓ This tasty dish uses less sugar, salt and fat. Recipe includes *Diabetic Exchanges.*

  6 pork loin chops (5 ounces *each*)
  1 tablespoon vegetable oil
  1 cup orange juice
  1 tablespoon brown sugar
  1/4 teaspoon ground mace
  1/4 to 1/2 teaspoon ground ginger
  1/4 teaspoon salt, optional
  1/8 teaspoon pepper
  2 large sweet potatoes (1-1/4 pounds)
  2 tablespoons butter *or* margarine, melted
  2 teaspoons cornstarch
  1 tablespoon water

In a skillet over medium heat, brown pork chops in oil. Place in a 13-in. x 9-in. x 2-in. baking pan. In a saucepan, combine orange juice, brown sugar, mace, ginger, salt if desired and pepper; bring to a boil. Pour over chops. Cover and bake at 350° for 30 minutes. Peel potatoes; cut into 1/3-in. slices. Brush with butter. Turn chops. Cover with potatoes; baste with pan juices. Cover and bake 40 minutes longer or until potatoes are tender. Remove chops and potatoes to a serving platter; cover and keep warm. Dissolve cornstarch in water; stir into pan juices. Bring to a boil; boil for 2 minutes, stirring constantly. Pour over pork chops and potatoes. **Yield:** 6 servings. **Diabetic Exchanges:** One serving (prepared with margarine and without salt) equals 3 lean meat, 1-1/2 starch; also, 271 calories, 100 mg sodium, 58 mg cholesterol, 21 gm carbohydrate, 22 gm protein, 11 gm fat.

ZUCCHINI PORK CHOP SUPPER

Linda Martin, Rhinebeck, New York

(Pictured below)

My mom gave me a recipe for zucchini casserole, and I added meat for a one-dish supper. Ever since, I've looked forward to having fresh zucchini each year.

> 1 package (14 ounces) seasoned cubed stuffing mix, *divided*
> 1/4 cup butter *or* margarine, melted
> 2 pounds zucchini, cut into 1/2-inch pieces
> 1/2 cup grated carrots
> 1 can (10-3/4 ounces) condensed cream of celery soup, undiluted
> 1/2 cup milk
> 1 cup (8 ounces) sour cream
> 1 tablespoon chopped fresh parsley *or* 1 teaspoon dried parsley flakes
> 1/2 teaspoon pepper
> 6 pork loin chops (1 inch thick)
> Water *or* additional milk

Combine two-thirds of the stuffing mix with butter; place half in a greased 13-in. x 9-in. x 2-in. baking dish. Combine the zucchini, carrots, soup, milk, sour cream, parsley and pepper; spoon over stuffing. Sprinkle remaining buttered stuffing on top. Crush remaining stuffing mix; dip pork chops in water or milk and coat with the stuffing crumbs. Place on top of casserole. Bake, uncovered, at 350° for 1 hour or until pork chops are tender. **Yield:** 6 servings.

BEEF 'N' RICE HOT DISH

Elma Katainen, Menahga, Minnesota

Ground beef and rice star in this hearty casserole. It's prepared on the stovetop, so dinner's ready in no time.

> 1 pound ground beef
> 1 medium onion, chopped
> 1/2 cup chopped green pepper
> 1/2 teaspoon salt
> Pinch pepper
> 1-1/2 cups uncooked instant rice
> 1 can (14-1/2 ounces) stewed tomatoes
> 1 can (8 ounces) tomato sauce
> 1-1/2 cups hot water
> 1 teaspoon prepared mustard

In a skillet, brown beef; drain. Add onion, green pepper, salt and pepper; cook and stir over medium heat until vegetables are tender. Add remaining ingredients; bring to a boil. Reduce heat; cover and simmer for 10 minutes. **Yield:** 4 servings.

Beefy Pie Turns Heat on High!

WHEN winter comes storming through her family's Canadian country place, Heather Thurmeier is happy to turn up the heat in her kitchen—with her spicy chili.

"This recipe is one of my husband Dwayne's favorites, especially during cooler weather," states Heather from Pense, Saskatchewan.

"The topping is crunchy, and the chili has just enough spice to warm you up inside in even the coldest weather! I add a simple side salad to complete the meal."

MEXICAN CHILI PIE

1 pound ground beef
1 medium onion, chopped
3 garlic cloves, minced
2 teaspoons chili powder
1 teaspoon dry mustard
1/4 teaspoon ground cumin
1/4 teaspoon crushed red
    pepper flakes
1/4 teaspoon dried oregano
1/4 teaspoon salt
1 can (14-1/2 ounces) diced
    tomatoes, undrained
1/2 cup diced green pepper
1 can (15-1/2 ounces)
    kidney beans, rinsed and
    drained

TOPPING:
3/4 cup cornmeal
1/2 cup all-purpose flour
1/2 teaspoon *each* baking
    soda, salt and sugar
1 cup (4 ounces) shredded
    cheddar cheese
3/4 cup buttermilk
1 egg, lightly beaten
2 tablespoons vegetable oil

In a skillet, brown beef, onion and garlic; drain. Add seasonings and tomatoes. Simmer, uncovered, for 20 minutes. Add green pepper. Spoon 2 cups into an ungreased 2-1/2-qt. shallow baking dish; top with half of the beans. Repeat layers. For topping, combine the dry ingredients in a large bowl. Stir in cheese. Combine the buttermilk, egg and oil; stir into dry ingredients just until moistened. Spread over filling. Bake at 450° for 15 minutes or until the topping is lightly browned and filling is bubbly. **Yield:** 4-6 servings.

SHEPHERD'S PIE

Diane Gillingham, Carman, Manitoba

As the second oldest of eight children in a busy farm family, I had plenty of opportunity to practice cooking while I was growing up. Now that our three children are grown, I am cooking just for my husband and me—though few weeks pass without visitors. For "country eaters", this hearty pie is perfect!

1 pound ground beef
3/4 cup chopped onion
2 garlic cloves, minced
3 tablespoons vegetable oil, *divided*
1 cup chopped fresh mushrooms
1 tablespoon tomato paste
1/2 cup beef broth
2 teaspoons prepared horseradish
1 teaspoon ground mustard
1-1/2 teaspoons salt, *divided*
1/4 teaspoon pepper
1/2 cup diced green pepper
1/2 cup diced sweet red pepper
8 medium potatoes, peeled and cubed
1/3 cup hot milk
1 cup (4 ounces) shredded cheddar cheese
2 egg whites

In a large skillet, brown beef, onion and garlic in 2 tablespoons of oil. Add the mushrooms. Cook and stir for 3 minutes; drain. Place the tomato paste in a bowl. Gradually whisk in broth until smooth. Stir in horseradish, mustard, 1 teaspoon salt and pepper. Add to meat mixture. Pour into a greased 11-in. x 7-in. x 2-in. baking pan; set aside. In the same skillet, saute the peppers in remaining oil until tender, about 3 minutes. Drain and spoon over meat mixture. Cook potatoes in boiling salted water until tender; drain. Mash with milk, cheese and remaining salt. Beat egg whites until stiff peaks form; gently fold into potatoes. Spoon over pepper layer. Bake, uncovered, at 425° for 15 minutes. Reduce heat to 350°; bake 20 minutes longer or until meat layer is bubbly. **Yield:** 4-6 servings.

Green Chili Pork Stew

Carrie Burton, Sierra Vista, Arizona

(Pictured below)

Anyone living in or visiting the Southwest knows green chilies are a staple. I grew up on this delicacy and thought everyone must know how delicious it is. It seems to be even more popular now in this area.

2-1/2 to 3 pounds boneless pork shoulder *or* butt, trimmed
   1 tablespoon vegetable oil
   1 cup chopped onion
   3 garlic cloves, minced
   2 cups water
   1 can (28 ounces) stewed tomatoes
   1 to 2 cans (4 ounces *each*) chopped green chilies
   2 cups cubed peeled potatoes
   1 tablespoon chopped fresh cilantro
   2 teaspoons ground cumin
   2 teaspoons dried oregano
   2 teaspoons fennel seed
   1 teaspoon salt
1/4 teaspoon pepper

   1 can (15 ounces) pinto beans, rinsed and drained

Cut pork into 1-in. cubes; brown in oil in a soup kettle or Dutch oven over medium heat. Add onion and garlic; saute for 3-5 minutes. Drain. Add water, tomatoes, chilies, potatoes and seasonings; bring to a boil. Reduce heat; cover and simmer for 45 minutes. Add beans; cover and simmer for 20-30 minutes or until the meat and vegetables are tender. **Yield:** 8-10 servings.

Robust Beef Sandwiches

Esther Hull, Buckley, Illinois

Before you go sledding or skating, be sure to prepare this dish. It will warm nicely in the oven while you play—and be ready to serve by the time you come in from the cold.

   1 boneless beef rump roast (3 to 4 pounds)
   2 cups water
   3 beef bouillon cubes
   3 hot yellow peppers, seeded and sliced
1/2 teaspoon *each* salt, onion salt and garlic salt
1/2 teaspoon *each* dried basil, oregano and Italian seasoning
 12 to 16 hard rolls

Place roast, water and bouillon in a roasting pan. Cover and bake at 350° for 2 hours or until meat is tender. Remove meat; strain broth. Chill broth and meat separately until meat is firm; cut into thin slices. Place in a 13-in. x 9-in. x 2-in. baking pan; set aside. In a saucepan, bring broth, peppers and seasonings to a boil. Reduce heat; simmer for 10 minutes. Pour over meat. Cover and bake at 325° for 1 hour, or refrigerate overnight before baking. Serve on rolls. **Yield:** 12-16 servings.

Turkey in Mushroom Sauce

Rose Maldet, Johnstown, Pennsylvania

If you like a traditional turkey dinner for Thanksgiving but don't like all the fuss, here's a recipe that fills the bill. It's easy to make and tastes very good.

3/4 cup all-purpose flour
   2 teaspoons salt
1/4 teaspoon pepper
   6 turkey thighs (4 to 5 pounds)
   3 tablespoons vegetable oil

2 cups chopped fresh mushrooms
3 green onions, sliced
1-1/2 teaspoons dried thyme
2 cups turkey *or* chicken broth
1/3 cup tomato paste
1 cup (8 ounces) sour cream
Hot cooked noodles

In a bowl or resealable plastic bag, combine flour, salt and pepper. Add turkey, one piece at a time; dredge or shake to coat. In a skillet, brown turkey in oil. Add mushrooms, onions and thyme. Combine the broth and tomato paste until smooth; pour over turkey. Cover and simmer for 1-1/2 hours or until the turkey juices run clear; skim fat. Stir in sour cream; heat through (do not boil). Serve over noodles. **Yield:** 6 servings.

HOT TAMALE PIE

Orilla Lawson, Independence, Missouri

You'll want to keep the ingredients for this dish on hand for last-minute meals. Ground beef lends itself to quick cooking.

1 pound ground beef
1 medium onion, chopped
2 cans (14-1/2 ounces *each*) stewed tomatoes
2 cans (2-1/4 ounces *each*) sliced ripe olives, drained
1 medium green pepper, chopped
2 to 3 teaspoons taco seasoning mix
Corn bread

In a skillet, cook the beef and onion until meat is browned; drain. Add tomatoes, olives, green pepper and taco seasoning. Cook and stir over low heat until hot and bubbly. Serve over corn bread. **Yield:** 6 servings.

CURRY CHICKEN DINNER

Marilyn Ausland, Columbus, Georgia

(Pictured above right)

This chicken dish was originated by a woman from our town, Mrs. W.L. Bullard, for a special party in honor of President Franklin D. Roosevelt. I really enjoy treating out-of-town relatives and friends to this dish when they come to visit.

8 boneless skinless chicken breast halves (about 2 pounds)

1/2 cup all-purpose flour
1/4 cup shortening
2 medium onions, chopped
2 medium green peppers, chopped
1 garlic clove, minced
2 to 3 teaspoons curry powder
1 teaspoon salt
1/2 teaspoon white pepper
2 cans (14-1/2 ounces *each*) diced tomatoes, undrained
1 teaspoon chopped fresh parsley
1/2 teaspoon dried thyme
1 cup water
3 tablespoons raisins *or* dried currants
Hot cooked rice
1/4 cup slivered almonds, toasted, optional

Dust chicken with flour. In a Dutch oven over medium heat, brown the chicken in shortening. Remove chicken and set aside. Saute onions, peppers and garlic in drippings for 3-4 minutes or until tender. Add curry powder, salt and pepper; mix well. Return chicken to the pan. Add tomatoes, parsley, thyme and water. Cover and bake at 375° for 45-50 minutes or until chicken is tender. Stir in raisins. Serve over rice; sprinkle with almonds if desired. **Yield:** 8 servings.

Recipes for Meat 'n' Potato Success

• I save and freeze little bits and pieces of leftover bacon, sausage and ham—they make my favorite quiche with tater tots more "meaty". To save time in the morning, I fix the quiche filling ahead and pour it into the crust right before baking. —*Lucy Mohlman Crete, Nebraska*

• Pouring tomato juice over the top of my favorite meat loaf recipe and baking as usual produces a very moist, flavorful and pretty loaf.

I prepare my top sirloin roast by rubbing it with paprika and pouring several tablespoons of Worcestershire sauce entirely over it. —*Mary Syphus St. George, Utah*

• When I'm in a hurry, I'll make my hash by browning a package of smoked sausage, a small onion and six sliced potatoes in a little oil. —*Donna Brandt Churubusco, Indiana*

• Give your beef stew "south-of-the-border" zest by adding canned green chilies, ground cumin and Mexican-style stewed tomatoes to the basic recipe. For more flavor, top each serving with shredded cheddar cheese. —*Anne Elmore-De Vinny Orlando, Florida*

• For a hearty but quick "one-pot" dinner, spread four or five medium sliced potatoes over the bottom of a large saucepan. Lightly salt and top with a pound of hamburger made into a large patty the size of the pan lid. Add a sliced onion and two or three sliced carrots. Cover and cook on low for 1 hour. —*Marj Ridgeway, Brashear, Texas*

• For a quick, easy potpie, combine leftover cooked beef, pork or chicken with leftover cooked potatoes, vegetables and gravy in a shallow baking pan. Sprinkle with your favorite herbs and seasonings and top with pastry.

I double my pie dough recipe and make several crusts at once…then I freeze them right in the pie plates. I roll out potpie tops, freeze them between layers of plastic wrap and place on a large tray. Whenever I need them in a hurry, I just have to defrost, fill and bake them. —*Shirley Lowes Peterborough, Ontario*

• Like barbecues? This complete meat-and-potato meal is an easy one to prepare out on the grill. Wrap husked corn and sliced potatoes in foil. Place over hot heat alongside hot dogs or hamburgers; grill until meat is done and vegetables are tender. —*Candace Robinson Frazeysburg, Ohio*

• To flavor a pork roast, insert slivers of garlic into small slits cut into its top. During the last 15 minutes of baking, brush the roast with a mixture of 3 tablespoons lemon juice and 1/2 cup maple syrup. Serve with oven-roasted potatoes. —*Beverly Borges Rockland, Massachusetts*

Bayou Chicken Pasta

Myrtle Anderson, Plaquemine, Louisiana

(Pictured at right)

This is a tasty main dish served in the bayou country of South Louisiana. Salsa and hot pepper sauce give this chicken its tempting zip. Add a tossed salad and French bread, and you have a hearty meal.

- 1 cup chopped onion
- 1 cup chopped celery
- 1/2 cup *each* chopped green and yellow pepper
- 3 tablespoons olive *or* vegetable oil
- 1 pound boneless skinless chicken breasts, cubed
- 2 teaspoons garlic powder
- 1 jar (16 ounces) salsa
- 1 tablespoon cornstarch
- 1 tablespoon water
- 1 tablespoon dried parsley flakes
- 1/2 teaspoon salt
- 1/4 teaspoon hot pepper sauce

Hot cooked pasta

In a large saucepan over medium-high heat, saute onion, celery and pepper in oil for 3-4 minutes or until crisp-tender. Add chicken and garlic powder; cook for 4-5 minutes or until chicken juices run clear. Stir in salsa. Combine cornstarch and water; stir into the chicken mixture. Bring to a boil; cook and stir for 2 minutes or until mixture is thickened and bubbly. Add the parsley, salt and hot pepper sauce; mix well. Serve over pasta. **Yield:** 4 servings.

Steak Potpie

Pattie Bonner, Cocoa, Florida

When I hear "meat and potatoes", this is the recipe that immediately comes to mind. I've made it for years, and everyone who's tried it has liked it. Most often, friends comment on its heartiness and on its combination of tastes.

- 3/4 cup sliced onions
- 4 tablespoons vegetable oil, *divided*
- 1/4 cup all-purpose flour
- 1 teaspoon salt
- 1/2 teaspoon pepper
- 1/2 teaspoon paprika

Pinch ground allspice
Pinch ground ginger
- 1 pound boneless round steak, cut into 1/2-inch pieces

- 2-1/2 cups boiling water
- 3 medium potatoes, peeled and diced

Pastry for single-crust pie

In a large skillet, saute the onions in 2 tablespoons oil until golden. Drain and set aside. In a plastic bag, combine dry ingredients; add meat and shake to coat. Brown meat in remaining oil in the same skillet. Add water; cover and simmer until meat is tender, about 1 hour. Add potatoes; simmer, uncovered, for 15-20 minutes or until the potatoes are tender. Pour into a greased 1-1/2-qt. baking dish. Top with onion slices. Roll pastry to fit baking dish. Place over hot filling; seal to edges of dish. Make slits in the crust. Bake at 450° for 25-30 minutes or until golden brown. If necessary, cover edges of crust with foil to prevent over-browning. **Yield:** 4-6 servings.

POTATO DELIGHT

Carol Klug, Boise, Idaho

(Pictured below)

Our state is, of course, synonymous with potatoes, so it should come as no surprise that my recipe features good ol' Idaho spuds.

✓ This tasty dish uses less sugar, salt and fat. Recipe includes *Diabetic Exchanges*.

    4 large baking potatoes (2 pounds)
    1 cup grated broccoli stems
  1/2 cup chopped fresh mushrooms
  1/4 cup sliced green onions
  1/4 cup grated carrot
  1/4 cup shredded red cabbage
1-1/2 cups diced fully cooked ham
  1/4 cup butter *or* margarine
Sour cream, optional

Bake potatoes in the oven or microwave until done. In a skillet, saute the next six ingredients in butter for 5 minutes or until vegetables are tender. Serve over hot potatoes. Top with sour cream if desired. **Yield:** 4 servings. **Diabetic Exchanges:** One serving (prepared with margarine and low-fat ham and without sour cream) equals 2 starch, 2 fat, 1 meat, 1 vegetable; also, 340 calories, 865 mg sodium, 25 mg cholesterol, 39 gm carbohydrate, 15 gm protein, 14 gm fat.

GRILLED STEAK PINWHEELS

Mary Hills, Scottsdale, Arizona

I've been serving this recipe to family and friends for 20 years, and very seldom do I have leftovers. We try to keep the house cool, so we grill out often. I get most of the herbs in this recipe from my son's garden.

    2 flank steaks (1 pound *each*), trimmed
  1/2 pound sliced bacon, cooked and
      crumbled
    1 cup finely chopped fresh mushrooms
    1 cup finely chopped green onions
  1/4 cup finely chopped fresh basil *or* 4
      teaspoons dried basil
    2 tablespoons minced fresh chives

Pound flank steaks on each side. Combine bacon, mushrooms, onions, basil and chives; spread evenly over steaks. Roll the meat up and secure with skewers or wooden picks. Cut each roll into 1/2- to 3/4-in. slices and secure with a wooden pick or skewer. Grill over hot coals for 4-6 minutes per side or until meat reaches desired doneness. Remove picks before serving. **Yield:** 6-8 servings.

ROASTED PORK AND POTATO ROSES

Linda Ault, Newberry, Indiana

A favorite with my family, this roast looks so lovely when embellished with the rose-shaped potatoes.

    4 garlic cloves, minced
  3/4 teaspoon grated lemon peel
  3/4 teaspoon dried rosemary, crushed
  3/4 teaspoon dried thyme
  1/2 teaspoon salt
  1/4 teaspoon pepper
4-1/2 teaspoons olive or vegetable oil
    4 medium red potatoes (about 1-1/2
      pounds)
    1 boneless pork loin roast (about 2 pounds)

In a small bowl, combine the first six ingredients; mash into a paste. Stir in oil; set aside. Peel potatoes. To achieve rose shape, cut a thin slice off the bottom so rose will sit flat. Begin petals about 1 in. from bottom of potato. Make a circular row of downward cuts, each about 3/4 in. long, but do not cut all the way through. To ex-

pose the petals, starting 1/4-in. above each petal, cut out a small wedge from behind each petal. Repeat with additional layers, positioning petals of new row between the lower row to create a true flower effect. Brush with herb mixture. Brush remaining mixture over pork. Place potatoes on a rack in a shallow roasting pan. Bake, uncovered, at 325° for 40 minutes. Place pork with fat side up on rack in pan. Bake for 1-1/4 hours or until a meat thermometer reads 160°-170° and potatoes are tender. Let roast stand 10 minutes before slicing. **Yield:** 4 servings.

⬛⬛⬛⬛⬛⬛⬛⬛⬛⬛

FARM-STYLE SAUSAGE BAKE

Catherine O'Hara, Bridgeton, New Jersey

(Pictured above)

This dish is a hearty meal all by itself. My family thinks it's fantastic. I hope yours does, too.

6 medium potatoes (about 2 pounds), peeled and cubed
3 to 4 green onions, sliced
2 garlic cloves, minced
2 tablespoons butter *or* margarine
3/4 cup milk
2 egg yolks
Dash *each* pepper and ground nutmeg
2 tablespoons dried parsley flakes
1 pound smoked sausage, sliced
1/2 cup diced mozzarella cheese
2 tablespoons grated Parmesan cheese
1 teaspoon dried thyme *or* sage

Cook potatoes in boiling salted water until tender. Drain and transfer to a mixing bowl; mash potatoes. Add onions, garlic, butter, milk, egg yolks, pepper and nutmeg; beat until light and fluffy. Stir in parsley, sausage and cheeses. Spoon into a greased 2-qt. baking dish. Sprinkle with thyme. Bake, uncovered, at 400° for 30 minutes or until lightly browned and heated through. **Yield:** 6 servings.

SAVORY BEEF STEW

Kay Fortier, Wildrose, North Dakota

(Pictured below)

Stew is one of my family's favorite dishes. Everyone is surprised that there's cranberry juice in this recipe—it really gives it a unique flavor.

✓ This tasty dish uses less sugar, salt and fat. Recipe includes *Diabetic Exchanges*.

  1/2 cup all-purpose flour
    1 teaspoon salt, optional
    2 pounds lean beef stew meat, cut into
      1-inch cubes
    4 bacon strips, cut into 1-inch pieces,
      optional
  10 small onions
    2 cups cranberry juice, *divided*
    1 can (14-1/2 ounces) beef broth
    4 whole cloves
    1 bay leaf
  1/2 teaspoon pepper
  1/2 teaspoon dried marjoram
  1/4 teaspoon dried thyme
  1/4 teaspoon garlic powder
    5 medium carrots, cut into chunks
    5 medium potatoes, peeled and cubed
    2 cups frozen peas, thawed

Combine flour and salt if desired; coat beef cubes. Reserve remaining flour mixture. Place beef in a Dutch oven. Add bacon if desired. Bake, uncovered, at 400° for 30 minutes. Add onions, 1-1/2 cups cranberry juice, broth and seasonings. Cover and bake at 350° for 1 hour. Add carrots and potatoes; bake 1 hour or until meat and vegetables are tender. Combine reserved flour mixture and remaining cranberry juice until smooth; stir into stew. Cover and bake 30 minutes longer. Remove bay leaf. Add peas; return to the oven for 5 minutes. **Yield:** 10 servings. **Diabetic Exchanges:** One 1-cup serving (prepared with low-sodium beef broth and without salt or bacon) equals 2 starch, 2 vegetable, 1-1/2 meat; also, 321 calories, 231 mg sodium, 56 mg cholesterol, 42 gm carbohydrate, 23 gm protein, 7 gm fat.

BARBECUED SPARERIBS

Christine Davis, Concord, California

The sauce for these ribs makes all the difference—it flavors the meat in a delightful way no one expects.

    8 pounds pork spareribs
    4 whole cloves
    2 medium onions
    2 bay leaves
PEACH BARBECUE SAUCE:
    2 cups chopped peeled fresh or frozen
      peaches, thawed
    1 can (10-3/4 ounces) condensed tomato
      soup, undiluted
  1/2 cup light corn syrup
  1/2 cup cider vinegar
  1/2 cup packed brown sugar
  1/4 cup vegetable oil
    1 tablespoon ground mustard
    1 tablespoon Worcestershire sauce
    2 teaspoons salt
1-1/2 teaspoons paprika
    1 teaspoon garlic powder
  1/2 teaspoon pepper

Cut ribs into serving-size pieces; place in a large kettle and cover with water. Insert cloves into onions; add to water with bay leaves. Bring to a boil. Reduce heat; cover and simmer for 30-45 minutes or until ribs are tender. Meanwhile, combine sauce ingredients in a saucepan; bring to a boil over medium heat, stirring constantly. Reduce heat; simmer, uncovered, for 20 minutes, stirring occasionally. Cool. Process in a blender until smooth. Drain ribs. Grill over medium-hot heat for 15-20 minutes or until browned, turning once. Brush generously with sauce. Grill 10-15 minutes longer. Heat any remaining sauce to serve with ribs if desired. **Yield:** 8-10 servings.

MANDARIN PORK MEDALLIONS

Dawn Doyle, Easton, Minnesota

(Pictured above)

My daughter demonstrated this recipe at the state fair and received lots of compliments. Since she is involved in both the food projects and the swine projects, she took great pleasure in promoting Minnesota pork.

- 1 pork tenderloin (about 1 pound)
- 1 tablespoon vegetable oil
- 3/4 cup orange juice
- 1 tablespoon cornstarch
- 1/4 cup orange marmalade
- 2 tablespoons lemon juice
- 1 teaspoon prepared horseradish
- 1/4 to 1/2 teaspoon salt
- Hot cooked noodles
- 1 can (11 ounces) mandarin oranges, drained

Cut tenderloin into four pieces; pound until 1/3 in. thick. Brown in a large skillet in hot oil for 3 minutes per side; remove and set aside. Combine orange juice and cornstarch; add to the skillet along with marmalade, lemon juice, horseradish and salt. Bring to a boil. Reduce heat; cook and stir until the sauce thickens, about 2 minutes. Return pork to skillet; cover and cook for 8-10 minutes or until pork is no longer pink. Serve over noodles; garnish with mandarin oranges. **Yield:** 4 servings.

PASTA WITH SAUSAGE AND TOMATOES

Michelle Fryer Dommel, Quakertown, Pennsylvania

I reach for this recipe whenever I crave spaghetti sauce but don't have the time to make my usual recipe.

- 1 pound bulk Italian sausage
- 2 cans (16 ounces *each*) diced tomatoes, undrained
- 1-1/2 teaspoons chopped fresh basil *or* 1/2 teaspoon dried basil
- 1 package (12 ounces) pasta, cooked and drained

In a skillet, cook sausage until browned; drain. Add tomatoes and basil. Simmer, uncovered, for 10 minutes. Serve immediately over pasta. **Yield:** 4 servings.

VARIETY'S not only the spice of life...it's also what seasons chili and soups! The dishes in this chapter have it all—ground beef, pork, chicken, vegetables, pasta and beans. For filling fare, you're in the right place.

KETTLE CREATIONS. Clockwise from top left: Meaty Three-Bean Chili (p. 42), Black Bean Sausage Chili (p. 41), Chili with Tortilla Dumplings (p. 41) and Santa Fe Chicken Chili (p. 42).

Chili & Soups

CHILI WITH TORTILLA DUMPLINGS

Shirley Logan, Houston, Texas

(Pictured at left)

Down here in Texas, we've always enjoyed Southwestern cooking. This chili is a special favorite—I've prepared it for a crowd and for just the two of us, too.

  1 medium onion, chopped
  2 garlic cloves, minced
  1 tablespoon vegetable oil
  2 pounds ground beef
  2 cans (15-1/2 ounces *each*) kidney beans, rinsed and drained
  1 can (28 ounces) diced tomatoes, undrained
  1 can (14-1/2 ounces) chicken broth
  2 to 3 tablespoons chili powder
  1 teaspoon ground cumin
  1 teaspoon dried oregano
1/2 teaspoon salt
  4 flour tortillas (7 inches)

In a 3-qt. saucepan over medium-high heat, saute onion and garlic in oil for 3 minutes. Add beef; cook until browned, about 6 minutes. Drain. Add the next seven ingredients; bring to a boil. Reduce heat; cover and simmer for 50 minutes. Halve each tortilla and cut into 1/4-in. strips. Gently stir into soup; cover and simmer for 8-10 minutes or until tortillas are softened. Serve immediately. **Yield:** 6-8 servings (2-1/4 quarts).

BLACK BEAN SAUSAGE CHILI

Nanci Keatley, Salem, Oregon

(Pictured at left)

I came up with this recipe one day when I wasn't sure what to do with a can of black beans I had. I just threw a bunch of things together, and out came a new chili that's become our favorite.

  1 pound bulk Italian sausage
  3 garlic cloves, minced
1/2 cup chopped green pepper
1/2 cup chopped onion
  1 can (15 ounces) black beans, rinsed and drained
  1 can (14-1/2 ounces) diced tomatoes, undrained
  1 can (11 ounces) whole kernel corn, drained
  1 can (8 ounces) tomato sauce
  1 can (6 ounces) tomato paste
1/2 cup water
  1 tablespoon chili powder
  1 teaspoon dried oregano
3/4 teaspoon salt
1/2 teaspoon dried basil
1/4 teaspoon pepper
Shredded cheddar cheese, optional

In a 3-qt. saucepan over medium heat, brown sausage and garlic. Add green pepper and onion. Cook and stir until onion is tender; drain. Add beans, tomatoes, corn, tomato sauce and paste, water, chili powder, oregano, salt, basil and pepper; bring to a boil. Reduce heat; cover and simmer for 30 minutes. Garnish with cheese if desired. **Yield:** 6 servings (1-3/4 quarts).

CHILI IN NO TIME

Pearl Johnson, Prior Lake, Minnesota

When your family's asking for chili and time is short, make this quick and easy variety. It gets a head start with store-bought spaghetti sauce.

1-1/2 pounds ground beef
  1 medium onion, chopped
  1 can (28 ounces) crushed tomatoes
  1 jar (30 ounces) spaghetti sauce
  2 cans (16 ounces *each*) kidney beans
  2 to 4 tablespoons chili powder

In a large kettle or Dutch oven, brown beef and onion; drain. Add remaining ingredients; simmer for at least 15 minutes, stirring occasionally. **Yield:** 10 servings (2-1/2 quarts).

This Chili's a Winner with Her Family

SPICED just right, Sandra Miller's Meaty Three-Bean Chili is easily adapted for different tastes. "Over the years, I've altered the recipe, heating it up or cooling it down as needed," shares this Lees Summit, Missouri cook.

Easily doubled or tripled, Sandra's recipe is a proven crowd-pleaser, too. "I've made this chili for as many as 50 people at a variety of potlucks," she says.

MEATY THREE-BEAN CHILI

(Pictured on page 40)

3/4 pound Italian sausage links, cut into 1/2-inch chunks
3/4 pound ground beef
1 large onion, chopped
1 medium green pepper, chopped
1 jalapeno pepper, seeded and minced
2 garlic cloves, minced
1 cup beef broth
1/2 cup Worcestershire sauce
1-1/2 teaspoons chili powder
1 teaspoon pepper
1 teaspoon ground mustard
1/2 teaspoon celery seed
1/2 teaspoon salt
6 cups chopped fresh plum tomatoes (about 2 pounds)
6 bacon strips, cooked and crumbled
1 can (15-1/2 ounces) kidney beans, rinsed and drained
1 can (15 ounces) pinto beans, rinsed and drained
1 can (15 ounces) garbanzo beans, rinsed and drained
Additional chopped onion, optional

In a 4-qt. kettle or Dutch oven over medium heat, brown the sausage and beef; drain, discarding all but 1 tablespoon drippings. Set meat aside. Saute onion, peppers and garlic in the drippings for 3 minutes. Add the broth, Worcestershire sauce and seasonings; bring to a boil over medium heat. Reduce heat; cover and simmer for 10 minutes. Add tomatoes, bacon, and browned sausage and beef; return to a boil. Reduce heat; cover and simmer for 30 minutes. Add all of the beans. Simmer for 1 hour, stirring occasionally. Garnish with chopped onion if desired. **Yield:** 10-12 servings (3 quarts).

SANTA FE CHICKEN CHILI

Sonia Gallant, St. Thomas, Ontario

(Pictured on page 40)

Stir up this chili on Sunday, and you'll be set for a couple weekday meals.

2 pounds boneless skinless chicken breasts, cut into 1/2-inch cubes
4 medium sweet red peppers, diced
4 garlic cloves, minced
2 large onions, chopped
1/4 cup olive *or* vegetable oil
3 tablespoons chili powder
2 teaspoons ground cumin
1/4 teaspoon cayenne pepper
1 can (28 ounces) diced tomatoes, undrained
2 cans (14-1/2 ounces *each*) chicken broth
2 cans (15-1/2 ounces *each*) kidney beans, rinsed and drained
1 jar (12 ounces) salsa
1 package (10 ounces) frozen corn
1/2 teaspoon salt
1/2 teaspoon pepper

In a 5-qt. kettle or Dutch oven over medium heat, saute chicken, peppers, garlic and onions in oil until the chicken is no longer pink and vegetables are tender, about 5-7 minutes. Add chili powder, cumin and cayenne pepper; cook and stir for 1 minute. Add the tomatoes and broth; bring to a boil. Reduce heat; simmer, uncovered, for 15 minutes. Stir in remaining ingredients; bring to a boil. Reduce heat; cover and simmer for 10-15 minutes or until the chicken is tender. **Yield:** 14-16 servings (4 quarts).

COUNTRY CARROT SOUP

Marlane Jones, Allentown, Pennsylvania

Ground beef adds some spark to traditional carrot soup. This easy creation always disappears quickly.

1 pound ground beef
1/4 cup chopped onion
2 cans (10-3/4 ounces *each*) condensed
   cream of celery soup, undiluted
3 cups tomato juice
2 cups grated carrots
1 cup water
1 bay leaf
1/2 teaspoon sugar
1/2 teaspoon dried marjoram
1/2 teaspoon salt
1/4 teaspoon garlic powder
1/4 teaspoon pepper

In a large saucepan over medium heat, brown the beef and onion until the beef is no longer pink; drain. Add all remaining ingredients; bring to a boil. Reduce heat; cover and simmer for 15 minutes or until the carrots are tender. Remove the bay leaf. **Yield:** 6-8 servings.

PARMESAN POTATO SOUP

Tami Walters, Kingsport, Tennessee

(Pictured at right)

Even my husband, who's not much of a soup eater, likes this. Our two boys do, too. With homemade bread and a salad, it's a satisfying meal.

4 medium baking potatoes (about 2
   pounds)
3/4 cup chopped onion
1/2 cup butter *or* margarine
1/2 cup all-purpose flour
1/2 teaspoon dried basil
1/2 teaspoon seasoned salt
1/4 teaspoon celery salt
1/4 teaspoon garlic powder
1/4 teaspoon onion salt
1/4 teaspoon pepper
1/4 teaspoon rubbed sage
1/4 teaspoon dried thyme
4-1/2 cups chicken broth
6 cups milk
3/4 to 1 cup grated Parmesan cheese
10 bacon strips, cooked and crumbled

Pierce potatoes with a fork; bake in the oven or microwave until tender. Cool, peel and cube; set aside. In a large Dutch oven or soup kettle over medium heat, saute onion in butter until tender. Stir in flour and seasonings. Gradually add broth, stirring constantly. Bring to a boil; cook and stir for 2 minutes. Add potatoes; return to a boil. Reduce heat; cover and simmer for 10 minutes. Add milk and cheese; heat through. Stir in bacon. **Yield:** 10-12 servings.

ROUND STEAK CHILI

Linda Goshorn, Bedford, Virginia

The addition of round steak gives this chili recipe a nice change of pace. Everyone in my family just loves it!

1 pound round steak
1 large onion, chopped
2 garlic cloves, minced
1 to 2 tablespoons vegetable oil
1 can (46 ounces) V-8 juice
1 can (28 ounces) crushed tomatoes
2 cups sliced celery
1 can (16 ounces) kidney beans, rinsed
   and drained
1 medium green pepper, chopped
1 bay leaf
2 tablespoons chili powder
1-1/2 teaspoons salt
1 teaspoon dried oregano
1 teaspoon brown sugar
1/2 teaspoon *each* celery seed, paprika and
   ground mustard and cumin
1/4 teaspoon cayenne pepper
1/4 teaspoon dried basil

Cut meat into 1/2-in. cubes. In a large kettle or Dutch oven, brown meat, onion and garlic in oil. Add remaining ingredients; bring to a boil. Reduce heat; simmer, uncovered, for 3 hours. Remove bay leaf before serving. **Yield:** 6-8 servings.

VEGETABLE BEAN CHILI

Rene Fry, Hampstead, Maryland

(Pictured on page 46)

Because it is so hearty, no one misses the meat in this chili. Both family and friends ask for it.

✓ This tasty dish uses less sugar, salt and fat. Recipe includes *Diabetic Exchanges*.

1 medium zucchini, sliced 1/4 inch thick
1 medium green pepper, chopped
1 cup chopped onion
1 cup shredded carrots
1/2 cup finely chopped celery
2 garlic cloves, minced
1/4 cup olive *or* vegetable oil
1 can (28 ounces) diced tomatoes, undrained
1 jar (8 ounces) picante sauce
1 teaspoon beef bouillon granules
1-1/2 teaspoons ground cumin
1 can (15 ounces) garbanzo beans, rinsed and drained
1 can (15-1/2 ounces) chili beans, undrained
1 can (2-1/4 ounces) sliced ripe olives, drained
1 cup (4 ounces) shredded cheddar cheese
Alfalfa sprouts, optional

In a 4-qt. kettle or Dutch oven, saute zucchini, green pepper, onion, carrots, celery and garlic in oil until tender. Stir in tomatoes, picante sauce, bouillon and cumin; bring to a boil. Reduce heat; simmer, uncovered, for 30 minutes, stirring occasionally. Add beans and olives; heat through. Garnish with cheese and alfalfa sprouts if desired. **Yield:** 9 servings (2-1/4 quarts). **Diabetic Exchanges:** One 1-cup serving (prepared with low-sodium bouillon and served with low-fat cheese) equals 1-1/2 starch, 1 meat, 1 vegetable, 1 fat; also, 250 calories, 863 mg sodium, 4 mg cholesterol, 33 gm carbohydrate, 11 gm protein, 10 gm fat.

GARDEN HARVEST CHILI

Debbie Cosford, Bayfield, Ontario

(Pictured on page 47)

Anytime you're looking for a way to use up your zucchini and squash, this recipe gives a different taste sensation. My husband really enjoys it—and, except for the zucchini, our two daughters do as well!

✓ This tasty dish uses less sugar, salt and fat. Recipe includes *Diabetic Exchanges*.

1 medium sweet red pepper, chopped
1 medium onion, chopped
4 garlic cloves, minced
2 tablespoons vegetable oil
1 tablespoon chili powder
1 teaspoon ground cumin
1 teaspoon dried oregano
2 cups cubed peeled butternut squash
1 can (28 ounces) diced tomatoes, undrained
2 cups diced zucchini
1 can (15 ounces) black beans, rinsed and drained
1 can (8-3/4 ounces) whole kernel corn, drained
1/4 cup minced fresh parsley

In a 3-qt. saucepan, saute red pepper, onion and garlic in oil until tender. Stir in chili powder, cumin, oregano, butternut squash and tomatoes; bring to a boil. Reduce heat; cover and simmer for 10-15 minutes or until squash is almost tender. Stir in remaining ingredients; cover and simmer 10 minutes more. **Yield:** 7 servings (1-3/4 quarts). **Diabetic Exchanges:** One 1-cup serving equals 1-1/2 starch, 1 vegetable, 1 fat; also, 193 calories, 167 mg sodium, 0 cholesterol, 33 gm carbohydrate, 8 gm protein, 5 gm fat.

ZESTY COLORADO CHILI

Beverly Bowman, Conifer, Colorado

(Pictured on page 47)

Chili is a hearty winter staple up here in the mountains—especially for a couple of outdoor lovers like my husband and me!

1 pound Italian sausage links
1 pound pork shoulder
2 pounds ground beef
2 medium onions, chopped
1 large green pepper, chopped
1 tablespoon minced garlic
1 can (29 ounces) tomato puree
1 can (28 ounces) diced tomatoes, undrained
1 cup beef broth
1 jalapeno pepper, seeded and minced
2 tablespoons brown sugar
1 tablespoon vinegar
2 teaspoons chili powder
2 teaspoons ground cumin
1 to 2 teaspoons crushed red pepper flakes
1 teaspoon dried basil
1 teaspoon dried oregano
1/2 teaspoon hot pepper sauce
2 cans (15-1/2 ounces *each*) kidney beans, rinsed and drained

Cut sausage into 1/2-in. pieces. Trim pork and cut into 1/2-in. pieces. In a 5-qt. kettle or Dutch oven over medium heat, brown sausage, pork and beef; drain, discarding all but 1 tablespoon drippings. Set meat aside. Saute onions, green pepper and garlic in drippings until tender. Add the next 12 ingredients. Return meat to the pan; bring to a boil. Reduce heat; cover and simmer for 1 hour. Add the beans and heat through. **Yield:** 12-14 servings (3-1/2 quarts).

BEEF BARLEY SOUP

Sharon Kolenc, Jasper, Alberta

(Pictured at right)

When making this soup, I tend to clean out the refrigerator by adding all kinds of leftovers. In fact, my family says they have to watch out for the kitchen sink!

  2 cups beef broth
  8 cups water
  2 cups chopped cooked roast beef
1/2 cup chopped carrots
  3 celery ribs, chopped
1/2 cup chopped onion
  1 can (14-1/2 ounces) diced tomatoes, undrained
  1 cup quick-cooking barley
  1 teaspoon dried oregano
1/2 teaspoon pepper
  1 can (10-3/4 ounces) condensed tomato soup, undiluted
1/2 cup frozen *or* canned peas
1/2 cup frozen *or* canned cut green *or* wax beans
Seasoned salt to taste

In a large kettle or Dutch oven, combine the first 10 ingredients; bring to a boil. Reduce heat; cover and simmer for 25 minutes, stirring occasionally. Add soup, peas and beans. Simmer, uncovered, for 10 minutes. Add seasoned salt. **Yield:** 12-14 servings (about 3-1/2 quarts).

TANGY OVEN CHILI

Sue O'Connor, Lucan, Ontario

(Pictured on page 46)

I never cared much for chili. But my husband does. So I played with ingredients until I came up with one I liked!

  1 pound dry red kidney beans
  2 pounds ground beef

  2 medium onions, chopped
  1 medium green pepper, chopped
  2 envelopes chili seasoning mix
1-1/2 teaspoons salt
1-1/2 teaspoons pepper
  1 teaspoon sugar
  2 cans (28 ounces *each*) diced tomatoes, undrained
  1 can (12 ounces) tomato paste
  2 cans (8 ounces *each*) crushed pineapple, undrained
  2 jars (4-1/2 ounces *each*) sliced mushrooms, drained
  3 to 5 fresh jalapeno peppers, seeded and minced
  3 cans (11-1/2 ounces *each*) V-8 juice

Rinse beans and place in a large kettle or Dutch oven; cover with water. Bring to a boil; boil for 2 minutes. Remove from the heat; let stand for 1 hour. Drain, discarding liquid; set beans aside. In a skillet, brown beef, onions and green pepper; drain. Stir in seasoning mixes, salt and pepper. Pour into an ovenproof 8-qt. Dutch oven. Add beans and remaining ingredients; mix well. Cover and bake at 350° for 1 hour. Reduce heat to 250°; bake for 5 hours or until beans are tender, stirring every 30 minutes. **Yield:** 18-20 servings (5 quarts).

YOUR FAMILY and friends will warm up to a steaming bowlful of hearty chili. There's a zesty chili, mild chili, traditional chili...plus some surprises, too!

CHILI FORECAST. Clockwise from lower left: Tangy Oven Chili (p. 45), Vegetable Bean Chili (p. 44), Chili for a Crowd (p. 49), Zesty Colorado Chili (p. 44), Garden Harvest Chili (p. 44), Chunky Beef Chili (p. 48), Spicy White Chili (p. 48) and Hearty Italian Chili (p. 48).

SPICY WHITE CHILI

Carlene Bailey, Bradenton, Florida

(Pictured on page 46)

As far as I was concerned, the original version of this dish was fine. But, with a son who can't get enough spice, I added green chilies and other seasonings until I "discovered" a quick and easy chili that he's wild about.

  2 medium onions, chopped
  1 tablespoon vegetable oil
  4 garlic cloves, minced
  2 cans (4 ounces *each*) chopped green
     chilies
  2 teaspoons ground cumin
  1 teaspoon dried oregano
1/4 teaspoon cayenne pepper
1/4 teaspoon ground cloves
  2 cans (14-1/2 ounces *each*) chicken
     broth
  4 cups cubed cooked chicken
  3 cans (15-1/2 ounces *each*) great
     northern beans, rinsed and drained
  2 cups (8 ounces) shredded Monterey Jack
     cheese
Sour cream and sliced jalapeno peppers,
     optional

In a 3-qt. saucepan, saute onions in oil until tender. Stir in garlic, chilies, cumin, oregano, cayenne and cloves; cook and stir 2-3 minutes more. Add broth, chicken and beans; simmer, uncovered, for 15 minutes. Remove from the heat. Stir in cheese until melted. Garnish with sour cream and jalapeno peppers if desired. **Yield:** 6-8 servings (2-1/4 quarts).

CHUNKY BEEF CHILI

Vicki Flowers, Knoxville, Tennessee

(Pictured on page 47)

When I first tasted this chili that originated with my brother, I couldn't wait to share it. It's the best I've ever had.

1/2 cup all-purpose flour
1-1/2 teaspoons *each* dried thyme and
     rosemary, crushed
1-1/2 pounds beef stew meat, cut into 1-inch
     cubes
1/2 pound ground beef
  1 can (14-1/2 ounces) beef broth
  1 large onion, finely chopped
1/2 cup chopped green pepper
  1 garlic clove, minced

  1 can (4 ounces) chopped green chilies
  1 to 2 jalapeno peppers, seeded and minced
  1 can (16 ounces) crushed tomatoes
  2 cans (15-1/2 ounces *each*) chili beans,
     undrained
  1 can (15-1/2 ounces) pinto beans, rinsed
     and drained
  1 can (15 ounces) white *or* red kidney
     beans, rinsed and drained
  1 can (6 ounces) tomato paste
  2 tablespoons ground cumin
  1 teaspoon dried oregano
1/2 teaspoon *each* pepper, white pepper and
     cayenne pepper
  3 to 4 drops hot pepper sauce
Shredded cheddar cheese, optional

In a plastic bag, combine flour, thyme and rosemary; add beef cubes and shake to coat. In a 4-qt. kettle or Dutch oven, brown ground beef and the beef cubes; drain. Add remaining ingredients except cheese. Cover and simmer for 5 hours. Garnish with cheese if desired. **Yield:** 10-12 servings (3 quarts).

HEARTY ITALIAN CHILI

Chloe Buckner, Edinburg, Pennsylvania

(Pictured on page 46)

I can't seem to follow a recipe without changing it! That's how this one came about when I got bored with plain chili. The first time I served it at a potluck, people passed around copies of the recipe.

  1 pound ground beef
1/2 pound bulk Italian sausage
  1 medium onion, chopped
1/2 cup chopped green pepper
  1 can *or* jar (26-1/2 to 30 ounces)
     spaghetti sauce
  1 can (15-1/2 ounces) kidney beans,
     rinsed and drained
  1 can (14-1/2 ounces) diced tomatoes,
     undrained
  1 jar (4-1/2 ounces) sliced mushrooms,
     drained
  1 cup water
1/3 cup halved sliced pepperoni
  5 teaspoons chili powder
1/2 teaspoon salt
Pinch pepper

In a 3-qt. saucepan, brown beef, sausage, onion and green pepper; drain. Add remaining ingredients; bring to a boil. Reduce heat; simmer, uncovered, for 30 minutes. **Yield:** 6-8 servings (2-1/4 quarts).

CHILI FOR A CROWD

Lisa Humphreys, Wasilla, Alaska

(Pictured on page 46)

My aunt got this recipe from a "grizzled Montana mountain man". I added some zesty ingredients on my own.

- 3 pounds ground beef
- 2 cans (28 ounces *each*) diced tomatoes, undrained
- 4 cans (15 to 16 ounces *each*) kidney, pinto *and/or* black beans, rinsed and drained
- 1 pound smoked kielbasa, sliced and halved
- 2 large onions, halved and thinly sliced
- 2 cans (8 ounces *each*) tomato sauce
- 2/3 cup hickory-flavored barbecue sauce
- 1-1/2 cups water
- 1/2 cup packed brown sugar
- 5 fresh banana peppers, seeded and sliced
- 2 tablespoons chili powder
- 2 teaspoons dry mustard
- 2 teaspoons instant coffee granules
- 1 teaspoon *each* dried oregano, thyme and sage
- 1/2 to 1 teaspoon cayenne pepper
- 1/2 to 1 teaspoon crushed red pepper flakes
- 2 garlic cloves, minced

In an 8-qt. kettle or Dutch oven, brown beef; drain. Add remaining ingredients; bring to a boil. Reduce heat; cover and simmer for 1 hour, stirring occasionally. **Yield:** 20-24 servings (6 quarts).

TOMATO DILL SOUP

Patty Kile, Greentown, Pennsylvania

(Pictured at right)

Most often, I make this soup ahead and keep it in the fridge. It's particularly good to take out and heat up with tuna or grilled cheese sandwiches, hard rolls or a salad. It would be fine to serve—hot or cold—at a soup supper as well.

- 1 medium onion, thinly sliced
- 1 garlic clove, minced
- 2 tablespoons vegetable oil
- 1 tablespoon butter *or* margarine
- 1/2 teaspoon salt
- Pinch pepper
- 3 large tomatoes, sliced
- 1 can (6 ounces) tomato paste
- 1/4 cup all-purpose flour
- 2 cups water, *divided*

- 3/4 cup whipping cream, whipped
- 1 to 2 tablespoons finely minced fresh dill *or* 1 to 2 teaspoons dill weed

In a large saucepan over low heat, cook onion and garlic in oil and butter until tender. Add salt, pepper and tomatoes; cook over medium-high heat for 3 minutes. Remove from the heat and stir in tomato paste. In a small bowl, combine flour and 1/2 cup of water; stir until smooth. Stir into saucepan. Gradually stir in remaining water until smooth; bring to a boil over medium heat. Cook and stir for 2 minutes. Place mixture in a sieve over a bowl. With the back of a spoon, press vegetables through the sieve to remove seeds and skin; return puree to pan. Add cream and dill; cook over low heat just until heated through (do not boil). **Yield:** 4 servings (1 quart).

Quick & Easy Chili Choices

SURE...a pot of chili slowly simmering on the stove usually makes a mighty appetizing image. But on the days that your schedule's hotter than the spiciest of varieties (or if you simply want to keep your kitchen cool), turn to these fast favorites. All can go from start to finish to table in 30 minutes or under.

ALL-AMERICAN CHILI

Cheryl Groenenboom, Rose Hill, Iowa

Pork and beans make this an all-American meal everyone enjoys.

> 1 pound ground beef
> 1 medium onion, chopped
> 1/4 teaspoon pepper
> 1 can (16 ounces) pork and beans, undrained
> 1 can (10-3/4 ounces) condensed tomato soup, undiluted
> 1 can (10-1/2 ounces) condensed vegetable beef soup, undiluted
Shredded mozzarella cheese

In a large saucepan, brown beef, onion and pepper; drain. Stir in the beans and soups. Simmer, uncovered, for 15 minutes. Garnish with cheese. **Yield:** 4-6 servings (1-1/2 quarts).

SPEEDY CHILI

Betty Ruenholl, Syracuse, Nebraska

(Pictured at right)

By using your microwave, this one-pot meal takes just minutes to prepare.

> 1 pound ground beef
> 1 large onion, chopped
> 1 garlic clove, minced

> 2 cans (8 ounces *each*) tomato sauce
> 1 tablespoon chili powder
> 1 tablespoon red wine vinegar
> 2 teaspoons baking cocoa
> 1/4 teaspoon ground cinnamon
Dash ground allspice
> 1 can (15-1/2 ounces) kidney beans, rinsed and drained
Hot cooked macaroni, shredded cheddar cheese and sliced green onions, optional

In a microwave oven, cook beef, onion and garlic on high for 3 minutes in a covered 2-qt. microwave-safe dish; stir to crumble meat. Cover and cook for 3 minutes; drain. Add the next six ingredients; cover and cook on high for 6 minutes. Stir in the beans. Cover and cook 4 minutes more. Let stand 3-5 minutes. If desired, serve over macaroni and top with cheese and onions. **Yield:** 4 servings (about 1 quart). **Editor's Note:** Recipe was tested using a 700-watt microwave.

MARGIE'S CHILI

Margaret Ganzel, Mankato, Minnesota

I simply spice up canned tomato soup to create a flavorful chili.

1 pound ground beef
2 small onions, chopped
1 can (10-3/4 ounces) condensed tomato soup, undiluted
1 can (15-1/2 ounces) kidney beans, rinsed and drained
3/4 cup chili sauce
2 teaspoons chili powder
1/4 teaspoon salt
1/4 teaspoon pepper

In a medium saucepan, brown beef and onions; drain. Add remaining ingredients; bring to a boil. Reduce heat; simmer, uncovered, for 5-10 minutes or until thickened. **Yield:** 4 servings (about 1 quart).

SAUSAGE ONION CHILI

Denise VonStein, Shiloh, Ohio

When people request this recipe, they're surprised to see onion soup as an ingredient.

1 pound bulk pork sausage
1 pound ground beef
1 can (10-1/2 ounces) condensed French onion soup, undiluted
2 tablespoons chili powder
1 teaspoon ground cumin
1/2 teaspoon salt
1/2 teaspoon pepper
1 can (15-1/2 ounces) kidney beans, rinsed and drained
1 can (8 ounces) tomato sauce
1 can (6 ounces) tomato paste
1/2 cup water

In a large saucepan, brown sausage and beef; drain. Add remaining ingredients and mix well; bring to a boil. Reduce heat; cook and stir for 10-

15 minutes or until thickened. **Yield:** 6 servings (about 1-1/2 quarts).

CORN AND BEAN CHILI

Mary Pitts, Powder Springs, Georgia

My family favors corn in a variety of dishes, including this one.

2 pounds ground beef
1 small onion, finely chopped
1 envelope chili seasoning mix
3 cans (16 ounces *each*) chili beans, undrained
1 can (46 ounces) V-8 juice
1/2 teaspoon salt
1 can (16 ounces) cream-style corn
Shredded cheddar cheese

In a 5-qt. kettle or Dutch oven, brown beef and onion. Stir in seasoning mix, beans, V-8 juice and salt. Simmer, uncovered, for 15 minutes. Stir in corn. Cook and stir over low heat for 15 minutes. Garnish with cheese. **Yield:** 14-16 servings (4 quarts).

ALOHA CHILI

Dyan Cornies, Vernon, British Columbia

Pineapple and brown sugar give this chili a unique tropical taste.

2 pounds ground beef
1 large onion, finely chopped
1 can (15-1/2 ounces) kidney beans, rinsed and drained
1 can (16 ounces) pork and beans, undrained
1 can (20 ounces) pineapple chunks, undrained
1 cup ketchup
1/4 cup packed brown sugar
1/4 cup vinegar

In a large saucepan, brown beef and onion; drain. Stir in remaining ingredients. Cover and simmer for 20 minutes. **Yield:** 8 servings (2-1/4 quarts).

Here's a Helping of Red-Hot Hints

• For convenience, I simmer my chili con carne on low all day in my slow cooker after first browning the hamburger.

I like to add a cup of shredded zucchini to my chili besides for additional bulk, nutrition and flavor.
—*Linda Sinclair*
Congress, Saskatchewan

• I always add a tablespoon or two of molasses and the grated peel of an orange to my deluxe chili recipe.
—*Martha Creech*
Kinston, North Carolina

• To take the bitter edge from tomato paste, I add a can of 7-Up to my bean and ground beef chili recipe. I also puree the celery, onions and red pepper to "hide" the vegetables from fussy eaters.
—*Alice Herring*
Havana, Florida

• As a mother of five, I need a chili with child appeal! So I stir in 1/4 cup chocolate syrup per 8-cup batch for a little sweetener.
—*Sandra Murray*
Marble Hill, Missouri

• Sometimes, I pour a can of kernel corn into my chili for color *and* flavor.
—*Catherine Johnston*
Stafford, New York

• At big family gatherings, I try to stretch my chili with what I call a "Mexican pile-up". To make it, I stack ingredients in this order: crushed tortilla chips, rice, chili, beans, chopped lettuce, chopped tomatoes, sliced black olives, sliced jalapenos, shredded cheese, salsa and sour cream.
—*Terri Gilmore, Roswell, New Mexico*

• Be creative with roast beef! Cube any that's left over and add all your favorite chili ingredients to it. To turn it into Cincinnati Chili, top with cooked spaghetti, shredded cheese and lettuce, chopped red onion and tomato.
—*Marie Hollada, Danville, Indiana*

• For a thick full-flavored chili, let it sit in the refrigerator a day or two before serving. —*Erna Nestegard*
Ellensburg, Washington

• I warm up leftover chili the next morning and fill everyone's thermoses with it so my family can have hot lunches. In addition, I pack little bags of shredded cheese and chopped onion to top off each serving.
—*Earline Campbell*
Pensacola, Florida

• For cold winter outings, I make a big batch of chili and freeze it in gallon ice cream pails. Often, I make my chili so thick it can be served on hamburger buns or over chunks of corn bread.
—*Eleanor Steg, Stuartburn, Manitoba*

• You can add interest to your chili recipes by substituting ground turkey, pork, veal or chicken for the ground beef.
—*Pamela Gregory*
Wantagh, New York

GARDEN TOMATO SOUP

Frances McFarlane, Winnipeg, Manitoba

(Pictured at right)

"Delicious" and "filling" are the words friends I've served this soup to use to describe it. Alone, it makes for a tasty lunch…or you can have it with a sandwich or crackers. Like an even heartier soup? Simply cube some of your leftover cooked chicken or roast and add.

> 1 cup chopped celery
> 1 small onion, chopped
> 1 medium carrot, shredded
> 1 small green pepper, chopped
> 1/4 cup butter *or* margarine
> 4-1/2 cups chicken broth, *divided*
> 4 cups chopped peeled tomatoes (about 7 medium)
> 2 teaspoons sugar
> 1/2 teaspoon curry powder
> 1/2 teaspoon salt
> 1/4 teaspoon pepper
> 1/4 cup all-purpose flour

In a 3-qt. saucepan, saute celery, onion, carrot and green pepper in butter until tender. Add 4 cups broth, tomatoes, sugar, curry, salt and pepper; bring to a boil. Reduce heat; simmer, uncovered, for 20 minutes. In a small bowl, stir flour and remaining broth until smooth. Gradually stir into tomato mixture; bring to a boil. Cook and stir until thickened and bubbly, about 2 minutes. **Yield:** 6 servings (1-3/4 quarts).

BEANS AND BARLEY CHILI

Gail Applegate, Myrtle Beach, South Carolina

Most folks have heard of barley soup, but this barley chili takes them by surprise. My variation features a delectable combination of beans and seasonings.

✓ This tasty dish uses less sugar, salt and fat. Recipe includes *Diabetic Exchanges*.

> 1 cup medium barley
> 2 cups chopped onion
> 2 cups chopped red pepper
> 1 tablespoon vegetable oil
> 1 tablespoon minced garlic
> 2 tablespoons chili powder
> 1-1/2 teaspoons ground cumin
> 1/8 teaspoon cayenne pepper
> 1 can (14-1/2 ounces) reduced-sodium fat-free chicken broth
> 1 can (14-1/2 ounces) no-salt-added stewed tomatoes
> 1 can (15-1/2 ounces) kidney beans, rinsed and drained
> 1 can (15 ounces) black beans, rinsed and drained
> 1 can (15-1/2 ounces) black-eyed peas, rinsed and drained

Cook barley without adding salt; drain. Saute onion and green pepper in oil for 5 minutes. Add barley and remaining ingredients; bring to a boil. Reduce heat; simmer 20 minutes. **Yield:** 12 servings. **Diabetic Exchanges:** One 1-cup serving equals 2 starch, 2 vegetable; also, 198 calories, 461 mg sodium, 0 cholesterol, 39 gm carbohydrate, 10 gm protein, 2 gm fat.

HUNGARIAN GOULASH SOUP

Julie Polakowski, West Allis, Wisconsin

(Pictured above)

This soup is similar to one made by my mother years ago. Brimming with potatoes, rutabagas, carrots and onions, it's a rich, flavorful meal in a bowl!

✓ This tasty dish uses less sugar, salt and fat. Recipe includes *Diabetic Exchanges*.

1-1/4 pounds beef stew meat, cut into 1-inch
    cubes
  2 tablespoons olive *or* vegetable oil, *divided*
  4 medium onions, chopped
  6 garlic cloves, minced
  2 teaspoons paprika
1/2 teaspoon caraway seed, crushed
1/2 teaspoon pepper
1/4 teaspoon cayenne pepper
  1 teaspoon salt, optional
  2 cans (14-1/2 ounces *each*) beef broth
  2 cups cubed peeled potatoes
  2 cups sliced carrots
  2 cups cubed peeled rutabagas
  2 cans (28 ounces *each*) diced
    tomatoes, undrained
  1 large sweet red pepper, chopped
Sour cream, optional

In a Dutch oven over medium heat, brown beef in 1 tablespoon oil. Remove beef; drain drippings.

Heat remaining oil in the same pan; saute onions and garlic for 8-10 minutes over medium heat or until lightly browned. Add paprika, caraway, pepper, cayenne and salt if desired; cook and stir 1 minute. Return beef to pan. Add broth, potatoes, carrots and rutabagas; bring to a boil. Reduce heat; cover and simmer for 1-1/2 hours or until vegetables are tender and meat is almost tender. Add tomatoes and red pepper; return to a boil. Reduce heat; cover and simmer 30-40 minutes or until meat and vegetables are tender. Serve with sour cream if desired. **Yield:** 15 servings. **Diabetic Exchanges:** One 1-cup serving (prepared with lean stew meat and low-sodium broth and without salt and sour cream) equals 2 lean meat, 1 vegetable, 1/2 starch; also, 185 calories, 330 mg sodium, 38 mg cholesterol, 16 gm carbohydrate, 15 gm protein, 7 gm fat.

SUMMERTIME MELON SOUP

Valerie Black, Fairfield Bay, Arkansas

My summertime soup always elicits a sweet response. Guests never fail to request the recipe. To make it look even better, I often serve it in cantaloupe "bowls".

  5 cups seeded cubed watermelon
  1 pint fresh strawberries

1/4 cup sour cream
2 tablespoons milk
2 tablespoons sugar
3 to 4 cantaloupes, optional
Additional fresh strawberries, optional

Combine watermelon and strawberries. Puree in batches in a blender, adding sour cream, milk and sugar to the last batch. Pour into a 2-qt. container; mix well. Cover and chill at least 3 hours. To serve soup in cantaloupe bowls, cut cantaloupes in half; hollow out melon and seeds, leaving about a 1/2-in. shell. Cut a decorative edge if desired. Add soup; garnish with a strawberry if desired. **Yield:** 6-8 servings.

BROCCOLI CHEESE SOUP

Carol Miller, Rittman, Ohio

Because I add different-shaped pasta to the soup each time I serve it, this soup always causes lively dinner conversation. My family never knows what kind they'll find—and that makes it extra fun.

1-1/2 cups chopped onion
2 tablespoons butter *or* margarine
6 cups water
6 chicken bouillon cubes
1/4 teaspoon garlic powder
8 ounces uncooked pasta
2 teaspoons salt
2 packages (10 ounces *each*) frozen chopped broccoli
6 cups milk
1 pound process American cheese, cubed

In a 5-qt. kettle, saute onion in butter until tender. Add water, bouillon and garlic powder; bring to a boil. Stir until bouillon is dissolved. Add pasta and salt; cook and stir for 3 minutes. Add broccoli; cook and stir for 3-4 minutes or until pasta is tender. Add milk and cheese; cook and stir over low heat until cheese is melted. **Yield:** 12-16 servings (4 quarts).

WILD WEST CHILI

Frances Hanson, Mills, Wyoming

(Pictured at right)

My sister-in-law, who has cooked for many years at the family ranch, shared this hearty recipe with me. I make it often during the winter—it sure can warm you up after being outside doing chores!

2 bacon strips, diced

1 pound ground beef *or* venison
2 teaspoons chili powder
1-1/2 teaspoons salt
1/4 teaspoon garlic salt
1/4 teaspoon dried oregano
1/8 teaspoon cayenne pepper
3 to 5 drops hot pepper sauce
1 can (14-1/2 ounces) diced tomatoes, undrained
1 cup *each* finely chopped celery, onion and carrots
1/2 cup finely chopped green pepper
1 can (16 ounces) chili beans, undrained

In a large saucepan over medium heat, brown bacon and the beef or venison; drain. Add the seasonings; cook and stir for 5 minutes. Stir in tomatoes, celery, onion, carrots and green pepper; bring to a boil. Reduce heat; cover and simmer for 40 minutes. Stir in beans; cook 30 minutes longer. **Yield:** 6 servings.

WHETHER *they feature meat, pasta, potatoes, vegetables or fruit, salads deliciously top off all of your favorite meals.*

PICK OF THE CROP. Clockwise from top left: Chicken Pasta Salad (p. 57), Sunflower Strawberry Salad (p. 57), Hearty Rice Salad (p. 58) and Tomato Cucumber Salad (p. 57).

Garden-Fresh Salads

CHICKEN PASTA SALAD

Jo Schiff, Weehawken, New Jersey

(Pictured on page 56)

My dad grows incredibly delicious tomatoes and red peppers. I created this combination to take advantage of the bounty from 1 year's especially abundant crop. My husband gave this recipe a "thumbs up".

- 1 package (16 ounces) bow tie *or* corkscrew pasta, cooked and drained
- 3 cups cubed cooked chicken
- 2 tablespoons olive *or* vegetable oil
- 1/4 to 1/2 teaspoon garlic powder
- 1 cup mayonnaise
- 1/2 cup Caesar *or* Parmesan salad dressing
- 1 tablespoon honey mustard *or* other prepared mustard
- 2 to 3 teaspoons curry powder
- 1 teaspoon salt
- 1/4 teaspoon pepper
- 1 sweet red pepper, chopped
- 1 large tomato, chopped
- 1 cup shredded carrot

In a large bowl, toss pasta, chicken, oil and garlic powder. Cover and chill. In a small bowl, combine mayonnaise, salad dressing, mustard, curry powder, salt and pepper; cover and chill. Just before serving, add the red pepper, tomato, carrot and dressing to pasta mixture; gently toss. **Yield:** 8-10 servings.

TOMATO CUCUMBER SALAD

Margery Richmond, Lacombe, Alberta

(Pictured on page 56)

When you need a salad in a snap, nothing can top this recipe. It nicely slices kitchen time without sacrificing quality! I like to make this dish a lot in summer, and my family never complains!

- 3 medium tomatoes, sliced
- 1 small cucumber, thinly sliced
- 1 green onion, chopped
- 3 tablespoons Italian salad dressing
- 1 tablespoon vinegar
- 1 teaspoon chopped fresh basil *or* 1/4 teaspoon dried basil
- 1/4 teaspoon salt
- Pinch pepper
- Pinch garlic salt

In a serving bowl, layer half the tomatoes, all of the cucumber, then remaining tomatoes. Sprinkle with onion. Combine remaining ingredients in a jar with tight-fitting lid; shake well. Pour over salad. Cover and chill for 25 minutes or until ready to serve. **Yield:** 4 servings.

SUNFLOWER STRAWBERRY SALAD

Betty Malone, Humboldt, Tennessee

(Pictured on page 56)

We have an annual Strawberry Festival in our town, so recipes with strawberries are popular here. I've served this salad at luncheons and have always received a lot of compliments. Sunflower seeds add just the right amount of crunch.

✓ This tasty dish uses less sugar, salt and fat. Recipe includes *Diabetic Exchanges*.

- 2 cups sliced fresh strawberries
- 1 medium apple, diced
- 1 cup seedless green grapes, halved
- 1/2 cup thinly sliced celery
- 1/4 cup raisins
- 1/2 cup strawberry yogurt
- 2 tablespoons sunflower seeds
- Lettuce leaves, optional

In a large bowl, combine strawberries, apple, grapes, celery and raisins. Stir in the yogurt. Cover and refrigerate for at least 1 hour. Add sunflower seeds and toss; serve on lettuce leaves if desired. **Yield:** 6 servings. **Diabetic Exchanges:** One 1-cup serving (prepared with sugar-free yogurt and unsalted sunflower seeds) equals 1 fruit, 1 fat; also, 98 calories, 23 mg sodium, 0 cholesterol, 18 gm carbohydrate, 2 gm protein, 3 gm fat.

HEARTY RICE SALAD

Donna Schmuland, Wetaskiwin, Alberta

(Pictured on page 56)

I enjoy experimenting with new recipes, and this is one of my creations. I like to serve this salad as a luncheon or light supper dish, accompanied by cold asparagus and pumpernickel rolls.

    4 cups chicken broth
1-1/2 teaspoons salt
    1/4 teaspoon ground turmeric
    2 cups uncooked long grain rice
    1 cup diced fully cooked ham
    5 to 6 green onions, sliced
    2 medium carrots, shredded
    1/4 cup chopped fresh parsley *or* 1
       tablespoon dried parsley
    1/2 cup fresh *or* frozen peas, thawed
    1 small sweet red pepper, diced
    1 small green pepper, diced
    2 tablespoons chopped fresh basil *or* 2
       teaspoons dried basil
    1/2 cup sliced stuffed olives
    1/4 teaspoon pepper
    1 cup diced Swiss *or* cheddar cheese
    1/3 cup olive *or* vegetable oil
    3 tablespoons white wine vinegar

In a large saucepan, bring broth, salt and turmeric to a boil; stir in the rice. Reduce heat; cover and simmer for 20 minutes. Remove from the heat; let stand, covered, for 5 minutes or until liquid is absorbed. Transfer to a large bowl; cool to room temperature. Stir in the next 11 ingredients. If desired, cover and refrigerate for up to 24 hours. Four hours before serving, combine oil and vinegar; pour over salad and toss well. Serve at room temperature. **Yield:** 10-12 servings.

ZIPPY RADISH SALAD

Carol Stevens, Basye, Virginia

(Pictured above right)

I admit to it—the first time I prepared this salad for my husband, he was skeptical! He loved it, though. Served with a rich entree or hot barbecue, it makes a light and refreshing side dish.

    2 cups thinly sliced radishes
    1/2 cup cubed Swiss cheese
    2 green onions, thinly sliced
    1 garlic clove, minced
    1 tablespoon tarragon vinegar
    1/2 teaspoon Dijon mustard
    1/4 teaspoon salt
    1/8 teaspoon pepper
    3 tablespoons olive *or* vegetable oil
Leaf lettuce

In a bowl, combine radishes, cheese and onions. In a small bowl, combine garlic, vinegar, mustard, salt and pepper; whisk in oil until smooth. Pour over radish mixture; toss to coat. Chill for 2 hours. Serve on a bed of lettuce. **Yield:** 4 servings.

THREE-PEPPER PASTA SALAD

Jan Malone, Arapaho, Oklahoma

(Pictured on cover)

I like to make this recipe during the summer when I can get the ingredients fresh from the garden. It not only tastes very good, but it's a pretty addition to any meal.

    1 package (12 ounces) tricolor spiral pasta
    2/3 cup olive *or* vegetable oil

3 tablespoons red wine vinegar
1/4 cup minced fresh basil *or* 1 tablespoon
    dried basil
2 tablespoons grated Parmesan cheese
1-1/4 teaspoons salt
1/4 teaspoon pepper
1 small sweet red pepper, julienned
1 small yellow pepper, julienned
1 small green pepper, julienned
1 medium tomato, cut into thin wedges
1 can (2-1/4 ounces) sliced ripe olives,
    drained
2 tablespoons sliced green onions
8 ounces mozzarella cheese, cubed

Cook pasta according to package directions. Meanwhile, in a blender or food processor, process the oil, vinegar, basil, Parmesan cheese, salt and pepper until smooth. Drain and rinse pasta; place in a large bowl. Add the peppers, tomato, olives and onions. Add dressing; toss to coat. Add mozzarella and toss. Serve at room temperature. **Yield:** 6-8 servings.

ROAST BEEF PASTA SALAD

Sandy Shields, Mead, Washington

I made this salad one year when a neighbor came over to help my husband put up hay. They both were hot and dusty, so this cool dish was well received. It's a meal in itself.

1 package (16 ounces) spiral pasta
2 cups julienned cooked roast beef
1 cup chopped green pepper
1 cup sliced celery
3/4 cup chopped red onion
1/2 cup chopped sweet red pepper
1/3 cup chopped dill pickle
2 to 3 green onions, sliced
DRESSING:
2 tablespoons beef bouillon granules
1/4 cup boiling water
1/2 cup milk
2 cups mayonnaise
1 cup (8 ounces) sour cream
1 teaspoon dill weed
Dash pepper

Cook the pasta according to package directions; drain and rinse in cold water. Place in a large bowl; add beef, green pepper, celery, onion, red pepper, pickle and green onions. For dressing, dissolve bouillon in water. Add milk, mayonnaise, sour cream, dill and pepper; mix well. Toss with pasta mixture. Cover and refrigerate until ready to serve. **Yield:** 12-16 servings.

BLUEBERRY SPINACH SALAD

Heidi Gilleland, Lees Summit, Missouri

(Pictured below)

I received this recipe from a co-worker's wife and it's become one of my favorites. The addition of blueberries gives this salad a different twist.

1/2 cup vegetable oil
1/4 cup raspberry vinegar
2 teaspoons Dijon mustard
1 teaspoon sugar
1/2 teaspoon salt
1 package (10 ounces) fresh spinach, torn
1 package (4 ounces) blue cheese,
    crumbled
1 cup fresh blueberries
1/2 cup chopped pecans, toasted

In a jar with tight-fitting lid, combine the first five ingredients and shake well. In a large salad bowl, toss the spinach, blue cheese, blueberries and pecans. Add dressing and toss gently; serve immediately. **Yield:** 6-8 servings.

PEACHY CHICKEN SALAD

Toni Crismon, Albany, Georgia

(Pictured below)

With peaches and pecans among the ingredients, I think this recipe definitely reflects my state. My family really enjoys it. Now I'm happy to share the recipe with you!

 1/3 cup mayonnaise
  2 tablespoons milk
 1/2 teaspoon salt
 1/4 teaspoon pepper
 1/4 teaspoon dried tarragon *or* 1 teaspoon
    chopped fresh tarragon
2-1/2 cups cubed cooked chicken
  1 cup seedless red grapes, halved
  1 cup frozen tiny peas, thawed
  2 large peaches, peeled and chopped
  1 cup pecan halves, toasted
Lettuce leaves, optional

In a large bowl, stir the mayonnaise, milk, salt, pepper and tarragon until smooth. Add chicken and toss to coat. Stir in the grapes, peas, peaches and pecans. Serve in a lettuce-lined bowl if desired. **Yield:** 4-6 servings.

ASPARAGUS MUSHROOM SALAD

Patsy Bell Hobson, Liberty, Missouri

Occasionally I'll use toasted walnut halves instead of tomatoes to give this salad some crunch.

  1 pound fresh asparagus
  1 pound fresh mushrooms, sliced 1/4 inch
    thick
  4 tablespoons lemon juice, *divided*
  1 cup whipping cream
 1/2 teaspoon paprika
 1/2 teaspoon salt
 1/4 teaspoon pepper
  1 bunch romaine, torn
Tomato wedges and additional paprika, optional

Cook asparagus in boiling salted water until crisp-tender; drain and rinse in cold water. In a bowl, toss mushrooms with 3 tablespoons of lemon juice. Combine cream, paprika, salt, pepper and remaining lemon juice; whisk until smooth. Pour over mushrooms; toss to coat. Line a large serving platter with romaine. Arrange the asparagus in spoke fashion with stems toward center. Spoon mushrooms into center. If desired, garnish with tomato wedges and paprika. **Yield:** 8-10 servings.

PICNIC PASTA SALAD

Luana Francis, Columbia Station, Ohio

I like recipes that use what we grow. This particular recipe has been handed down in our family for years. I can't go to a picnic without it.

  3 cups tricolor spiral pasta, cooked and
    drained
  1 package (10 ounces) frozen corn,
    thawed
  2 cups cherry tomatoes, halved
  2 small zucchini, sliced
  1 cup small pitted ripe olives
DRESSING:
 1/3 cup tarragon vinegar
 1/2 cup olive *or* vegetable oil
  2 teaspoons dill weed
  1 teaspoon salt

1/2 teaspoon sugar
1/2 teaspoon ground mustard
1/4 teaspoon pepper
1/4 teaspoon garlic powder

In a large bowl, toss pasta, corn, tomatoes, zucchini and olives; set aside. In a jar with tight-fitting lid, combine all of the dressing ingredients; shake well. Pour over salad; toss lightly. Cover and refrigerate for at least 2 hours or overnight. **Yield:** 6-8 servings.

ITALIAN POTATO SALAD

Ardis Kohnen, Rudolph, Wisconsin

With six grown daughters who visit us frequently, I have plenty of chances to serve this family favorite—whether we are making steaks, burgers or bratwurst.

3 pounds potatoes
1/3 cup Italian salad dressing
4 hard-cooked eggs, chopped
3/4 cup chopped celery
1/3 cup chopped onion
1/4 cup chopped cucumber
1/4 cup chopped green pepper
1/2 cup mayonnaise
1/4 cup sour cream
1 teaspoon prepared horseradish
Chopped fresh tomatoes

Place potatoes in a saucepan; cover with water. Bring to a boil and cook until tender; drain and cool. Peel and cube potatoes; place in a large bowl. Add dressing and toss to coat. Cover and chill for 2 hours. Add eggs, celery, onion, cucumber and green pepper; mix well. In a small bowl, combine mayonnaise, sour cream and horseradish; mix well. Pour over potato mixture and toss to coat. Chill for at least 1 hour. Top with tomatoes. **Yield:** 8-10 servings.

HOT GERMAN POTATO SALAD

Inez Senner, Glendive, Montana

(Pictured above right)

I enjoy sharing favorite dishes at church and family potlucks. This one has won raves whenever I've served it. I've also found it makes a good lunch that's better the second time around!

9 medium potatoes
1-1/2 pounds smoked sausage *or* precooked bratwurst
6 bacon strips
3/4 cup chopped onion
2 tablespoons all-purpose flour
1 teaspoon salt
1/2 teaspoon celery seed
1/8 teaspoon pepper
1/4 cup sugar
1-1/3 cups water
2/3 cup cider vinegar

In a saucepan, cook potatoes in boiling salted water until tender. Meanwhile, cut sausage into 1/2-in. slices; saute in a skillet until browned. Drain and place in a large bowl. Drain potatoes; peel and cut into 3/4-in. cubes. Add to sausage; keep warm. Cook bacon until crisp; crumble and set aside. Drain all but 3 tablespoons of drippings; saute onion in drippings until tender. Stir in the flour, salt, celery seed and pepper; blend well. Add sugar, water and vinegar; bring to a boil. Boil for 2 minutes. Pour over potato mixture and stir gently to coat. Sprinkle with bacon. Serve warm. **Yield:** 12-14 servings.

Getting the Most from Tomatoes

● For a quick but attractive salad, place thickly sliced tomatoes on shredded lettuce. Sprinkle with chopped green onions. Border tomato slices with cucumber and radishes. Drizzle with your favorite homemade or bottled salad dressing. *—Edan Havens Wann, Oklahoma*

● To season plain hoagies or hamburgers, marinate tomato slices with Italian or French dressing. Top sandwiches just before serving.
—Nancy Ray, Williamsburg, Pennsylvania

● To preserve fresh garden tomatoes for use in future casseroles and soups, wash and remove stems. Place whole tomatoes in plastic freezer bags in recipe-size quantities. Freeze. After defrosting, skins will easily peel off and the tomatoes can be diced and added to your dishes. *—Bev Graaff Hull, Iowa*

● *Don't* throw out that excess liquid at the bottom of the salsa jar. Instead, add it to ground beef—for hamburgers with extra zip! *—Wendy Nowakowski Rama, Saskatchewan*

● To balance the acid of tomatoes, I add a tablespoon of grape jelly to my spaghetti sauce. *—Shirley Prejean Cut Off, Louisiana*

● When I don't have time to can or freeze tomatoes, I chop or puree them in the blender with the skins on. Then I pour the tomatoes directly into the skillet or kettle with my other ingredients. This saves me time and adds extra nutrition as well. *—Debra Wolf Crawfordsville, Indiana*

● Removing the skins from tomatoes before canning is easy if you dip them in boiling water, then cold water. They slip right off! *—Irene Madden Thayer, Missouri*

● Here's a speedy salad for using up a bounty of garden "cherries": Cut cherry tomatoes in half and arrange in a pretty dish or shallow bowl. Sprinkle with garlic powder, seasoned salt and dried basil. Chill several hours; serve. *—Eulalie Haas Swanton, Ohio*

● As a garnish for my tomato-basil salad, I add edible flowers from my garden. Pansies and nasturtiums are both colorful *and* flavorful.
—Denise Butler Mantua, New Jersey

● Here's a quick way to remove tomato skins: Heat tomatoes, a few at a time, in an uncovered microwave-safe bowl on high power for 30-45 seconds. Let stand 2 minutes and peel.
—Eileen Smith, Sumner, Texas

● If you want a chunky spaghetti sauce, do *not* puree the green peppers, onions or celery in a blender or food mill. Instead, add them directly to the sauce after the tomatoes have started to thicken. Then cook until vegetables are tender. *—Kathi Richards, Dundee, Ohio*

Two-Bean Rice Salad

Lois Kodada, Northfield, Minnesota

(Pictured at right)

I've had many people tell me how much they like this salad. It's a great dish to take to a potluck dinner. I especially appreciate its make-ahead convenience.

✓ This tasty dish uses less sugar, salt and fat. Recipe includes *Diabetic Exchanges*.

- 3 cups cooked wild rice
- 1 can (15 ounces) pinto beans, rinsed and drained
- 1 can (15 ounces) black beans, rinsed and drained
- 1 package (10 ounces) frozen peas, thawed
- 1 cup sliced celery
- 1 medium onion, chopped
- 1 can (4 ounces) chopped green chilies
- 1/4 cup chopped fresh parsley *or* cilantro
- 1/2 cup white wine vinegar
- 1/4 cup olive *or* vegetable oil
- 2 tablespoons water
- 3/4 teaspoon salt, optional
- 1/2 teaspoon garlic powder
- 1/2 teaspoon pepper

In a large salad bowl, combine the rice, beans, peas, celery, onion, chilies and parsley; mix well. Combine the remaining ingredients in a jar with tight-fitting lid; shake well. Pour over rice mixture; toss to coat. Cover and refrigerate for at least 1 hour. **Yield:** 18 servings. **Diabetic Exchanges:** One 1/2-cup serving (prepared without salt) equals 1 starch, 1 fat; also, 117 calories, 308 mg sodium, 0 cholesterol, 18 gm carbohydrate, 5 gm protein, 3 gm fat.

Ruby Slaw

Eunice Juckett Meeker, East Hampton, New York

Red cabbage is one of the crops grown here on Long Island, and this recipe is one of the ways I most like to use it. This salad is a pretty addition to any meal.

- 1 medium head red cabbage (about 1-1/2 pounds)
- 1 medium head green cabbage (about 1-1/2 pounds)
- 5 tablespoons vinegar, *divided*
- 1 medium onion, chopped
- 2 medium red apples, chopped
- 2 tablespoons brown sugar
- 1 tablespoon Dijon mustard
- 1/2 cup sour cream
- 1/2 cup mayonnaise
- 2 tablespoons crumbled blue cheese
- 1 tablespoon chopped fresh *or* dried chives
- 1 tablespoon chopped fresh parsley *or* 1 teaspoon dried parsley flakes
- 1/2 teaspoon salt
- 1/2 teaspoon pepper

Thinly slice or shred cabbage; place in an 8-qt. Dutch oven. Add 2 tablespoons vinegar. Cover and cook over medium heat for 8-10 minutes or until cabbage is crisp-tender, stirring occasionally. Add onion, apples, sugar, mustard and remaining vinegar. Cook, uncovered, for 2-3 minutes. Place mixture in a large bowl; cover and refrigerate for 1 hour or until completely cool. Add remaining ingredients; toss to coat. Cover and refrigerate at least 6 hours. **Yield:** 20-24 servings.

HERBED CHERRY TOMATOES

Dianne Bahn, Yankton, South Dakota

(Pictured below)

My recipe's a good one for when you want a little fancier salad dish but one that's still quick to fix. I find it's especially popular served with grilled steak, baked potatoes and corn on the cob.

1 pint cherry tomatoes, halved
1/4 cup vegetable oil
3 tablespoons vinegar
1/4 cup minced fresh parsley
1-1/2 teaspoons minced fresh basil *or* 1/2 teaspoon dried basil
1-1/2 teaspoons minced fresh oregano *or* 1/2 teaspoon dried oregano

1/2 teaspoon salt
1/2 teaspoon sugar
Leaf lettuce, optional

Place tomatoes in a medium bowl; set aside. In a small bowl, combine oil and vinegar. Add parsley, basil, oregano, salt and sugar; mix well. Pour over the tomatoes. Cover and refrigerate for at least 3 hours. Drain; serve on lettuce if desired. **Yield:** 4-6 servings.

FROZEN FRUIT SALAD

Faye Hintz, Springfield, Missouri

The thought of something chilled was so appealing to me one hot day. So I combined frozen and fresh ingredients. It's a treat we eat often now.

6 large firm bananas, sliced
1/4 cup lemon juice
4 cans (8 ounces *each*) crushed pineapple, undrained
1 package (20 ounces) frozen unsweetened strawberries, thawed
2-1/2 cups water
1 can (12 ounces) frozen orange juice concentrate, thawed
1 cup sugar

In a medium bowl, toss bananas with lemon juice; set aside. In a large bowl, combine remaining ingredients; mix well. Add bananas. Pour into an ungreased 14-cup mold or plastic freezer containers. Freeze for several hours or overnight. Unmold 20 minutes before serving. **Yield:** 12-16 servings.

MARINATED ONION SALAD

Michelle Wrightsman, Linwood, Kansas

Everyone knows how sweet onions flavor all kinds of food. But in this recipe, they take center stage! This salad is a nice addition to any table.

3 medium sweet onions, thinly sliced
4 cups boiling water
4 medium cucumbers, thinly sliced
1 cup (8 ounces) plain yogurt
1 teaspoon lemon juice
1-1/2 teaspoons salt
1/8 teaspoon pepper
Dash Worcestershire sauce
Dash vinegar

1 teaspoon dill weed, optional
2 tablespoons minced fresh parsley

Separate onions into rings and place in a large bowl; pour water over onions. Let stand 1 minute; drain. Add cucumbers. In a small bowl, combine the yogurt, lemon juice, salt, pepper, Worcestershire sauce, vinegar and dill if desired; mix well. Pour over onion mixture; toss to coat. Chill until ready to serve. Sprinkle with parsley. Serve with a slotted spoon. **Yield:** 16-20 servings.

TART CHERRY SALAD

Bea Wittman, Ridgway, Pennsylvania

This recipe has been in my family for years; we especially use it during the holiday season. It's pleasantly tart and a perfect complement to any meal.

    2 cans (16 ounces *each*) tart red cherries
    2 cans (8 ounces *each*) crushed pineapple
    1 cup sugar
    2 packages (6 ounces *each*) cherry gelatin
    3 cups ginger ale
3/4 cup flaked coconut
    1 cup chopped nuts, optional

Drain cherries and pineapple, reserving juices. Set fruit aside. Add enough water to combined juices to make 3-1/4 cups; pour into a saucepan. Add sugar; bring to a boil. Remove from the heat; stir in gelatin until dissolved. Add cherries, pineapple and ginger ale. Chill until partially set. Stir in coconut and nuts if desired. Pour into an oiled 3-qt. mold or 13-in. x 9-in. x 2-in. pan. Chill until firm, about 3 hours. **Yield:** 16-18 servings.

MAKE-AHEAD VEGETABLE MEDLEY

Ramona Hook Wysong, Barlow, Kentucky

(Pictured above right)

I like experimenting with different combinations and this is one of my most popular creations. I make it often for potlucks and seldom is there any left over.

    1 can (16 ounces) kidney beans, rinsed
        and drained
    1 can (15-1/4 ounces) lima beans, rinsed
        and drained
    1 can (15 ounces) garbanzo beans, rinsed
        and drained
    1 can (14-1/2 ounces) wax beans, drained

    1 can (14-1/2 ounces) green beans,
        drained
    1 can (15 ounces) small peas, drained
    1 can (11 ounces) white shoepeg corn,
        drained
1-1/2 cups chopped onion
    1/2 cup chopped green pepper
    1 large cucumber, chopped
    1 jar (2 ounces) diced pimientos, drained
    2 cups cider vinegar
1-1/2 cups sugar
    2/3 cup vegetable oil
    1/2 teaspoon seasoned salt
    1/2 teaspoon pepper
    1/4 teaspoon garlic powder

In a large bowl, combine all of the beans, peas, corn, onion, green pepper, cucumber and pimientos. Combine the remaining ingredients; pour over vegetables and mix well. Cover and refrigerate overnight. **Yield:** 16-18 servings.

IT'S EASY *to enhance any main entree with this chapter's appealing assortment of vegetable, bean, pasta and rice dishes.*

SPECTACULAR SIDE SHOWS. Clockwise from top right: Zesty Grilled Corn (p. 67), Orange Rice Pilaf (p. 67), Root Vegetable Medley (p. 67) and Fried Onion Rings (p. 68).

Vegetables & Side Dishes

ORANGE RICE PILAF

Joyce Sitz, Wichita, Kansas

(Pictured at left)

For a delicious and different way to serve rice, I usually make this recipe whenever I have guests. It makes a fabulous side dish served with any entree.

- 1 cup diced celery
- 3 tablespoons chopped onion
- 1 tablespoon grated orange peel
- 1/4 cup butter *or* margarine
- 1/2 teaspoon salt
- 3 tablespoons orange juice
- 1-1/3 cups water
- 1-1/2 cups uncooked instant rice

In a 3-qt. saucepan, saute celery, onion and orange peel in butter until tender but not brown. Add salt. Combine orange juice and water; add to celery mixture. Bring to a boil. Stir in the rice. Remove from the heat; cover and let stand for 10 minutes. Fluff with a fork. **Yield:** 4-6 servings.

ZESTY GRILLED CORN

Deb McCaffery, Danville, Pennsylvania

(Pictured at left)

This recipe is a definite crowd-pleaser at summer gatherings. It's easy to make the day before and just pop on the grill during the picnic.

- 1/3 cup butter *or* margarine
- 2 tablespoons prepared mustard
- 2 tablespoons prepared horseradish
- 1 teaspoon Worcestershire sauce
- 1/4 to 1/2 teaspoon lemon-pepper seasoning
- 6 ears sweet corn, husked

In a small saucepan, melt butter; add the mustard, horseradish, Worcestershire sauce and lemon-pepper. Place each ear of corn on a 13-in. x 12-in. piece of heavy-duty foil. Drizzle with butter mixture. Fold in edges of foil and seal, leaving space for expansion of steam. Grill over medium heat for 15-20 minutes or until corn is tender. Carefully unwrap foil. **Yield:** 6 servings.

ROOT VEGETABLE MEDLEY

Marilyn Smudzinski, Peru, Illinois

(Pictured at left)

Equally good with pork or beef roast—or with a Thanksgiving turkey—this dish is one my husband requests at least once a month.

✓ This tasty dish uses less sugar, salt and fat. Recipe includes *Diabetic Exchanges*.

- 6 small red potatoes, quartered
- 1 medium rutabaga, peeled and cut into 1-inch cubes
- 1/2 teaspoon salt, optional
- 3 medium carrots, cut into 1/2-inch slices
- 1 medium turnip, peeled and cut into 1-inch cubes
- 1 to 2 medium parsnips, peeled and cut into 1/2-inch slices
- 1 medium onion, cut into eighths

GLAZE:
- 1 tablespoon butter *or* margarine
- 3 tablespoons brown sugar
- 1 teaspoon cornstarch
- 1/4 cup water
- 3 tablespoons lemon juice
- 1/2 teaspoon dill weed
- 1/8 teaspoon pepper
- 1/2 teaspoon salt, optional

Place potatoes and rutabaga in a large saucepan; cover with water. Add salt if desired. Bring to a boil. Reduce heat; cover and simmer for 8 minutes. Add remaining vegetables; return to a boil. Reduce heat; cover and simmer for 10 minutes or until vegetables are tender; drain. For glaze, melt butter in a saucepan; stir in brown sugar and cornstarch. Stir in water, lemon juice, dill, pepper and salt if desired; bring to a boil. Cook and stir for 2 minutes. Pour over vegetables and toss to coat. **Yield:** 8 servings. **Diabetic Exchanges:** One 1-cup serving (prepared with margarine and without salt) equals 1 starch; also, 85 calories, 41 mg sodium, 0 cholesterol, 17 gm carbohydrate, 1 gm protein, 2 gm fat.

stuffing mixture and toss. Spoon over broccoli. Bake, uncovered, at 350° for 25-30 minutes. **Yield:** 6 servings.

FRIED ONION RINGS

Marsha Moore, Poplar Bluff, Missouri

(Pictured on page 66)

Try these as an accompaniment to hamburgers or fried fish, or with steaks on the grill. The recipe's from my mom, and it's one of her most popular.

- 2 large sweet onions
- 1 egg, lightly beaten
- 2/3 cup water
- 1 tablespoon vegetable oil
- 1 teaspoon lemon juice
- 1 cup all-purpose flour
- 1-1/2 teaspoons baking powder
- 1 to 1-1/4 teaspoons salt
- 1/8 to 1/4 teaspoon cayenne pepper
- Vegetable oil for deep-fat frying

Cut onions into 1/2-in. slices; separate into rings. Place in a bowl; cover with ice water and soak for 30 minutes. Meanwhile, combine egg, water, oil and lemon juice in a bowl; mix well. Combine flour, baking powder, salt and cayenne; stir into egg mixture until smooth. Drain onion rings; dip into batter. In an electric skillet or deep-fat fryer, heat 1 in. of oil to 375°. Fry onion rings, a few at a time, for 1 to 1-1/2 minutes per side or until golden brown. Drain on paper towels. **Yield:** 4-6 servings. **Editor's Note:** Onion rings may be kept warm in a 300° oven while frying remainder of batch.

BROCCOLI-HAZELNUT BAKE

Florence Snyder, Hillsboro, Oregon

(Pictured above)

Oregon's fertile Willamette Valley produces a lot of hazelnuts, and this is one of my favorite recipes that calls for them. I love to experiment with recipes, and my vegetable dish is the result of one of my experiments.

- 8 cups chopped fresh broccoli *or* 2 packages (10 ounces *each*) chopped frozen broccoli
- 5 tablespoons butter *or* margarine, *divided*
- 3 tablespoons all-purpose flour
- 1-1/2 cups milk
- 2 teaspoons chicken bouillon granules
- 1 cup herb-seasoned stuffing mix
- 1/4 cup water
- 2/3 cup chopped hazelnuts *or* filberts, toasted

Cook broccoli on the stove or in the microwave until crisp-tender. Meanwhile, in a saucepan over medium heat, melt 3 tablespoons butter. Stir in flour to form a smooth paste. Gradually add milk and bouillon, stirring constantly. Cook and stir until thickened and bubbly; cook and stir 2 minutes more. Drain broccoli; add to sauce and mix well. Pour into a greased 9-in. square baking dish. In a bowl, combine the stuffing mix, water and nuts. Melt the remaining butter; pour over

CRANBERRY-GLAZED BEETS

Louise Piper, Rolfe, Iowa

Why serve ordinary beets when you can dress them up with an extraordinary cranberry glaze? Folks who don't care for beets will find them irresistible.

- 1 can (15 ounces) sliced beets
- 4 teaspoons cornstarch
- 1 tablespoon sugar
- 1 tablespoon white wine vinegar
- 1/8 teaspoon salt
- 1 cup cranberry juice
- 1/3 cup raisins

Drain the beets, reserving 1/4 cup juice; set aside. In a saucepan, combine cornstarch, sugar, vinegar and salt; mix until smooth. Stir in beet juice and cranberry juice; bring to a boil. Cook and stir for 2 minutes or until thickened. Remove from the heat; stir in raisins and let stand for 5 minutes. Add beets; cook over low heat for 2 minutes or until heated through. **Yield:** 4-6 servings.

PARSNIP SAUTE

Janice Van Wassehnova, South Rockwood, Michigan

My family fondly follows the "Eat your veggies" command when this dish appears on the table!

   3 large parsnips, peeled and diced
1/2 cup diced carrot
1/2 cup sliced celery
1/2 cup diced onion
   2 tablespoons butter *or* margarine
3/4 teaspoon salt
1/8 teaspoon pepper

Place parsnips in a saucepan and cover with water. Cook until crisp-tender; drain. Meanwhile, in a skillet over medium heat, saute carrot, celery and onion in butter until crisp-tender, about 6 minutes. Add the parsnips, salt and pepper; cook and stir for 4 minutes or until vegetables are tender. **Yield:** 6 servings.

CREAMY MUSHROOM-POTATO BAKE

Kathy Smith, Granger, Indiana

The day I first made this, we'd invited a bachelor farmer over, and I wanted to fix something hearty. It was a hit instantly. These days, we enjoy it as a change from regular mashed potatoes.

2-1/2 to 3 pounds white potatoes, peeled
   1 medium onion, finely chopped
1/2 pound fresh mushrooms, chopped
   3 tablespoons butter *or* margarine, *divided*
1/2 cup sour cream
1/2 teaspoon salt
1/4 teaspoon pepper
1/4 cup grated Parmesan cheese

Cook potatoes in salted water until tender; drain and mash (do not add butter or milk). In a skillet, saute onion and mushrooms in 2 tablespoons butter for 3-4 minutes or until just tender. Stir into potatoes along with sour cream, salt and pepper. Spoon into a greased 2-qt. baking dish. Sprinkle with cheese; dot with remaining butter. Bake, uncovered, at 400° for 20-25 minutes or until heated through and golden brown. **Yield:** 10 serv-

ings. **Editor's Note:** Potatoes can be prepared the day before and refrigerated overnight. Remove from refrigerator 30 minutes before baking.

GREEN TOMATOES PARMESAN

Clara Mifflin, Creal Springs, Illinois

(Pictured below)

If you follow the recipe directions, you should end up with firm tomatoes. It's been a tried-and-true method for me. They look so pretty and taste so good!

   3 medium green tomatoes, sliced 1/4 inch thick
Salt
1/4 cup cornmeal
1/4 cup grated Parmesan cheese
   2 tablespoons all-purpose flour
3/4 teaspoon garlic salt
1/2 teaspoon dried oregano
1/8 teaspoon pepper
   1 egg, beaten
1/4 cup vegetable oil

Lightly sprinkle tomatoes with salt; drain on paper towels for 30-60 minutes. Meanwhile, combine cornmeal, Parmesan, flour, garlic salt, oregano and pepper in a shallow plate. Dip each tomato slice into egg, then into cornmeal mixture. In a medium skillet, heat oil over medium-high. Fry tomatoes, a few at a time, for 2 minutes per side or until golden brown. Drain on a paper towel-lined wire rack. Serve immediately. **Yield:** 4-6 servings.

Root-Vegetable Secrets That Work

● My husband has to have salt-free foods, so I substitute lemon-pepper seasoning for table salt in many of my potato dishes.

For convenience and to save energy, bake your potato casserole right along with your roast.
—Joyce Gelle
Rice, Minnesota

● To prepare fried parsnips, trim roots and wash; do not peel. Thinly slice and fry in a small amount of oil until tender and well browned. There's no need to season—the sweetness of the parsnips is flavor enough. Serve immediately.
—Donna Christensen
Superior, Nebraska

● For a quick scalloped potato, combine frozen French fries with a homemade cheese sauce and bake until it's bubbly. You'll save all of the time peeling and cutting the potatoes normally takes you!
—Monna Buckley
McKinney, Texas

● The best way I've found to preserve garden-fresh carrots is this: Dig carrots from the ground in fall and wash well. Allow to dry on the counter overnight, then pack in plastic bags and close securely. Store in the refrigerator and enjoy all winter long.
—Susan Gullikson
Gilby, North Dakota

● Freeze your onion bounty! Simply slice or dice onions and bake in a covered casserole at 350° until they're tender, about 20-30 minutes. Cool and pack them in freezer containers in recipe-sized portions. Freeze for up to 6 months. To use, thaw and warm with a little butter until light golden brown—perfect for casseroles, over burgers or in cream gravy.
—Martha Unger
Altona, Manitoba

● One of my favorite methods of fixing sweet potatoes is to treat them like white potatoes. Just wash, prick with a fork and bake at 350° until soft. Simply serve with butter and a little salt for a wholesome addition to a meal.

Since whole sweet potatoes often drip their sticky juices while baking, lay a piece of foil on the rack beneath the potatoes to keep your oven clean.
—Aimee Steffes
Chilton, Wisconsin

● Here's a simple but different way to make mashed potatoes. Cook equal amounts of peeled potatoes and turnips in boiling salted water until tender. Mash as usual with milk or cream and a little butter. Delicious!
—Harriet Bennett
Hodgkins, Illinois

● To make a speedy German-style potato salad, layer sliced cooked potatoes, onion that has been sauteed in bacon drippings and crumbled bacon in a casserole dish. Pour your favorite garlic and herb salad dressing over all and let marinate overnight. Warm in a skillet or in the microwave before serving.
—Maureen Dart, Middletown, New York

SCALLOPED CABBAGE CASSEROLE

Alice Nulle, Woodstock, Illinois

If your children won't eat cabbage, try making this recipe for them (but don't tell them what's in it!).

8 cups thinly sliced cabbage (2 to 2-1/2 pounds)
2 large carrots, shredded
1 medium onion, finely chopped
5 tablespoons butter *or* margarine, *divided*
3 tablespoons all-purpose flour
1/2 teaspoon salt
1/8 teaspoon pepper
1-1/2 cups milk
1-1/2 cups (6 ounces) shredded process American cheese
1/2 cup seasoned dry bread crumbs
1 teaspoon dried marjoram
1 teaspoon dried thyme

Cook the cabbage and carrots in boiling salted water until crisp-tender. Meanwhile, in a saucepan, saute the onion in 3 tablespoons of butter until tender. Stir in flour, salt and pepper; cook until bubbly. Gradually add milk; cook and stir until thickened. Drain cabbage and carrots; place half in a greased 2-1/2-qt. baking dish. Top with half of the sauce; sprinkle with half of the cheese. Repeat layers. In a small skillet, melt remaining butter. Add crumbs, marjoram and thyme; cook and stir until lightly browned. Sprinkle over casserole. Bake, uncovered, at 350° for 30-35 minutes or until the cabbage is tender and the top is browned. **Yield:** 8-10 servings.

CHILI CHEESE GRITS

Martha Lee, Foley, Alabama

This zesty dish is a real crowd-pleaser. It's great as a side dish and can also be served as a cold appetizer.

3 cups water
1 teaspoon salt
1 garlic clove, minced
1 cup quick-cooking grits
1/2 cup butter *or* margarine
1-1/2 cups (6 ounces) shredded cheddar cheese, *divided*
3 tablespoons canned chopped green chilies
2 eggs
1/2 cup milk

In a medium saucepan, bring water, salt and garlic to a boil; slowly stir in grits. Reduce heat; cook and stir for 3-5 minutes or until thickened. Remove from the heat. Add butter, 1 cup cheese and

chilies; stir until butter melts. Beat eggs and milk; add to the grits and mix well. Pour into a greased 2-qt. baking dish. Bake, uncovered, at 350° for 45 minutes. Sprinkle with remaining cheese. **Yield:** 6 servings.

ZUCCHINI-GARLIC PASTA

Shelley Smail, Chico, California

(Pictured below)

My Italian neighbor gave me the ingredients for this salad, but he didn't have the measurements written down. I experimented and came up with this recipe.

1 package (16 ounces) wagon wheel pasta *or* other specialty shape pasta
1/2 pound sliced bacon, diced
1 medium onion, chopped
4 to 6 garlic cloves, minced
2 to 3 medium zucchini (about 1-1/2 pounds), halved and sliced
1/2 teaspoon salt
3 tablespoons lemon juice
1/4 cup grated Romano *or* Parmesan cheese

Cook pasta according to package directions. Meanwhile, in a large skillet over medium heat, cook bacon until crisp. Remove with a slotted spoon and set aside to drain; discard all but 2 tablespoons of drippings. Saute onion and garlic in drippings until tender, about 3 minutes. Add the zucchini and salt; cook until tender, about 6 minutes. Drain pasta and add to the zucchini mixture. Add lemon juice and bacon; toss. Transfer to a serving bowl or platter; sprinkle with cheese. **Yield:** 6-8 servings.

TWICE-BAKED SWEET POTATOES

Miriam Christophel, Battle Creek, Michigan

(Pictured below)

When I prepare these sweet potatoes, I like to serve them with ham. Those two different tastes always team really well.

 6 large sweet potatoes (3-1/2 to 4 pounds)
1/4 cup orange juice
 6 tablespoons cold butter *or* margarine, divided
1/4 cup all-purpose flour
1/4 cup packed brown sugar
1/4 teaspoon ground cinnamon
1/4 teaspoon ground ginger
1/8 teaspoon ground mace
1/4 cup chopped pecans

Pierce potatoes with a fork. Bake at 375° for 40-60 minutes or until tender. Allow potatoes to cool to the touch. Cut them in half lengthwise; carefully scoop out pulp, leaving a 1/4-in. shell. Place pulp in a large bowl. Add orange juice. Melt 3 tablespoons butter; add to pulp and beat until smooth. Stuff the potato shells; place in an ungreased 15-in. x 10-in. x 1-in. baking pan. In a small bowl, combine flour, brown sugar, cinnamon, ginger and mace. Cut in remaining butter until crumbly. Stir in pecans. Sprinkle over potatoes. Bake at 350° for 20-25 minutes or until golden and heated through. **Yield:** 12 servings.

SPICED BAKED BEETS

Margery Richmond, Lacombe, Alberta

Especially during fall and winter, this recipe is a favorite. With its red color, it looks great served at Christmastime. It's nice for taking to potlucks as well.

✓ This tasty dish uses less sugar, salt and fat. Recipe includes *Diabetic Exchanges.*

 4 cups shredded peeled beets
  (about 4 to 5 medium)
 1 medium onion, shredded
 1 medium potato, shredded
 3 tablespoons brown sugar
 3 tablespoons vegetable oil
 2 tablespoons water
 1 tablespoon vinegar
1/2 teaspoon salt, optional
1/4 teaspoon pepper
1/4 teaspoon celery seed
1/8 to 1/4 teaspoon ground cloves

In a large bowl, combine beets, onion and potato; set aside. In a small bowl, combine brown sugar, oil, water, vinegar and seasonings. Pour over vegetables; toss to coat. Pour into a greased 1-1/2-

qt. baking dish. Cover and bake at 350° for 45 minutes, stirring occasionally. Uncover and bake 15-25 minutes longer or until vegetables are tender. **Yield:** 8-10 servings. **Diabetic Exchanges:** One 1/2-cup serving (prepared without salt) equals 1 vegetable, 1/2 starch, 1/2 fat; also, 84 calories, 42 mg sodium, 0 cholesterol, 12 gm carbohydrate, 1 gm protein, 4 gm fat.

ONION POTATO PIE

Gwyn Frasco, Walla Walla, Washington

(Pictured at right)

I found the basic potato pie recipe in a cookbook and added the sweet onions, for which our area is famous. I've used this recipe for brunches and as a side dish for a main meal.

- **8 cups frozen shredded hash brown potatoes, thawed**
- **6 tablespoons butter *or* margarine, *divided***
- **3/4 teaspoon salt, *divided***
- **1 cup diced sweet onion**
- **1/4 cup chopped sweet red pepper**
- **1 cup (4 ounces) shredded cheddar cheese**
- **3 eggs, lightly beaten**
- **1/3 cup milk**

Gently squeeze potatoes to remove excess water. Melt 5 tablespoons butter; add to potatoes along with 1/2 teaspoon salt. Press in bottom and up sides of a greased 9-in. pie plate to form a crust. Bake at 425° for 25-30 minutes or until edges are browned. Cool to room temperature. In a saucepan over medium heat, saute the onion and red pepper in remaining butter until tender, about 6-8 minutes. Spoon into crust; sprinkle with cheese. Combine the eggs, milk and remaining salt; pour over onion mixture. Bake at 350° for 20-25 minutes or until a knife inserted near the center comes out clean. Let stand 5 minutes before serving. **Yield:** 6-8 servings.

CARROT-APPLE SIDE DISH

Martina Knowles, Grand Forks, North Dakota

Whenever this dish makes an appearance at a family gathering or church potluck, folks always comment on the interesting combination of carrots and apple. Then they ask for the recipe!

1-1/2 cups diced carrots (about 6 medium)
2 cups water

- **1 tablespoon butter *or* margarine**
- **1/4 cup packed brown sugar**
- **1 tablespoon lemon juice**
- **1/8 teaspoon ground cinnamon**
- **1 cup diced peeled apple**
- **1 tablespoon cornstarch**
- **2 tablespoons cold water**

In a saucepan, cook carrots in water until crisp-tender; drain. Add butter, brown sugar, lemon juice and cinnamon; mix well. Stir in apple. Cover and simmer for 10 minutes, stirring occasionally. Combine cornstarch and cold water; stir into carrot mixture. Bring to a boil; cook and stir for 1 minute or until thickened. Simmer, uncovered, for 2 minutes or until glazed, stirring constantly. **Yield:** 4 servings.

baking dish. Sprinkle with croutons. Melt remaining butter; drizzle over croutons. Bake, uncovered, at 350° for 20-25 minutes. **Yield:** 10-12 servings.

ROASTED ROOT VEGGIES

Rebecca Dornfeld, Grass Lake, Michigan

Baking root vegetables in the oven instead of steaming them in the microwave makes them especially tender. Plus, they give my house a wonderful aroma.

✓ This tasty dish uses less sugar, salt and fat. Recipe includes *Diabetic Exchanges*.

  3 large red potatoes, cut into 1-inch cubes
  1 large red onion, cut into wedges
  2 medium turnips, peeled and quartered
  5 medium carrots, halved and quartered
  2 medium parsnips, peeled and cut into
    1/4-inch strips
  1 small rutabaga, peeled and cut into
    3/4-inch cubes
  2 tablespoons vegetable oil
  1 teaspoon dried thyme
1/8 teaspoon pepper

Toss all of the ingredients in a large bowl; transfer to a 15-in. x 10-in. x 1-in. baking pan that has been coated with nonstick cooking spray. Bake, uncovered, at 375° for 1 to 1-1/2 hours or until vegetables are tender, stirring frequently. **Yield:** 15 servings. **Diabetic Exchanges:** One 1-cup serving equals 1/2 starch, 1/2 fat; also, 54 calories, 24 mg sodium, 0 cholesterol, 9 gm carbohydrate, 1 gm protein, 2 gm fat.

BARBECUED BUTTER BEANS

Mrs. W.L. Doolittle, Crossville, Tennessee

These are a proven crowd-pleaser. The secret's in the seasoning and in the butter beans you use. They're a nice change from usual baked beans.

  3 cans (15 ounces *each*) butter beans,
    rinsed and drained
  1 can (15 ounces) lima beans, rinsed and
    drained
1/2 cup ketchup
1/2 cup beef broth
1/2 cup packed brown sugar
  3 tablespoons vegetable oil
  2 tablespoons chopped onion
  1 tablespoon dried parsley flakes
Dash liquid smoke, optional

CARROT CASSEROLE

Lois Hagen, Stevens Point, Wisconsin

(Pictured above)

Each time I make this dish, people rave about how good it is. One friend told me, "I don't usually eat carrots, but this is delicious!" That made my day.

  8 cups sliced carrots
  2 medium onions, sliced
  5 tablespoons butter *or* margarine, *divided*
  1 can (10-3/4 ounces) condensed cream of
    celery soup, undiluted
1/2 teaspoon salt
1/4 teaspoon pepper
  1 cup (4 ounces) shredded cheddar cheese
  1 cup seasoned croutons

Place carrots in a saucepan and cover with water; bring to a boil. Cook until crisp-tender. Meanwhile, in a skillet, saute onions in 3 tablespoons butter until tender. Stir in the soup, salt, pepper and cheese. Drain carrots; add to the onion mixture. Pour into a greased 13-in. x 9-in. x 2-in.

Combine all ingredients. Pour into an ungreased 2-qt. baking dish. Bake, uncovered, at 375° for 1 hour or until bubbly. **Yield:** 10 servings.

CREAMED ASPARAGUS AND TOMATO

Phyllis Clinehens, Maplewood, Ohio

Sometimes I just don't have the time to prepare an authentic cream sauce for asparagus. That's when this recipe comes in handy.

> 2 pounds fresh asparagus spears, trimmed
> 1/3 cup mayonnaise *or* salad dressing
> 1-1/4 teaspoons lemon juice
> 1/4 teaspoon salt
> Pinch pepper
> 1 medium tomato, peeled, diced and drained

Cook the asparagus in boiling salted water until tender, about 10 minutes. Meanwhile, in a small saucepan over low heat, combine mayonnaise, lemon juice, salt and pepper; heat through. Stir in tomato and remove from the heat. Drain the asparagus and place in a serving dish; top with tomato mixture. **Yield:** 6-8 servings.

POTATO CHEESE CASSEROLE

Maryann Sanregret, Nevada City, California

(Pictured at right)

My sister shared this recipe with me. The combination of cheeses is wonderful. It's a side dish that will dress up any dinner and one of my favorites to serve family and friends.

> 6 large red potatoes (about 2-1/2 pounds), peeled and cut into 3/4-inch cubes
> 2 cups cubed mozzarella cheese
> 1 carton (15 ounces) ricotta cheese
> 1 cup grated Romano cheese
> 1 cup (8 ounces) sour cream
> 1/4 cup finely chopped green onions
> 3 tablespoons chopped fresh parsley
> 1 teaspoon dried basil
> 1 garlic clove, minced
> 1 teaspoon salt
> 1/4 teaspoon pepper
> 1-1/2 cups (6 ounces) shredded Swiss cheese, divided
> 1/2 cup shredded cheddar cheese
> 1/4 teaspoon paprika

Cook potatoes in boiling salted water for 8-10 minutes or until tender; drain and set aside. In a large bowl, combine the next 10 ingredients and 1 cup of Swiss cheese; mix well. Fold in the potatoes. Spoon into a greased 13-in. x 9-in. x 2-in. baking dish. Bake, uncovered, at 350° for 30-35 minutes or until bubbly and lightly brown. Top with cheddar and remaining Swiss; sprinkle with paprika. Let stand 5 minutes. **Yield:** 10-12 servings. **Editor's Note:** Fat-free and imitation sour cream and cheese products are not recommended for this recipe.

IT'S OFTEN SAID that "man cannot live by bread alone". But your family might be tempted to test that truism when you begin baking up these oven-fresh goodies!

BEST BREADS. Clockwise from top left: Christmas Bread (p. 77), Three-Day Yeast Rolls (p. 77), Caramel Pecan Rolls (p. 78) and Cranberry Eggnog Braid (p. 78).

Breads & Rolls

CHRISTMAS BREAD

Betty Jean McLaughlin, La Vista, Nebraska

(Pictured at left)

Some of my friends prefer this slightly sweet bread to fruitcake. My family enjoys it at Christmastime.

1 package (1/4 ounce) active dry yeast
3/4 cup warm water (110° to 115°)
3/4 cup evaporated milk
1/3 cup sugar
1/3 cup shortening
1/2 teaspoon salt
2 eggs
4 to 4-1/2 cups all-purpose flour, *divided*
1 cup chopped mixed candied fruit
1 cup confectioners' sugar
1 to 2 tablespoons milk
1/4 teaspoon vanilla extract
Additional candied fruit, optional

In a mixing bowl, dissolve yeast in water. Add evaporated milk, sugar, shortening, salt, eggs and 2 cups of flour; beat until smooth. Stir in fruit and enough remaining flour to form a soft dough (do not knead). Place in a greased bowl. Cover and let rise in a warm place until doubled, about 1-1/4 hours. Punch dough down. Turn onto a floured surface; knead 3-4 minutes. Pat evenly into a greased 10-in. tube pan. Cover and let rise in a warm place until nearly doubled, about 45 minutes. Bake at 375° for 30-35 minutes or until golden brown. Remove from pan to cool on a wire rack. Combine confectioners' sugar, milk and vanilla; drizzle over bread. Garnish with candied fruit if desired. **Yield:** 1 loaf.

THREE-DAY YEAST ROLLS

Kelly Hardgrave, Hartman, Arkansas

(Pictured at left)

These rolls are excellent for any time you have a special occasion to celebrate. I especially like them because I can prepare the batter days in advance.

2 packages (1/4 ounce *each*) active dry yeast
2 cups warm water (110° to 115°), *divided*
1 cup butter *or* margarine, softened
3/4 cup sugar
2 eggs
2 teaspoons salt
7-1/2 to 8 cups all-purpose flour
Additional butter, melted, optional

In a mixing bowl, dissolve yeast in 1/4 cup water. Add butter, sugar, eggs, salt and remaining water; mix well. Add 2 cups flour; beat until smooth. Gradually stir in enough remaining flour to form a soft dough (do not knead). Place in a greased bowl. Cover and refrigerate for up to 3 days. When ready to use, turn out onto a floured board; knead until smooth and elastic, about 6-8 minutes. Shape into rolls as desired. Place in greased muffin cups or on baking sheets. Cover and let rise until nearly doubled, about 1 hour. Bake at 375° for 10-15 minutes or until golden brown. Brush with butter if desired. Immediately remove to wire racks to cool. **Yield:** 3-4 dozen.

BREAKFAST SCONES

Kate Carpenter, Callahan, Florida

(Pictured on page 128)

Don't let the name of these scones fool you...they're great to serve around the clock.

2 cups all-purpose flour
1 cup whole wheat flour
1/2 cup packed brown sugar
1 tablespoon baking powder
1/2 teaspoon baking soda
3/4 cup butter *or* margarine
1 cup buttermilk

In a bowl, combine flours, brown sugar, baking powder and baking soda. Cut in butter until mixture resembles coarse crumbs. Stir in buttermilk until a soft dough forms. Turn onto a lightly floured board and knead gently 10-12 times or until no longer sticky. Divide dough in half; gently pat or roll each half into an 8-in. circle 1/2 in. thick. Cut each circle into eight wedges. Separate wedges and place on an ungreased baking sheet. Bake at 400° for 15-18 minutes. **Yield:** 16 scones.

SOFT AND SWEET, Caramel Pecan Rolls from Carolyn Buschkamp will evoke lip-smacking smiles from all.

"These rolls rise nice and high and hold their shape. And the gooey caramel sauce is scrumptious," assures this Emmetsburg, Iowa cook.

CARAMEL PECAN ROLLS

(Pictured on page 76)

2 cups milk
1/2 cup water
1/2 cup sugar
1/2 cup butter *or* margarine
1/3 cup cornmeal
2 teaspoons salt
7 to 7-1/2 cups all-purpose flour, *divided*
2 packages (1/4 ounce *each*) active dry yeast
2 eggs

TOPPING:
2 cups packed brown sugar
1/2 cup butter *or* margarine
1/2 cup milk
1/2 to 1 cup chopped pecans
FILLING:
1/4 cup butter *or* margarine, softened
1/2 cup sugar
2 teaspoons ground cinnamon

In a saucepan, combine the first six ingredients; bring to a boil, stirring frequently. Set aside to cool to 120°-130°. In a mixing bowl, combine 2 cups flour and yeast. Add cooled cornmeal mixture; beat on low until smooth. Add eggs and 1 cup of flour; mix for 1 minute. Stir in enough remaining flour to form a soft dough. Turn onto a floured board; knead until smooth and elastic, about 6-8 minutes. Place in a greased bowl, turning once to grease top. Cover and let rise in a warm place until doubled, about 1 hour. Combine the first three topping ingredients in a saucepan; bring to a boil, stirring occasionally. Pour into two greased 13-in. x 9-in. x 2-in. baking pans. Sprinkle with pecans; set aside. Punch dough down; divide in half. Roll each into a 12-in. x 15-in. rectangle; spread with butter. Combine sugar and cinnamon; sprinkle over butter. Roll up dough from one long side; pinch seams and turn ends under. Cut each roll into 12 slices. Place 12 slices, cut side down, in each baking pan. Cover and let rise in a warm place until nearly doubled, about 30 minutes. Bake at 375° for 20-25 minutes or until golden brown. Let cool 1 minute; invert onto a serving platter. **Yield:** 2 dozen.

CRANBERRY EGGNOG BRAID

Mary Lindow, Florence, Wisconsin

(Pictured on page 76)

Whether at Thanksgiving, Christmas or New Year's, this is a good party bread.

3 to 3-1/2 cups all-purpose flour, *divided*
1/4 cup sugar
1/2 teaspoon salt
1 package (1/4 ounce) active dry yeast
1/2 teaspoon ground nutmeg
1-1/4 cups eggnog
1/4 cup butter *or* margarine
1/2 cup dried cranberries
GLAZE:
1 cup confectioners' sugar
1 to 2 tablespoons eggnog*
1/4 teaspoon vanilla extract
Dash nutmeg

In a mixing bowl, combine 1-1/2 cups of flour, sugar, salt, yeast and nutmeg; set aside. In a saucepan, heat eggnog and butter to 120°-130° (the butter does not need to melt); add to flour mixture. Beat on low until moistened; beat on medium for 3 minutes. Stir in cranberries and enough remaining flour to make a soft dough. Turn onto a floured surface; knead until smooth and elastic, about 6-8 minutes. Place in a greased bowl, turning once to grease top. Cover and let rise in a warm place until doubled, about 1 hour. Punch dough down; divide into thirds. Shape each third into a 16-in. rope. Braid ropes on a greased baking sheet; seal ends. Cover and let rise until nearly doubled, about 30 minutes. Bake at 350° for 25-30 minutes or until golden. Immediately remove from pan to a wire rack to cool completely. Combine the first three glaze ingredients; drizzle over braid. Dust with nutmeg. **Yield:** 1 loaf. *Ed- itor's Note:** This recipe was tested with commercially prepared eggnog.

PUMPKIN BREAD

Dorothy Schumacher, Barnesville, Ohio

Every autumn, our farm becomes a large-scale operation when we harvest our pumpkins. Then we reap our rewards in recipes like this.

- 3 cups sugar
- 1-3/4 cups canned or cooked pumpkin
- 1 cup vegetable oil
- 4 eggs
- 2/3 cup cold water
- 3-1/2 cups all-purpose flour
- 2 teaspoons baking soda
- 1-1/2 teaspoons salt
- 1-1/2 teaspoons ground cinnamon
- 1 teaspoon ground nutmeg

In a mixing bowl, beat the sugar, pumpkin, oil, eggs and water until well mixed. Combine remaining ingredients; gradually add to pumpkin mixture and mix well. Pour into two greased 8-in. x 4-in. x 2-in. loaf pans. Bake at 325° for 75-80 minutes or until bread tests done. Cool in pans for 10 minutes before removing to a wire rack. **Yield:** 2 loaves.

OVERNIGHT FRENCH TOAST

Sue Marsteller, Gouldsboro, Pennsylvania

(Pictured below right)

This is a great dish to make ahead of time and refrigerate; then you'll have a fancy but easy-to-prepare breakfast to offer your overnight guests.

- 9 eggs
- 3 cups half-and-half cream
- 1/3 cup sugar
- 1-1/2 teaspoons rum extract, optional
- 1-1/2 teaspoons vanilla extract
- 1/2 teaspoon ground nutmeg
- 24 to 30 slices French bread (3/4 inch thick)

PRALINE SYRUP:
- 1-1/2 cups packed brown sugar
- 1/2 cup light corn syrup
- 1/2 cup water
- 1/2 cup chopped pecans, toasted
- 2 tablespoons butter *or* margarine

In a large bowl, lightly beat eggs. Mix in cream, sugar, rum extract if desired, vanilla and nutmeg. Place the bread in a single layer in two well-greased 15-in. x 10-in. x 1-in. baking pans. Pour the egg mixture over bread in each pan. Turn bread over to coat both sides. Cover and refrigerate overnight. Bake, uncovered, at 400° for 20-22 minutes or until golden. Meanwhile, for syrup, bring brown sugar, corn syrup and water to a boil in a saucepan. Re-

duce heat and simmer for 3 minutes. Add pecans and butter; simmer 2 minutes longer. Serve with the French toast. **Yield:** 10-12 servings.

LEMON TEA CAKES

Suzanne McKinley, Lyons, Georgia

These mini-muffins may be bite-size, but they're packed with a slightly sweet lemon taste.

- 1/2 cup butter *or* margarine, softened
- 1/2 cup sugar
- 2 eggs
- 3 tablespoons lemon juice
- 1 tablespoon grated lemon peel
- 1 cup all-purpose flour
- 1 teaspoon baking powder
- 1/8 teaspoon salt

TOPPING:
- 2 tablespoons sugar
- 1/4 teaspoon ground cinnamon

In a large mixing bowl, cream butter and sugar. Add eggs, one at a time, beating well after each addition. Beat in lemon juice and peel. Combine flour, baking powder and salt; add to creamed mixture just until moistened. Fill greased or paper-lined mini-muffin cups two-thirds full. Combine sugar and cinnamon; sprinkle on top. Bake at 375° for 12-15 minutes or until the top springs back when touched lightly. Cool in pan 10 minutes before removing to a wire rack. **Yield:** about 2-1/2 dozen.

Tips for Baking Best Bread

• I decorate my Christmas yeast coffee cakes by brushing them before baking with a lightly beaten egg white... then sprinkling with slivered almonds and white or colored sugar.
—*Janice Mathews, St. Joseph, Michigan*

• Quick breads will slice better if you prepare them a day ahead of serving, then wrap tightly and refrigerate. You'll love the rich flavor, moist texture *and* perfect slices!
—*Cathy Burgdoerfer*
Connersville, Indiana

• Dough will rise better if it is kept out of drafts. I like to set my dough bowl over the pilot lights on my stove and cover it with a towel.
Be sure to let your dough "rest" a few minutes before rolling it out to shape it—it will be less elastic and easier to handle.
You'll know bread is baked perfectly if it sounds hollow when you tap it with your fingers. —*Arlene Bontrager*
Haven, Kansas

• If you want your bread to have a crisp crust, brush the unbaked loaf with a lightly beaten egg white. For a soft crust, brush the baked loaf with melted butter when you remove it from the oven. —*Mrs. David Yarnell*
Homer City, Pennsylvania

• For an easy-to-prepare (and easy-to-spread) spread for quick breads or for muffins, combine softened cream cheese, a small can of drained crushed pineapple, 3/4 cup chopped walnuts and a little milk or pineapple juice.
—*Dorothy Jasper*
Washington, Missouri

• During the holidays, I often shape my favorite cinnamon rolls into a festive tree or wreath. Then I tint the icing and top with candied red and green cherries.
I put foil over heavy cardboard and place my fancy breads on it to give as gifts. All I have to do is cover the bread with plastic wrap or slip it into a plastic bag and tie with a pretty bow. Some breads will even freeze well wrapped this way!
—*Judi Haydu*
Bloomington, Illinois

• My pumpkin quick bread is even more delicious when I add butterscotch chips to the batter instead of raisins.
—*Star Strahle*
Copperopolis, California

• Turn your basic recipe for two or three loaves of whole wheat bread into one for herb bread by adding 1/4 teaspoon *each* marjoram, thyme, oregano and garlic powder and 1 tablespoon grated onion. Mix into the warm water or milk before adding the flour.
—*Vera Chalfant, Parker City, Indiana*

PUMPKIN SPICE BREAD

Delora Lucas, Belle, West Virginia

(Pictured at right)

This recipe is at least 40 years old. It makes a very moist bread. It's been described as tasting like pumpkin pie without the crust.

  3 cups sugar
  1 cup vegetable oil
  4 eggs, lightly beaten
  1 can (16 ounces) solid-pack pumpkin
3-1/2 cups all-purpose flour
  2 teaspoons baking soda
  1 teaspoon baking powder
  1 teaspoon salt
  1 teaspoon ground cinnamon
  1 teaspoon ground nutmeg
  1/2 teaspoon ground cloves
  1/2 teaspoon ground allspice
  1/2 cup water

In a large bowl, combine sugar, oil and eggs. Add pumpkin and mix well. Combine dry ingredients; add to the pumpkin mixture alternately with water. Pour into two greased 9-in. x 5-in. x 3-in. loaf pans. Bake at 350° for 60-70 minutes or until bread tests done. Cool in pans 10 minutes before removing to a wire rack; cool completely. **Yield:** 2 loaves.

A-TO-Z BREAD

Marcelle Okawa, Carson City, Nevada

When I tell my family I'm making this bread, they never know what the first bite will be like! That's because I add whatever ingredients I have on hand. The results are delicious every time.

  2 cups sugar
  1 cup vegetable oil
  3 eggs, lightly beaten
  2 cups A-to-Z ingredients (choose from
    list below)
  1 tablespoon vanilla extract
  3 cups all-purpose flour
  2 teaspoons ground cinnamon
  1 teaspoon baking powder
  1 teaspoon baking soda
  1 teaspoon salt
  1 cup chopped walnuts

A-TO-Z INGREDIENTS:
Apples, peeled and shredded
Applesauce
Apricots (dried), chopped
Banana, mashed
Carrots, shredded
Coconut
Dates, pitted and chopped
Figs (dried), chopped
Grapes (seedless), chopped
Oranges, peeled and chopped
Peaches, peeled and chopped
Pears, peeled and chopped
Pineapple (canned), crushed and drained
Prunes, pitted and chopped
Pumpkin, canned
Raisins
Raspberries, unsweetened fresh *or* frozen
Rhubarb, chopped fresh *or* frozen
Strawberries, fresh *or* frozen
Sweet potatoes, cooked and mashed
Zucchini, peeled and grated

In a mixing bowl, combine the sugar, oil and eggs; mix well. Stir in A-to-Z ingredients of your choice and vanilla. Combine flour, cinnamon, baking powder, baking soda and salt; stir into liquid ingredients just until moistened. Stir in nuts. Pour into two greased 8-in. x 4-in. x 2-in. loaf pans. Bake at 325° for 55-65 minutes or until a wooden pick inserted near the center comes out clean. Cool in pan 10 minutes before removing to a wire rack. **Yield:** 2 loaves.

French Crescent Rolls

Betty Ann Wolery, Joplin, Montana

(Pictured on page 85)

Whenever we have rolls and coffee after church, these come along with me.

  1 package (1/4 ounce) active dry yeast
1/4 cup warm water (110° to 115°)
3/4 cup warm milk (110° to 115°)
  1 egg
  2 tablespoons sugar
  1 tablespoon shortening
  1 teaspoon salt
2-1/2 cups all-purpose flour
  3 tablespoons butter *or* margarine, softened, *divided*
ICING:
1-1/2 cups confectioners' sugar
  2 tablespoons milk
  3 tablespoons butter *or* margarine
1/2 teaspoon almond extract
1/2 teaspoon vanilla extract
1/2 cup chopped walnuts

In a mixing bowl, dissolve yeast in water. Add milk, egg, sugar, shortening and salt; mix well. Add flour; mix until smooth. Place in a greased bowl, turning once to grease top. Cover and chill for at least 1 hour. On a floured surface, roll dough to 1/4-in. thickness. Spread with 1 tablespoon softened butter. Fold corners to the middle and then fold in half. Wrap dough in waxed paper; chill for 30 minutes. Repeat rolling, buttering, folding and chilling steps twice. Divide dough in half. On a floured surface, roll each into an 11-in. circle, 1/8 in. thick. Cut each circle into eight wedges; roll up from wide edge to tip of dough and pinch to seal. Place rolls, tip down, on greased baking sheets and curve to form crescent. Cover and let rise in a warm place until doubled, about 30 minutes. Bake at 400° for 10 minutes or until lightly browned. For icing, combine sugar, milk, butter and extracts; spread over warm rolls. Sprinkle with nuts. **Yield:** 16 rolls.

Festive Fruited Scones

Helen Carpenter, Marble Falls, Texas

(Pictured on page 85)

I've found you don't need to put butter on these scones...they're delicious plain and simple. I especially enjoy them in the wintertime with coffee or tea.

  2 cups all-purpose flour
  1 tablespoon sugar
  1 tablespoon baking powder
1/4 teaspoon baking soda
1/4 teaspoon salt
  3 tablespoons cold butter *or* margarine
1/2 cup diced dried fruit (apricots, apples *or* prunes)
1/2 teaspoon grated orange peel
3/4 cup buttermilk
  1 tablespoon milk
Additional sugar

In a bowl, combine flour, sugar, baking powder, baking soda and salt. Cut in butter until the mixture resembles fine crumbs. Add fruit and orange peel. Stir in buttermilk until a soft dough forms. Turn onto a floured board; knead gently for 2-3 minutes. Shape into a ball. Roll into a 7-in. circle. Cut into 10 wedges; place on a greased baking sheet. Brush with milk and sprinkle with sugar. Bake at 425° for 12-15 minutes or until lightly browned. Serve warm. **Yield:** 10 scones.

Cherry Apricot Tea Bread

Patty Bourne, Owings, Maryland

(Pictured on page 85)

This recipe makes three loaves of delicious bread. My family enjoys one loaf right away, then I give one loaf to a family member or friend and freeze the other to enjoy later.

FILLING:
  1 package (8 ounces) dried apricots, chopped
  2 cups boiling water
  1 jar (16 ounces) maraschino cherries, drained and chopped
BREAD:
  2 packages (1/4 ounce *each*) active dry yeast
1/2 cup warm water (110° to 115°)
  2 cups (16 ounces) sour cream
1/3 cup sugar
1-1/2 teaspoons salt
1/4 cup butter *or* margarine, melted
  2 eggs
6-1/2 to 7 cups all-purpose flour
GLAZE:
  1 cup confectioners' sugar
  1 tablespoon milk
Additional maraschino cherries and dried apricots, optional

In a small bowl, combine apricots and water; let stand for 1 hour. Drain. Add cherries; set aside. In a mixing bowl, dissolve yeast in water; let stand for 5 minutes. Add sour cream, sugar, salt, butter, eggs and 2 cups flour; beat until smooth. Stir in enough remaining flour to form a soft dough. Turn onto a floured board; knead until smooth and elastic, about 6-8 minutes. Place in a greased bowl, turning once to grease top. Cover and let rise in a warm place until doubled, about 1 hour. Punch dough down; divide into thirds. On a floured board, roll each third into a 15-in. x 6-in. rectangle. Place each on a greased baking sheet. Spoon a third of the filling down the center of each rectangle. On each long side, cut 1-in.-wide strips 2 in. into the center. Starting at one end, fold alternating strips at an angle across filling. Seal end. Cover and let rise until almost doubled, about 30 minutes. Bake at 375° for 15-20 minutes or until golden brown. Cover with foil if browning too fast. Cool. Combine sugar and milk; drizzle over bread. Garnish with cherries and apricots if desired. **Yield:** 3 loaves.

🮕🮕🮕🮕🮕🮕🮕🮕🮕🮕

TRIPLE-CHOCOLATE QUICK BREAD

Karen Grimes, Stephens City, Virginia

(Pictured on page 85)

Every year around Christmas, I'll make these breads for my family. I've also given a few as homemade gifts. They're pretty wrapped in colored foil or put in a tin.

1/2 cup butter *or* margarine, softened
2/3 cup packed brown sugar
2 eggs
1 cup (6 ounces) miniature semisweet chocolate chips, melted
1-1/2 cups applesauce
2 teaspoons vanilla extract
2-1/2 cups all-purpose flour
1 teaspoon baking powder
1 teaspoon baking soda
1 teaspoon salt
1/2 cup miniature semisweet chocolate chips
GLAZE:
1/2 cup miniature semisweet chocolate chips
1 tablespoon butter *or* margarine
2 to 3 tablespoons half-and-half cream
1/2 cup confectioners' sugar
1/4 teaspoon vanilla extract
Pinch salt

In a mixing bowl, cream butter and sugar. Add eggs and melted chocolate; mix well. Add applesauce and vanilla. Set aside. Combine flour, baking powder, baking soda and salt; add to creamed mixture and mix well. Stir in chocolate chips. Spoon the batter into four greased 5-1/2-in. x 3-in. x 2-in. loaf pans. Bake at 350° for 35-40 minutes or until done. Cool in pans 10 minutes before removing to wire racks to cool completely. For

glaze, melt chocolate chips and butter in a saucepan; stir in cream. Remove from the heat; stir in sugar, vanilla and salt. Drizzle over warm bread. **Yield:** 4 mini-loaves.

🮕🮕🮕🮕🮕🮕🮕🮕🮕🮕

GERMAN STOLLEN

Valeria Mauk, Elkhart Lake, Wisconsin

(Pictured on page 84)

My family and friends agree that the holidays just wouldn't be the same without this traditional bread.

3/4 cup raisins
1/2 cup chopped mixed candied fruit
1/4 cup dried currants
3/4 cup apple juice
4-1/2 to 5 cups all-purpose flour, *divided*
2 packages (1/4 ounce *each*) active dry yeast
1/4 cup sugar
1 teaspoon salt
1 cup milk
1/2 cup butter *or* margarine
2 eggs
2 tablespoons grated orange peel
1 tablespoon grated lemon peel
1/2 teaspoon almond extract
1/2 cup chopped almonds
Confectioners' sugar, optional
GLAZE (optional):
1 cup confectioners' sugar
3 to 4 tablespoons milk

In a bowl, soak raisins, fruit and currants in apple juice for 1 hour; drain and set aside. In a mixing bowl, combine 1-1/2 cups of flour, yeast, sugar and salt; mix well. In a saucepan, heat milk and butter to 120°-130° (butter does not need to melt). Add to flour mixture; mix well. Add eggs, grated peels and extract. Beat on low speed until moistened; beat on medium for 3 minutes. Stir in almonds, fruit mixture and enough remaining flour to form a soft dough. Turn onto a floured board; knead until smooth and elastic, about 6-8 minutes. Place in a greased bowl, turning once to grease top. Cover and let rise in a warm place until doubled, about 1-1/2 hours. Punch dough down; divide in half. Cover and let rest for 10 minutes. On a lightly floured surface, roll each half into a 12-in. x 8-in. oval. Fold one of the long sides over to within 1 in. of the opposite side; press edges lightly to seal. Place on greased baking sheets. Cover and let rise until almost doubled, about 45 minutes. Bake at 350° for 25-30 minutes or until golden brown. Cool on wire racks. Dust with confectioners' sugar or combine glaze ingredients and drizzle over stollen. **Yield:** 2 loaves.

ITALIAN SNACK BREAD

Joan Nowacki, Pewaukee, Wisconsin

(Pictured on page 84 and cover)

This snack bread's very versatile—I've served it with spaghetti, as an appetizer and as a main dish. Because it stays so moist, I often bake it a day before.

2-1/2 cups all-purpose flour, *divided*
   1 package (1/4 ounce) active dry yeast
2-1/2 teaspoons dried oregano
   1/2 teaspoon salt
   1 cup warm water (120° to 130°)
   2 tablespoons olive *or* vegetable oil
   1 egg, beaten
TOPPING:
1-1/2 cups thinly sliced onion
   1/4 cup olive *or* vegetable oil
   1 teaspoon dried rosemary, crushed
   1 teaspoon coarse salt, optional

In a large bowl, combine 1-1/2 cups flour, yeast, oregano and salt. Stir in water, oil and egg; mix well. Stir in enough remaining flour to form a soft dough. Cover and let rest 10 minutes. Pat into a greased 13-in. x 9-in. x 2-in. baking pan; set aside. In a skillet, saute onion in oil until tender. Spoon evenly over dough. Sprinkle with rosemary and salt if desired. Cover and let rise in warm place until doubled, about 30 minutes. Bake at 400° for 25-30 minutes or until lightly browned. Cut into small squares. Serve warm or at room temperature. **Yield:** about 8 servings.

ROSEMARY ORANGE BREAD

Deidre Fallavollita, Vienna, Virginia

(Pictured on page 84)

Of all the herbs, rosemary is my favorite. This bread goes great with a roast, chicken or pasta with red sauce. It's especially festive to serve at holiday time.

   1 package (1/4 ounce) active dry yeast
3/4 cup warm water (110° to 115°)
3/4 cup orange juice
   2 tablespoons honey
   1 tablespoon vegetable oil
   1 tablespoon minced fresh rosemary *or*
     1 teaspoon dried rosemary, crushed
   2 teaspoons salt
   1 teaspoon grated orange peel
3-3/4 to 4-1/2 cups all-purpose flour
   1 egg white
Additional fresh rosemary and whole
  peppercorns, optional

In a mixing bowl, dissolve yeast in warm water. Add orange juice, honey, oil, rosemary, salt, orange peel and 2 cups flour; beat until smooth. Stir in enough remaining flour to form a soft dough. Turn onto a floured board; knead until smooth and elastic, about 6-8 minutes. Place in a greased bowl, turning once to grease top. Cover and let rise in a warm place until doubled, about 1 hour. Punch dough down. Roll into a 15-in. x 10-in. rectangle. Starting at the short end, roll up jelly-roll style. Pinch edges to seal and shape into an oval. Place with seam side down on a greased baking sheet. Cover and let rise until nearly doubled, about 30 minutes. Bake at 375° for 20 minutes. Whisk egg white; brush over loaf. Place small sprigs of rosemary and peppercorns on top if desired. Bake 25 minutes longer or until brown. Cool on a wire rack. **Yield:** 1 loaf.

CHOCOLATE CHIP COFFEE RING

Laura Hertel, Columbia, Missouri

(Pictured on page 85)

When I was a girl, my mother served this only once a year—for Christmas-morning brunch. But it could easily be served as dessert or as a snack packed in a lunch. It travels very well.

1/2 cup butter *or* margarine, softened
   1 cup sugar
   2 eggs
   1 cup (8 ounces) sour cream
   1 teaspoon vanilla extract
   2 cups all-purpose flour
   1 teaspoon baking powder
   1 teaspoon baking soda
1/2 teaspoon salt
3/4 cup semisweet chocolate chips
TOPPING:
1/2 cup all-purpose flour
1/2 cup packed brown sugar
1-1/2 teaspoons baking cocoa
   1/4 cup cold butter *or* margarine
   1/2 cup chopped pecans
   1/4 cup semisweet chocolate chips

In a mixing bowl, cream butter and sugar until fluffy. Beat in eggs. Add sour cream and vanilla; mix just until combined. Set aside. Combine flour, baking powder, baking soda and salt; add to creamed mixture. Stir in the chocolate chips. Pour into a greased 8-cup fluted tube pan. For topping, combine flour, sugar and cocoa; cut in butter until mixture resembles coarse crumbs. Stir in pecans and chocolate chips. Sprinkle over batter. Bake at 350° for 55-60 minutes or until cake tests done. Cool in pan 20 minutes before removing to a wire rack to cool completely. **Yield:** 8-10 servings. **Editor's Note:** A greased 9-in. square baking pan can be used instead of the tube pan; bake for 45-50 minutes.

APRICOT CHEESE DANISH

Florence Schafer, Jackson, Minnesota

(Pictured below)

My family thinks this delicious Danish is a real treat. It's a treat to make, too, since you mix it up at night, then just roll it out and bake the next morning.

    1 package (1/4 ounce) active dry yeast
1/4 cup warm water (110° to 115°)
    3 tablespoons sugar
1/2 cup butter *or* margarine, softened
    2 eggs
1/2 cup sour cream
1/4 teaspoon salt
    3 cups all-purpose flour
FILLING:
    2 packages (8 ounces *each*) cream cheese, softened

1/2 cup sugar
    2 egg yolks
    2 teaspoons vanilla extract
1/4 cup apricot preserves
Confectioners' sugar

In a large mixing bowl, dissolve yeast in water. Add sugar, butter, eggs and sour cream. Gradually add salt and 2 cups flour; beat until smooth. Stir in remaining flour (the dough will be soft and sticky). Place in a greased bowl. Cover and refrigerate overnight. Next day, prepare filling. Beat cream cheese, sugar, egg yolks and vanilla in a mixing bowl until smooth. Turn dough onto a floured board; knead two to three times. Divide in half. Roll each half into a 16-in. x 10-in. oval and place on greased baking sheets. Spread 1-1/4 cups filling over each oval to within 1 in. of edges. Fold longest side over filling; pinch edges to seal. Cover and let rise in a warm place until doubled, about 1 hour. Bake at 375° for 20-22 minutes or until golden brown. Cool on a wire rack. Spread preserves on top. Dust with confectioners' sugar. Store in the refrigerator. **Yield:** 2 loaves.

RAISIN MINI-SCONES

Andrea Pflughaupt, Seward, Nebraska

Just because you're watching your waistline doesn't mean you can't indulge in fresh-from-the-oven goodies! These low-fat scones are full of flavor.

✓ This tasty dish uses less sugar, salt and fat. Recipe includes *Diabetic Exchanges*.

    2/3 cup margarine, melted
1-1/2 cups quick-cooking oats
Egg substitute equivalent to 2 eggs
    1 teaspoon vanilla extract
Artificial sweetener equivalent to 1 cup sugar
1-1/2 cups all-purpose flour
    1 teaspoon baking powder
1/2 teaspoon salt
1/2 cup skim milk
1/2 cup raisins

In a large bowl, combine margarine and oats. Stir in egg substitute, vanilla and sweetener. Combine flour, baking powder and salt; add to oat mixture alternately with milk. Stir in raisins. Drop by rounded tablespoonfuls onto baking sheets coated with nonstick cooking spray. Bake at 400° for 12-15 minutes or until browned. **Yield:** 3 dozen. **Editor's Note:** Use an artificial sweetener recommended for baking, such as Sweet 'N Low or Sweet One. **Diabetic Exchanges:** One scone equals 1 fat, 1/2 starch; also, 77 calories, 83 mg sodium, trace cholesterol, 9 gm carbohydrate, 2 gm protein, 4 gm fat.

Quick & Easy Festive Breads

INSTEAD of the 2 to 3 hours a yeast bread often requires, these abbreviated bread recipes take a mere 30 to 60 minutes in most cases.

CHOCOLATE TEA BREAD

Geri Davis, Prescott, Arizona

When people sample this chocolaty moist bread, they're surprised that biscuit mix is an ingredient.

    1 egg
    2/3 cup sugar
    3/4 cup orange juice
    2 cups biscuit/baking mix
    2 squares (1 ounce *each*) unsweetened
      chocolate, melted
    1/2 cup chopped nuts
    1 teaspoon vanilla extract
Cream cheese *or* orange marmalade, optional

In a mixing bowl, beat egg. Gradually add sugar; mix well. Add orange juice alternately with biscuit mix. Fold in chocolate, nuts and vanilla. Pour into a greased 8-in. x 4-in. x 2-in. loaf pan. Bake at 350° for 40-45 minutes or until bread tests done. Cool for 10 minutes before removing to a wire rack. Serve with cream cheese or marmalade if desired. **Yield:** 1 loaf.

FRUIT 'N' NUT BREAD

Mary Hansen, St. Louis, Missouri

I keep frozen bread dough on hand during the holidays so I can bake this favorite in brisk fashion!

    1/2 cup chopped pecans
    1/2 cup raisins
    1/2 cup chopped dates
    1/2 cup halved candied cherries
    2 teaspoons orange juice

    1 loaf (1 pound) frozen bread dough,
      thawed
    1 tablespoon butter *or* margarine, melted
GLAZE:
    1/2 cup confectioners' sugar
    1 tablespoon butter *or* margarine, melted
    1 tablespoon orange juice
    1/8 teaspoon grated orange peel
Pecan halves

In a bowl, combine the first five ingredients; set aside. Shape bread dough into ball. Turn onto a floured board; roll out to about 1 in. thick. Spread pecan mixture onto dough; fold over and knead well until the fruit and nuts are evenly mixed into dough. Shape into a flattened ball; place on a greased baking sheet. Brush with butter. Cover and let rise until doubled, about 1 hour. Bake at 375° for 20-25 minutes or until golden brown. Cool on a wire rack. Combine glaze ingredients; spread over bread. Top with pecan halves. **Yield:** 1 loaf.

BERRY CREAM COFFEE CAKE

Marjorie Miller, Haven, Kansas

Feel free to substitute your family's favorite preserves in this tried-and-true recipe.

    1 package (3 ounces) cream cheese
    1/4 cup butter *or* margarine
    2 cups biscuit/baking mix
    1/3 cup milk
    1/2 cup raspberry preserves
GLAZE:
    1 cup confectioners' sugar
    1 to 2 tablespoons milk
    1/2 teaspoon vanilla extract

With a pastry blender, cut cream cheese and butter into biscuit mix until mixture resembles coarse crumbs. Stir in milk just until moistened. Turn onto a floured board; knead 8-10 times or until dough is smooth. On waxed paper, roll dough into a 12-in. x 8-in. rectangle. Turn onto a greased 15-in. x 10-in. x 1-in. baking pan. Remove waxed paper. Spread preserves down center third of rectangle. On each long side, cut 1-in.-wide strips about 2-1/2 in. into center. Starting at one end, fold alternating strips at an angle across preserves. Seal end. Bake at 425° for 12-15 minutes. Combine glaze ingredients and drizzle over top. **Yield:** 8-10 servings.

HERBED MONKEY BREAD

Donna Gordon, Averill Park, New York

This pull-apart bread tastes especially good alongside a plate of saucy spaghetti!

   1/2 cup butter *or* margarine, melted
   1 garlic clove, minced
   2 teaspoons dried parsley flakes
   1 teaspoon dried chives
   1/2 teaspoon dried basil
   1/2 teaspoon dried oregano
   2 packages (12 ounces *each*) refrigerated
      buttermilk biscuits

Combine the first six ingredients in a bowl. Dip biscuits in the butter mixture; arrange in a greased 10-in. fluted tube pan. Bake at 400° for 20 minutes or until golden brown. Cool 10 minutes before removing to a wire rack. Serve warm. **Yield:** 1 loaf.

CHERRY ALMOND BRAID

Darcy Hebert, Argyle, Minnesota

(Pictured at right)

If you want to impress guests with homemade bread but are short on time, reach for this recipe.

   1 package (8 ounces) cream cheese,
      softened
   1/4 cup sugar

   1/2 teaspoon almond extract
   1/4 cup slivered almonds
   1/3 cup chopped maraschino cherries
   2 packages (8 ounces *each*) refrigerated
      crescent rolls
GLAZE:
   1 cup confectioners' sugar
   1 to 2 tablespoons milk
   1 tablespoon butter *or* margarine, melted
**Additional slivered almonds and red and
   green maraschino cherries**

In a mixing bowl, beat cream cheese and sugar until light and fluffy. Add extract. Fold in almonds and cherries; set aside. Unroll crescent rolls on an ungreased baking sheet; overlap long sides to make a 12-in. square. Press perforations to seal. Spread the cream cheese mixture down center third of square to within 1 in. of top and bottom; fold top and bottom edge over filling. Bring long sides over filling and overlap. Pinch seam to seal. Bake at 375° for 25-30 minutes or until golden brown. Cool completely on a wire rack. Combine the confectioners' sugar, milk and butter; pour over top of loaf. Garnish with almonds and cherries if desired. **Yield:** 8-10 servings.

RASPBERRY STREUSEL MUFFINS

Catherine Johnston, Stafford, New York

(Pictured below)

As a child, I would go out with my sister and pick wild raspberries. We'd help our mom make jellies, jams, pies and muffins with the berries. Now, I like to make these muffins on weekend mornings when I have a few extra moments to enjoy them with a cup of tea.

> 1/2 cup butter *or* margarine, softened
> 1/2 cup sugar
> 1 egg
> 1/2 cup sour cream
> 1/2 cup milk
> 1 teaspoon vanilla extract
> 2 cups all-purpose flour
> 1/2 teaspoon baking powder
> 1/2 teaspoon baking soda
> 1/2 teaspoon ground cinnamon
> 1/4 teaspoon salt
> 1 cup fresh *or* frozen raspberries
> STREUSEL:
> 1/4 cup all-purpose flour
> 1/4 cup quick-cooking oats
> 3 tablespoons sugar
> 1/4 teaspoon ground cinnamon
> 1/8 teaspoon salt
> 3 tablespoons cold butter *or* margarine
> Confectioners' sugar

In a mixing bowl, cream butter and sugar until light and fluffy; beat in egg. In a small bowl, mix sour cream, milk and vanilla. Combine dry ingredients; stir into creamed mixture alternately with sour cream mixture just until moistened. Gently fold in raspberries. Fill greased or paper-lined muffin cups two-thirds full. Combine flour, oats, sugar, cinnamon and salt; mix well. Cut the butter until crumbly. Sprinkle over muffins. Bake at 400° for 18-22 minutes or until muffins test done. Cool in pan 10 minutes before removing to a wire rack. Dust with confectioners' sugar. **Yield:** 1-1/2 dozen.

ENGLISH MUFFIN BREAD

Donna Meyer, Dayton, Ohio

You can bake the bread either in coffee cans for a change of pace or regular loaf pans. This bread is really delicious when toasted.

✓ This tasty dish uses less sugar, salt and fat. Recipe includes *Diabetic Exchanges*.

> 6 cups all-purpose flour, *divided*
> 2 packages (1/4 ounce *each*) active dry yeast
> 1 tablespoon sugar
> 2 teaspoons salt
> 1/4 teaspoon baking soda
> 2 cups warm skim milk (120° to 130°)
> 1/2 cup warm water (120° to 130°)
> Cornmeal

In a bowl, combine 3 cups flour, yeast, sugar, salt and baking soda. Stir in milk and water; mix well. Stir in remaining flour (batter will be soft). Do not knead. Spray three 13-oz. coffee cans or 8-1/2-in. x 4-in. x 2-in. loaf pans with nonstick cooking spray. Sprinkle with cornmeal. Spoon batter into pans; sprinkle cornmeal on top. Cover and let rise in a warm place until doubled, about 45 minutes. Bake at 400° for 20-25 minutes or until golden brown. Remove from pans to cool on wire racks. **Yield:** 3 loaves (16 slices each). **Diabetic Exchanges:** One slice equals 1 starch; also, 62 calories, 101 mg sodium, trace cholesterol, 13 gm carbohydrate, 2 gm protein, trace fat.

SWEET POTATO BISCUITS

Lauren McMann, Blairsville, Georgia

Sweet potatoes give these wholesome biscuits a pretty orange color that is sure to add a fun and festive touch to your holiday table. My family gobbles them up!

1-1/2 cups self-rising flour*
2 teaspoons brown sugar
1/3 cup shortening
1 egg
1/2 cup mashed cooked sweet potatoes
   (without added butter or milk)
2 tablespoons milk

In a bowl, combine the flour and brown sugar; cut in shortening until mixture resembles coarse crumbs. In another bowl, beat egg; add sweet potatoes and milk. Stir in crumb mixture just until moistened. Turn onto a floured board; knead 10-12 times or until smooth. Roll dough to 1/2-in. thickness. Cut with a 2-1/2-in. biscuit cutter; place on an ungreased baking sheet. Bake at 425° for 10-12 minutes or until bottoms are lightly browned. Serve warm. **Yield:** 10 biscuits. ***Editor's Note:** As a substitute for self-rising flour, place 2-1/4 teaspoons baking powder and 3/4 teaspoon salt in a 2-cup measuring cup. Add enough all-purpose flour to equal 1-1/2 cups.

SPRINGTIME COFFEE CAKE

Hilda Garey, St. Albans, Vermont

(Pictured at right)

I like the fresh fruit flavor in this coffee cake. The strawberries and rhubarb make a nice combination. Use frozen fruit during the winter months.

2 cups unsweetened fresh or frozen
   strawberries
1-1/2 cups diced fresh or frozen rhubarb
3/4 cup sugar
3 tablespoons cornstarch
3 tablespoons cold water
CAKE:
1-1/2 cups all-purpose flour
3/4 cup sugar
1 teaspoon ground cinnamon
1/2 teaspoon ground nutmeg
1/2 teaspoon salt
1/2 teaspoon baking powder
1/2 teaspoon baking soda
3/4 cup cold butter or margarine
2 eggs

3/4 cup buttermilk
1/2 teaspoon almond extract
TOPPING:
1/2 cup sugar
1/2 teaspoon ground cinnamon
1 tablespoon cold butter or margarine
1/2 cup chopped walnuts

In a saucepan, combine strawberries, rhubarb and sugar; let stand for 15 minutes. Combine cornstarch and water; stir into the fruit mixture. Bring to a boil over medium heat, stirring constantly. Cook and stir for 2 minutes. Cool to room temperature. Combine flour, sugar, cinnamon, nutmeg, salt, baking powder and baking soda; cut in butter until crumbly. In a small mixing bowl, beat eggs, buttermilk and extract; add to flour mixture and mix well. Spread half of the batter into a greased 9-in. square baking pan. Carefully spoon the fruit mixture on top. Spoon remaining batter over fruit mixture. For topping, combine sugar and cinnamon; cut in butter until crumbly. Stir in walnuts. Sprinkle over batter. Bake at 350° for 40-45 minutes or until a wooden pick inserted near the center comes out clean. **Yield:** 9-12 servings.

ture. Stir in oil, sugar, molasses, salt and 5 cups flour; beat until smooth. Add enough remaining flour to form a soft dough. Turn onto a floured board; knead until smooth and elastic, about 6-8 minutes. Place in a greased bowl, turning once to grease top. Cover and let rise in a warm place until doubled, about 1 hour. Punch dough down. Shape into 48 balls. Place 2 in. apart on greased baking sheets. Cover and let rise until almost doubled, about 1 hour. Bake at 350° for 18-20 minutes or until browned. **Yield:** 4 dozen.

AUTUMN PEAR BREAD

Mary Lynn Wilson, Linden, Texas

Pears give this bread a delicious taste and help keep it nice and moist. I bake small loaves and present them to friends and family for holidays all year long.

> 2 cups all-purpose flour
> 1 cup sugar
> 1 teaspoon baking powder
> 1/2 teaspoon baking soda
> 1/2 teaspoon salt
> 1/8 teaspoon ground nutmeg
> 1/2 cup butter *or* margarine
> 2 eggs
> 1/4 cup buttermilk
> 1 teaspoon vanilla extract
> 1 cup finely chopped peeled ripe pears

In a large bowl, combine dry ingredients; cut in butter until mixture resembles coarse crumbs. In a small bowl, beat eggs, buttermilk and vanilla; stir into dry ingredients just until moistened. Fold in the pears. Spoon into three greased 5-in. x 2-1/2-in. x 2-in. mini-loaf pans. Bake at 350° for 35-40 minutes or until a wooden pick inserted near the center comes out clean. Cool in pans 10 minutes before removing to wire racks to cool completely. **Yield:** 3 mini-loaves.

GOLDEN CARROT BUNS

Katharine Groine, Altona, Manitoba

(Pictured above)

These rolls have a nice flavor...folks usually don't guess that carrots are one of the ingredients. My family really likes them; see if yours will, too!

> 4 cups sliced carrots
> 2 eggs, beaten
> 1 cup warm water (110° to 115°), *divided*
> 2 packages (1/4 ounce *each*) active dry yeast
> 3/4 cup vegetable oil
> 1/2 cup sugar
> 1 tablespoon molasses
> 2 teaspoons salt
> 8-1/2 to 9 cups all-purpose flour

Place carrots in a saucepan and cover with water; cook until tender. Drain and place in a blender or food processor. Add eggs and 1/2 cup water; puree until smooth. In a large mixing bowl, dissolve yeast in remaining water. Add carrot mix-

COUNTRY CRUNCH PANCAKES

Anita Harmala, Howell, Michigan

I adapted this from a regular pancake recipe. They're simply delicious! My kids especially like them.

> 2 cups all-purpose flour
> 1/3 cup whole wheat flour
> 1/3 cup quick-cooking oats
> 2 tablespoons sugar
> 2 teaspoons baking powder

Breads & Rolls

1 teaspoon baking soda
1 teaspoon salt
1 teaspoon ground cinnamon
2-1/4 cups buttermilk
2 eggs, lightly beaten
2 tablespoons vegetable oil
1 cup fresh *or* frozen blueberries, optional
CRUNCHY TOPPING:
1/2 cup quick-cooking oats
1/4 cup chopped slivered almonds
1/4 cup packed brown sugar
1 teaspoon ground cinnamon

In a mixing bowl, combine flours, oats, sugar, baking powder, baking soda, salt and cinnamon. Combine buttermilk, eggs and oil; stir into dry ingredients just until blended. Fold in blueberries if desired. Combine topping ingredients; sprinkle about 1 teaspoon for each pancake onto a lightly greased hot griddle; pour 1/4 cup of batter over topping. Immediately sprinkle with another teaspoonful of topping; turn when bubbles form on top of pancake. Cook until second side is golden brown. **Yield:** 14-16 pancakes.

LOW-FAT CINNAMON ROLLS

Heather Cliften-Champagne, Brockville, Ontario

Not only are these sweet rolls low in fat, they're convenient. Instead of making a yeast bread from scratch, this recipe calls for frozen bread dough.

✓ This tasty dish uses less sugar, salt or fat.

1 loaf (1 pound) frozen bread dough, thawed
1 tablespoon margarine, melted
1 tablespoon sugar
1 teaspoon ground cinnamon
GLAZE:
1/2 cup confectioners' sugar
1/4 teaspoon grated orange peel
2 to 3 teaspoons orange juice

Punch dough down. On a lightly floured surface, roll dough into a 12-in. x 8-in. rectangle. Brush with margarine. Sprinkle with sugar and cinnamon. Roll up, jelly-roll style, starting at a narrow end. Slice into 1-in. rolls. Place in a 9-in. round baking pan coated with nonstick cooking spray. Cover and let rise until doubled, about 45 minutes. Bake at 375° for 15-20 minutes or until golden brown. Combine glaze ingredients; drizzle over warm rolls. Serve warm. **Yield:** 1 dozen. **Nutritional Analysis:** One roll equals 138 calories, 219 mg sodium, 0 cholesterol, 26 gm carbohydrate, 4 gm protein, 3 gm fat.

MILK-AND-HONEY WHITE BREAD

Kathy McCreary, Goddard, Kansas

(Pictured below)

My dad has been a wheat farmer all his life, and my state is the wheat capital, so this recipe represents my region and my family well. This bread never lasts too long at our house.

1 package (1/4 ounce) active dry yeast
2-1/2 cups warm milk (110° to 115°)
1/3 cup honey
1/4 cup butter *or* margarine, melted
2 teaspoons salt
8 to 8-1/2 cups all-purpose flour

In a large mixing bowl, dissolve yeast in warm milk. Add honey, butter, salt and 5 cups of flour; beat until smooth. Add enough remaining flour to form a soft dough. Turn onto a floured board; knead until smooth and elastic, about 6-8 minutes. Place in a greased bowl, turning once to grease top. Cover and let rise in a warm place until doubled, about 1 hour. Punch dough down and shape into two loaves. Place in greased 9-in. x 5-in. x 3-in. loaf pans. Cover and let rise until doubled, about 30 minutes. Bake at 375° for 30-35 minutes or until golden brown. Cover with foil if necessary to prevent overbrowning. Remove from pans and cool on wire racks. **Yield:** 2 loaves.

OF ALL the sweet aromas of autumn, *nothing's* more irresistible than the mouth-watering scent of homemade bread baking. Of course, the flavor's equally unbeatable.

What's more, with the right information, anyone can produce a prize-winning loaf. So, if you've always wanted to make your own bread, now's the time to rise to the challenge! Here the experts at Fleischmann's Yeast share some basic how-to tips...along with recipes that both new *and* seasoned bakers are sure to savor.

KNEADING DOUGH

The trick to kneading is to add only enough flour to keep the dough from sticking to your hands or the work surface. Expert bakers work with slightly sticky dough; as a result, their breads turn out moist and light. Here are simple kneading techniques to guide you:

• Start with a large cutting board or flat surface at a comfortable height for you to extend your arms, with palms resting on work surface.

• Sprinkle work surface with a small amount of flour, and rub some flour on your hands.

• Pat dough into a ball. At this stage, it's usually a "shaggy", fairly sticky mass.

• Flatten the dough slightly, and fold it toward you.

• Using the heels of your hands, push dough away with a rolling motion.

• Rotate dough a quarter turn and vigorously repeat the fold, push and turn steps.

• Knead dough until it is smooth and elastic. If the dough becomes sticky, sprinkle work surface with a small amount of flour and work into dough, adding flour to your hands, too.

• Kneading takes from 4 to 10 minutes. When sufficiently kneaded, the dough will be smooth, satiny and elastic. When shaped into a ball, the dough will spring back when gently punched.

RISING

Dough made with Active Dry Yeast generally requires a first rise in a bowl and a second rise after shaping.

• Lightly grease the top, exposed surface of the dough before the first rising.

• An easy way to grease the top of the dough is to place the dough in a large greased bowl, then turn the dough over. Or coat the bowl and dough with nonstick cooking spray.

• Cover the top loosely with a damp clean cloth or plastic wrap sprayed with nonstick cooking spray.

• Set the dough in a warm (80° to 85°), draft-free place. Another method is to place the dough on a rack with a large pan of steaming water set underneath.

• Or place the dough inside an unlit oven with a large pan of steaming water beneath it.

• Check your owner's manual for methods of letting dough rise in a microwave oven or a convection oven.

RESTING

Dough made with RapidRise Yeast according to the Quick, One-Rise Method is given a 10-minute rest instead of a first rise.

• Cover the kneaded dough with a clean cloth or plastic wrap. Let the dough rest on a floured surface for 10 minutes. The RapidRise dough is then shaped, allowed to rise until doubled in size and baked.

TESTING FOR "DOUBLED IN SIZE"

Press the tips of two fingers lightly and quickly 1/2 inch into the dough. If the dents stay, the dough is doubled.

Now that the dough has doubled, it's full of air pockets, and the gluten is

strong and elastic. The fermentation has generated heat and moisture and has allowed flavors to develop.

PUNCHING DOWN

Punching down the dough will get rid of excess carbon dioxide and redistribute the yeast. To punch down the dough, simply make a fist and push it

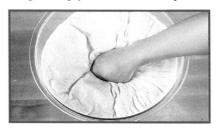

into the center of the dough. Pull the edges of the dough to the center, and turn the dough over. Now, it's ready to rise again or be shaped.

SHAPING

Recipes indicate how to shape special breads and rolls.

● For regular bread loaves, lightly flour the work surface and, after shap-

ing the dough into a smooth ball, roll into a rectangle using a rolling pin. Beginning at the short end, roll tightly to make a loaf shape.

● With fingers, pinch seam of rolled dough to seal. Then pinch each end.

● Pat into a uniform loaf shape.

● Place dough, seam side down, in a greased baking pan.

● After dough has been shaped, it must rise until doubled in size. This step can take about 20 to 60 minutes.

● In most instances, the second rising usually takes less time than the first.

● Cover the dough and set in a warm draft-free place.

BAKING

Always preheat the oven. There's a reason: During the first 10 to 15 minutes of baking, heat causes the dough to expand quickly, form the crust and give shape to the loaf.

If the oven isn't preheated, the dough may overrise before the crust is formed. This will result in a misshapen loaf.

Place the baking pans several inches apart on the center rack of the oven and bake according to the recipe.

TESTING FOR DONENESS

Oven temperatures can vary, so check your loaves about 10 minutes before the completed baking time.

● If loaves are getting overbrowned before the completion of the baking time, shield the loaves with aluminum foil and return them to the oven for the remainder of the baking time.

● Use an oven thermometer to gauge oven temperature.

● Baked loaves should be nicely browned and easy to remove from the baking pan. Most coffee cakes should be golden in appearance and solid to the touch.

● After turning bread out of the pan, tap the bottom or sides of the loaf; if it sounds hollow, the bread is done.

COOLING

It's important to remove most baked yeast products from the baking pan to cool on a wire rack. This prevents the bread from becoming soggy due to steam accumulating on the bottom of the baking pan.

MASTER BREAD DOUGH

6 to 6-1/2 cups all-purpose flour
3 tablespoons sugar

2 packages Active Dry *or* RapidRise Yeast
2 teaspoons salt
1-1/2 cups water
1/2 cup milk
2 tablespoons butter *or* margarine

In a large bowl, combine 2-1/2 cups of flour, sugar, undissolved yeast and salt. Heat water, milk, and butter until very warm (120°-130°). Gradually add mixture to dry ingredients; beat 2 minutes at medium speed of electric mixer, scraping bowl occasionally. Add 1/2 cup flour; beat 2 minutes at high speed, scraping bowl occasionally. With spoon, stir in enough remaining flour to make a soft dough. Knead on lightly floured surface until smooth and elastic, about 8-10 minutes. Place kneaded dough in a greased bowl, turning to grease top. Cover; let rise in a warm draft-free place until doubled in size, about 30-60 minutes. (With RapidRise Yeast, cover kneaded dough and let rest on floured surface for 10 minutes.) Shape, let rise and bake according to options below:

LOAF (use half of dough): Roll dough into a 12-in. x 7-in. rectangle. Beginning at short end, roll up tightly as for jelly roll. Pinch seam and ends to seal. Place, seam side down, in a greased 8-1/2-in. x 4-1/2-in. x 2-1/2-in. loaf pan. Cover; let rise in a warm draft-free place until doubled in size, about 1 to 1-1/2 hours. Bake at 400° for 30 minutes or until done. Remove from pan; let cool on wire rack. **Yield:** 1 loaf.

ONION ROLLS (use half of dough): Divide dough into 10 equal pieces; shape into smooth balls. Place in a greased 8-in. round cake pan. Cover; let rise in a warm draft-free place until doubled in size, about 30-60 minutes. Beat 1 egg with 1 tablespoon water; brush over rolls. Sprinkle with 2 tablespoons dried minced onion. Bake at 375° for 25 minutes or until done, covering with foil during the last 5 minutes of baking to prevent excess browning. Remove from pan; let cool on wire rack. **Yield:** 10 rolls.

SOFT HERB BREADSTICKS (use half of dough): Divide dough into 12 equal pieces; roll each into a 15-in. rope. Twist each rope several times if desired. Place on two greased baking sheets. Cover; let rise in a warm draft-free place until risen slightly, about 10-20 minutes. Lightly beat 1 egg white; brush over breadsticks. Sprinkle with herbs or herb blends such as oregano, dill weed or Italian herb seasoning. Bake at 400° for 15 minutes or until done. Remove from sheets; let cool on wire rack. **Yield:** 1 dozen.

SCANDINAVIAN CINNAMON ROLLS

Jean Vander Hoek, Hudsonville, Michigan

(Pictured below)

These rolls are so easy to make because they require no kneading.

    1 package (1/4 ounce) active dry yeast
1/4 cup warm water (110° to 115°)
    4 cups all-purpose flour
1/4 cup sugar
    1 teaspoon salt
    1 cup butter *or* margarine
    1 cup warm milk (110° to 115°)
    3 egg yolks, lightly beaten
FILLING:
    3 tablespoons butter *or* margarine,
       softened
1/2 cup sugar
    2 teaspoons ground cinnamon
GLAZE:
1-1/2 cups confectioners' sugar
    2 tablespoons butter *or* margarine,
       softened
1-1/2 teaspoons vanilla extract
    2 tablespoons milk

In a small bowl, dissolve yeast in water; set aside. In a large bowl, combine flour, sugar and salt; cut in the butter until crumbly. Add yeast mixture, milk and egg yolks; stir to form a soft dough. Cover and refrigerate 4 hours or overnight. Divide dough in half; roll each half into a 12-in. x 10-in. rectangle. Spread with butter. Combine sugar and cinnamon; sprinkle half over each piece. Roll up, jelly-roll style, starting at the long end. Cut each roll into 12 slices. Place in greased muffin cups. Cover and let rise until doubled, about 1 hour. Bake at 375° for 20-25 minutes or until golden brown. For glaze, cream sugar and butter in a mixing bowl. Add vanilla and milk; beat until smooth. Remove rolls to a wire rack; spread with glaze. **Yield:** 2 dozen.

BLACKBERRY MUFFINS

Candy Woelk, Lexington, Missouri

Our farm is the only commercial blackberry patch in this area. The fruits of our labor show up on the kitchen table—in pies, cobblers, jams, jellies and these muffins!

1/4 cup butter *or* margarine, softened
1/2 cup sugar
    1 egg, lightly beaten
3/4 cup milk
1/4 teaspoon vanilla extract
1-3/4 cups plus 1 tablespoon all-purpose flour,
       divided
2-1/2 teaspoons baking powder
1/4 teaspoon salt
    1 cup fresh blackberries
Honey, optional

In a mixing bowl, cream butter and sugar. Add egg and mix well. Beat in milk and vanilla until almost smooth, about 1 minute. Combine 1-3/4 cups flour, baking powder and salt; stir into creamed mixture just until combined (batter will be thick). Toss blackberries with the remaining flour until coated; fold into batter. Fill greased or paper-lined muffin cups half full. Bake at 425° for 20-25 minutes or until muffins are golden and test done. Serve warm with honey if desired. **Yield:** 1 dozen.

OAT-BRAN BREAD

Wanda Cutler, Canby, Oregon

I was a novice at bread making when a neighbor gave me this recipe many years ago. Now bread making is one of my favorite things to do.

✓ This tasty dish uses less sugar, salt and fat. Recipe includes *Diabetic Exchanges.*

    2 packages (1/4 ounce *each*) active dry yeast
4-1/2 cups warm water (110° to 115°), *divided*
3/4 cup vegetable oil
3/4 cup sugar
1/4 cup molasses

2 teaspoons salt
1/4 cup wheat germ
1/4 cup oat bran
2 cups quick-cooking oats
3 cups whole wheat flour
7 to 7-1/2 cups all-purpose flour

In a large mixing bowl, dissolve yeast in 1/2 cup warm water. Add oil, sugar, molasses, salt, wheat germ, bran and remaining warm water; mix well. Add oats, whole wheat flour and 2 cups all-purpose flour; beat until smooth. Add enough remaining all-purpose flour to form a soft dough. Turn onto a floured board; knead until smooth and elastic, about 6-8 minutes. Place in a greased bowl, turning once to grease top. Cover and let rise in a warm place until doubled, about 1 hour. Punch dough down and shape into four loaves. Place in greased 8-in. x 4-in. x 2-in. loaf pans. Cover and let rise until doubled, about 30 minutes. Bake at 350° for 30-35 minutes. Remove from pans and cool on wire racks. **Yield:** 4 loaves (16 slices each). **Diabetic Exchanges:** One slice equals 1-1/2 starch; also, 116 calories, 68 mg sodium, 0 cholesterol, 20 gm carbohydrate, 3 gm protein, 3 gm fat.

CRANBERRY COFFEE CAKE

Elta Croft, Two Harbors, Minnesota

(Pictured above right)

I saw a contest in a local newspaper and worked up this recipe. It won first prize in the dessert category! Cranberries grow in this region of the country, so I use them in a variety of recipes.

3 cups fresh *or* frozen cranberries
1 cup chopped walnuts
2 cups sugar, *divided*
3/4 cup butter *or* margarine, softened
3 eggs, lightly beaten
1 teaspoon vanilla extract
1-1/2 cups all-purpose flour
1 teaspoon baking powder
1/2 teaspoon salt
TOPPING:
1 tablespoon sugar
1/2 teaspoon ground cinnamon

In a greased 9-in. square baking pan, combine cranberries, walnuts and 1 cup of sugar. In a mixing bowl, cream butter and the remaining sugar. Add eggs and vanilla; mix well. Combine flour, baking powder and salt; add to creamed mixture and mix well. Drop batter by large tablespoonfuls over cranberry mixture; carefully spread to cover. For topping, combine sugar and cinnamon; sprinkle over batter. Bake at 350° for 50-60 min-

utes or until a wooden pick inserted near the center comes out clean. **Yield:** 8-10 servings.

FINNISH BREAD

Arthur Luama, Red Lodge, Montana

This recipe was brought over from Finland by pioneers who settled the area. We make this bread for a local festival that features foods from different countries.

1 package (1/4 ounce) active dry yeast
2 cups warm water (110° to 115°)
1 cup whole wheat flour
1/4 cup butter *or* margarine, melted, *divided*
1 tablespoon brown sugar
2 teaspoons salt
4-1/2 to 5 cups all-purpose flour

In a large mixing bowl, dissolve yeast in water. Add whole wheat flour, 2 tablespoons of butter, brown sugar, salt and 2 cups of flour; beat until smooth. Add enough remaining flour to form a soft dough. Turn onto a floured board; knead until smooth and elastic, about 6-8 minutes. Place in a greased bowl, turning once to grease top. Cover and let rise in a warm place until doubled, about 1 hour. Punch the dough down. Shape into two 6-in. rounds; place on a greased baking sheet. Cut slashes in top with a knife. Cover and let rise in a warm place until doubled, about 40 minutes. Bake at 400° for 40-45 minutes or until golden brown. Brush with remaining butter. **Yield:** 2 loaves.

PIES, cakes, cookies and an assortment of other treats are sure to please anytime—for a coffee break, a snack or dessert.

PALATE PLEASERS. Clockwise from top right: Creamy Pineapple Pie (p. 99), Glazed Apple Tart (p. 99), Cherry Torte (p. 101) and Banana Streusel Pie (p. 100).

Sweet Treats

CREAMY PINEAPPLE PIE

Priscilla Wortman, Belmont, Vermont

(Pictured at left)

A local radio station sponsored a contest that required recipes with three different products from the dairy case. I entered this recipe and won a prize!

  1 package (8 ounces) cream cheese,
      softened
  1 cup sugar, *divided*
  1/2 teaspoon salt
  2 eggs
  1/2 cup milk
  1/2 teaspoon vanilla extract
  1 tablespoon cornstarch
  1 can (8 ounces) crushed pineapple,
      undrained
  1 unbaked pastry shell (9 inches)
  1/4 cup chopped pecans

In a mixing bowl, beat the cream cheese, 1/2 cup sugar and salt until smooth. Add eggs, one at a time, beating well after each addition. Blend in milk and vanilla; set aside. In a small saucepan, combine cornstarch and remaining sugar. Stir in pineapple; bring to a boil, stirring constantly. Boil for 2 minutes. Pour into pastry shell; spoon cream cheese mixture over top. Sprinkle with pecans. Bake at 400° for 10 minutes. Reduce heat to 325°; bake 45-50 minutes more or until center is set. Cool completely; chill before serving. **Yield:** 8 servings.

GLAZED APPLE TART

Judi Brinegar, Liberty, North Carolina

(Pictured at left)

This is one of my favorite desserts, and a primary reason is because it's so easy to prepare. I've taken it to numerous gatherings, where it's received rave reviews.

  2 cups all-purpose flour
  1/2 cup sugar, *divided*
  3/4 cup butter *or* margarine

  1 egg yolk, lightly beaten
  3 tablespoons cold water
  6 medium baking apples, peeled and
      chopped
1-1/2 cups granola with raisins
  1/2 cup slivered almonds
  1 cup confectioners' sugar
  2 tablespoons lemon juice

In a bowl, combine flour and 1/4 cup of sugar; cut in butter until mixture resembles coarse crumbs. Combine egg yolk and water; stir into flour mixture and mix lightly. Form dough into a ball; press onto bottom and up sides of an ungreased 15-in. x 10-in. x 1-in. baking pan. Bake at 350° for 15 minutes. Sprinkle the apples over crust. Combine granola, almonds and remaining sugar; sprinkle over apples. Bake at 350° for 50 minutes or until apples are tender. Cool on wire rack. Combine confectioners' sugar and lemon juice until smooth; drizzle over pie. **Yield:** 16-20 servings.

WATERMELON SHERBET

Lisa McAdoo, Rush Springs, Oklahoma

My family has been harvesting watermelons for generations. Our church group often serves this refreshing treat at the town's watermelon festival.

  8 cups diced seeded watermelon
1-1/2 cups sugar
  1/2 cup lemon juice
  2 envelopes unflavored gelatin
  1/2 cup cold water
  2 cups milk

In a large bowl, combine watermelon, sugar and lemon juice. Chill for 30 minutes; place half in a blender. Blend until smooth; pour into a large bowl. Repeat with the other half; set aside. In a saucepan, cook and stir gelatin and water over low heat until gelatin dissolves. Add to watermelon mixture; mix well. Stir in the milk until well blended. Freeze in an ice cream freezer according to the manufacturer's directions. Serve immediately or freeze and allow to thaw about 20 minutes before serving. **Yield:** 1/2 gallon.

FESTIVE FRUITCAKE
Xylpha Saunders, Letart, West Virginia

(Pictured below)

I usually make this dessert when I have plenty of time and won't be interrupted. It takes a while to make, but it's definitely worth it! This is a well-known regional recipe in our area. We make it every year and enjoy putting it together as much as we do eating it.

  1 cup butter (no substitutes), softened
  1 cup sugar
  3 eggs, *separated*
  2 tablespoons lemon extract
1-1/2 cups all-purpose flour
1-1/4 cups golden raisins

1-1/4 cups red and green candied cherries, halved
1-1/2 cups chopped candied pineapple
  2 cups whole pecans

In a large mixing bowl, cream butter, sugar and egg yolks. Add lemon extract; mix well. Gradually add flour. Fold in fruit and nuts. Beat the egg whites until soft peaks form; fold into batter and mix well. Spoon into a greased 10-in. tube pan lined with waxed paper. Bake at 200° for 1-1/2 hours. Increase heat to 250° and bake for 1 hour. Increase heat to 300° and bake for 30 minutes. Remove from the oven; cool completely in pan. **Yield:** 20-24 servings.

BANANA STREUSEL PIE
Gayle Kuipers, Holland, Michigan

(Pictured on page 98)

I obtained this recipe from my mom, who is a great cook. It's been in the family for years. We usually serve it at holiday meals—it's always a crowd-pleaser.

  1 unbaked pastry shell (9 inches)
1/4 cup sugar
1/2 teaspoon ground cinnamon
  1 teaspoon cornstarch
1/2 cup pineapple juice
  2 tablespoons lemon juice
1-1/2 teaspoons grated lemon peel
  4 cups sliced ripe bananas (5 to 6 medium)
STREUSEL:
1/2 cup all-purpose flour
1/2 cup packed brown sugar
1/3 cup chopped macadamia nuts *or* almonds
  1 teaspoon ground cinnamon
1/4 cup butter *or* margarine

Line the unpricked pastry shell with a double thickness of foil. Bake at 450° for 10 minutes. Remove the foil and bake 2 minutes more or until pastry is golden brown; set aside. Reduce heat to 375°. In a saucepan, combine the sugar, cinnamon and cornstarch. Add the pineapple juice, lemon juice and peel; mix well. Cook and stir until thickened and bubbly; cook and stir 2 minutes more. Remove from the heat. Fold in bananas; pour into crust. For streusel, combine flour, brown sugar, nuts and cinnamon; cut in butter until the mixture resembles coarse crumbs. Sprinkle over the filling. Cover edges of pie with foil. Bake at 375° for 40 minutes or until topping is golden and filling is bubbly. Cool on a wire rack. **Yield:** 6-8 servings.

DEVIL'S FOOD SHEET CAKE

James Crabb, Greeley, Colorado

(Pictured at right)

I like this cake because it's so moist and rich. It's great for large gatherings because it's so easy to make. Don't be surprised if your guests ask for seconds—it's that good!

1-1/2 cups water
   2 cups sugar
  3/4 cup butter *or* margarine
   2 eggs, lightly beaten
   1 teaspoon vanilla extract
   2 cups all-purpose flour
  1/2 cup baking cocoa
   2 teaspoons baking soda
  1/2 teaspoon salt
FROSTING:
  1/4 cup butter *or* margarine, softened
   2 cups confectioners' sugar
   2 tablespoons baking cocoa
  1/2 teaspoon vanilla extract
   2 to 3 tablespoons milk

In a large saucepan, bring water to a boil. Remove from the heat. Stir in sugar and butter until butter is melted. Add eggs and vanilla; mix well. Combine flour, cocoa, baking soda and salt; add to butter mixture and mix thoroughly. Pour into a greased and floured 15-in. x 10-in. x 1-in. baking pan. Bake at 350° for 30-35 minutes or until a wooden pick inserted near the center comes out clean. Cool completely on a wire rack. For frosting, beat butter, confectioners' sugar, cocoa, vanilla and enough milk to reach a spreading consistency. Frost cake. **Yield:** 16-20 servings.

CHERRY TORTE

Marsha Cook, Broken Arrow, Oklahoma

(Pictured on page 98)

As a pastor's wife, I am invited to many good dinners and get the chance to collect lots of recipes. This dessert comes from a cookbook put together years ago by my home church in Arkansas.

1-1/2 cups all-purpose flour
  1/4 teaspoon salt
  3/4 cup butter-flavored shortening
   1 to 2 tablespoons cold water
   1 package (8 ounces) cream cheese,
    softened
  1/2 cup sugar
   2 eggs
   1 teaspoon vanilla extract
   2 cans (21 ounces *each*) cherry pie filling
  3/4 teaspoon almond extract
   1 carton (8 ounces) frozen whipped
    topping, thawed
  1/4 cup chopped pecans

In a medium bowl, combine the flour and salt; cut in shortening until the mixture resembles coarse crumbs. Add enough water to shape dough into a ball. On a lightly floured surface, roll dough to fit a 12-in. pizza pan. Flute edges; prick bottom and sides with a fork. Bake at 425° for 10-12 minutes or until lightly browned; remove from the oven. Reduce heat to 350°. In a large mixing bowl, beat cream cheese, sugar, eggs and vanilla until smooth; pour into crust. Bake for 10-12 minutes or until center is set. Cool completely on a wire rack. Combine pie filling and almond extract; spoon over the cream cheese layer. Spread whipped topping over filling. Chill until ready to serve. Sprinkle with pecans. **Yield:** 10-12 servings.

PEANUT BUTTER CHOCOLATE CAKE

Dorcas Yoder, Weyers Cave, Virginia

(Pictured at left)

In our chocolate-loving house, this cake disappears very quickly! Cream cheese and peanut butter combine to create a finger-licking-good frosting.

  2 cups all-purpose flour
  2 cups sugar
2/3 cup baking cocoa
  2 teaspoons baking soda
  1 teaspoon baking powder
1/2 teaspoon salt
  2 eggs
  1 cup milk
2/3 cup vegetable oil
  1 teaspoon vanilla extract
  1 cup brewed coffee, room temperature
PEANUT BUTTER FROSTING:
  1 package (3 ounces) cream cheese, softened
1/4 cup creamy peanut butter
  2 cups confectioners' sugar
  2 tablespoons milk
1/2 teaspoon vanilla extract
Miniature semisweet chocolate chips, optional

In a mixing bowl, combine dry ingredients. Add eggs, milk, oil and vanilla; beat for 2 minutes. Stir in coffee (batter will be thin). Pour into a greased 13-in. x 9-in. x 2-in. baking pan. Bake at 350° for 35-40 minutes or until a wooden pick inserted near the center comes out clean. Cool completely on a wire rack. For frosting, beat the cream cheese and peanut butter in a mixing bowl until smooth. Beat in sugar, milk and vanilla. Spread over cake. Sprinkle with chocolate chips if desired. Store in the refrigerator. **Yield:** 12-16 servings.

PUMPKIN-PECAN CAKE

Joyce Platfoot, Wapakoneta, Ohio

(Pictured at left)

With our eight children, I do a lot of cooking. But I have to admit I enjoy baking much more. This cake is one of my family's favorites.

  2 cups crushed vanilla wafers (about 50)
  1 cup chopped pecans
3/4 cup butter *or* margarine, softened
CAKE:
  1 box (18-1/4 ounces) spice cake mix
  1 can (16 ounces) solid-pack pumpkin

1/4 cup butter *or* margarine, softened
  4 eggs
FILLING/TOPPING:
2/3 cup butter *or* margarine, softened
  1 package (3 ounces) cream cheese, softened
  3 cups confectioners' sugar
  2 teaspoons vanilla extract
1/2 cup caramel ice cream topping

In a mixing bowl on medium speed, beat the wafers, pecans and butter until crumbly, about 1 minute. Press into three greased and floured 9-in. round cake pans. In another mixing bowl, beat cake mix, pumpkin, butter and eggs for 3 minutes. Spread over crust in each pan. Bake at 350° for 30 minutes or until a wooden pick inserted near the center comes out clean. Cool in pans 10 minutes; remove to wire racks and cool completely. For filling, combine butter and cream cheese in a small mixing bowl. Add sugar and vanilla; beat on medium until light and fluffy, about 3 minutes. Thinly spread between layers (crumb side down) and on the sides of cake. Spread caramel topping over top of cake, allowing some to drip down the sides. Store in the refrigerator. **Yield:** 16-20 servings.

ICE CREAM PEACHES

Helen Banycky, Carterville, Illinois

You'll be struck by how the shape of the scoops suggests actual peaches. To expand that look, roll the scoops in gelatin for a fuzzy appearance.

  4 cups sliced peeled fresh *or* frozen peaches, thawed
  3 cups half-and-half cream
1-1/4 cups sugar
1-1/2 teaspoons lemon juice
1/2 teaspoon vanilla extract
1/4 teaspoon almond extract
1/8 teaspoon salt
  1 package (3 ounces) peach gelatin
Whole cloves and fresh mint, optional

In a large bowl, mash peaches until smooth. Stir in the next six ingredients until sugar is dissolved. For best results, chill for at least 3 hours. Freeze in an ice cream freezer according to manufacturer's directions. Shape by 2/3 cupfuls into balls, forming a crease down one side to resemble a peach if desired. Cover and freeze for at least 8 hours. Place gelatin in a large resealable plastic bag; add ice cream balls, one at a time, and roll until coated. Place in serving dishes. If desired, insert cloves to resemble peach stems and mint for leaves. Freeze or serve immediately. **Yield:** 12 servings.

Carroty Creation Suits Any Occasion

TURN any meal into a celebration with Carrot Layer Cake from Linda Van Holland of Innisfail, Alberta.

"When they cut into it, people are bowled over by this moist not-too-sweet cake," Linda explains. "The pecan filling is another unexpected treat."

Adds Linda, "My sister gave me this recipe for what she called 'the ultimate carrot cake'."

CARROT LAYER CAKE

(Pictured on page 102)

FILLING:
- 1 cup sugar
- 2 tablespoons all-purpose flour
- 1/4 teaspoon salt
- 1 cup whipping cream
- 1/2 cup butter *or* margarine
- 1 cup chopped pecans
- 1 teaspoon vanilla extract

CAKE:
- 1-1/4 cups vegetable oil
- 2 cups sugar
- 2 cups all-purpose flour
- 2 teaspoons ground cinnamon
- 2 teaspoons baking powder
- 1 teaspoon baking soda
- 1 teaspoon salt
- 4 eggs
- 4 cups finely shredded carrots
- 1 cup raisins
- 1 cup chopped pecans

FROSTING:
- 3/4 cup butter *or* margarine, softened
- 2 packages (3 ounces *each*) cream cheese, softened
- 1 teaspoon vanilla extract
- 3 cups confectioners' sugar

In a heavy saucepan, combine sugar, flour and salt. Stir in cream; add butter. Cook and stir over medium heat until the butter is melted; bring to a boil. Reduce heat. Simmer, uncovered, for 30 minutes, stirring occasionally. Stir in nuts and vanilla. Set aside to cool. In a mixing bowl, beat oil and sugar for 1 minute. Combine flour, cinnamon, baking powder, baking soda and salt; add to the creamed mixture alternately with eggs. Mix well. Stir in carrots, raisins and nuts. Pour into three greased and floured 9-in. round baking pans. Bake at 350° for 35-40 minutes or until a wooden pick inserted near the center comes out clean. Cool in pans 10 minutes; remove to wire racks and cool completely. For frosting, beat butter, cream cheese and vanilla until smooth. Gradually beat in sugar. Spread filling between cake layers. Frost sides and top of cake. Store in the refrigerator. **Yield:** 16-20 servings.

CRANBERRY-ORANGE POUND CAKE

Sheree Swistun, Winnipeg, Manitoba

(Pictured on page 102)

This is a favorite at the summer resort my husband and I operate in Ontario. We prepare all the meals for our guests, so I'm always looking for new recipes.

- 1-1/2 cups butter (no substitutes), softened
- 2-3/4 cups sugar
- 6 eggs
- 1 teaspoon vanilla extract
- 2-1/2 teaspoons grated orange peel
- 3 cups all-purpose flour
- 1 teaspoon baking powder
- 1/2 teaspoon salt
- 1 cup (8 ounces) sour cream
- 1-1/2 cups chopped fresh *or* frozen cranberries

VANILLA BUTTER SAUCE:
- 1 cup sugar
- 1 tablespoon all-purpose flour
- 1/2 cup half-and-half cream
- 1/2 cup butter (no substitutes), softened
- 1/2 teaspoon vanilla extract

In a mixing bowl, cream butter. Gradually beat in sugar until light and fluffy, about 5-7 minutes. Add eggs, one at a time, beating well after each addition. Stir in vanilla and orange peel. Combine flour, baking powder and salt; add to the creamed mixture alternately with sour cream. Beat on low just until blended. Fold in cranberries. Pour into a greased and floured 10-in. fluted tube pan. Bake at 350° for 65-70 minutes or until a wooden pick inserted near the center comes out clean. Cool in pan for 10 minutes; remove to a wire rack and cool completely. In a small saucepan, combine sugar and flour. Stir in cream and butter; bring to a boil over medium heat, stirring constantly. Boil for 2 minutes. Remove from the heat and stir in vanilla. Serve warm over cake. **Yield:** 16 servings (1-1/2 cups sauce).

SUNFLOWER SEED COOKIES

Connie White, Stirum, North Dakota

We grow 800 acres of sunflowers and use the nutritious seeds in a variety of recipes.

> 1 cup butter *or* margarine, softened
> 3/4 cup shortening
> 2 cups sugar
> 1 tablespoon water
> 1 teaspoon vanilla extract
> 3 cups all-purpose flour
> 1 teaspoon baking soda
> 1 teaspoon baking powder
> 1 teaspoon salt
> 1 cup roasted salted sunflower seeds

In a mixing bowl, cream butter, shortening and sugar. Add water and vanilla; mix well. Combine flour, baking soda, baking powder and salt; add to creamed mixture and mix well. Stir in sunflower seeds. Shape into 1-in. balls; place 2 in. apart on greased baking sheets. Flatten with a glass dipped in sugar. Bake at 350° for 11-13 minutes or until lightly browned. Remove to a wire rack to cool. **Yield:** about 10 dozen.

CARAMEL-CRUNCH APPLE PIE

Debbie Roach, Grant City, Missouri

(Pictured below right)

My mom taught me how to make all kinds of pies from scratch, and this is one of my favorites.

TOPPING:
> 1/4 cup all-purpose flour
> 1/3 cup packed brown sugar
> 2 tablespoons butter *or* margarine, softened
> 1/2 teaspoon ground cinnamon

PIE:
> 6 cups sliced peeled baking apples
> 1 tablespoon lemon juice
> 1/2 cup sugar
> 3 tablespoons all-purpose flour
> 1/2 teaspoon ground cinnamon
> 1 unbaked pastry shell (9 inches)
> 28 caramels
> 1 can (5 ounces) evaporated milk

Combine flour, brown sugar, butter and cinnamon; spread into an ungreased 8-in. square baking pan. Bake at 400° for 6-8 minutes or until golden brown. Cool; crumble and set aside. Sprinkle apples with lemon juice. Combine sugar, flour and cinnamon; toss with apples. Place apples in pie shell. Cut a circle of foil to cover apples but not the edge of pastry; place over pie. Bake at 425° for 10 minutes. Reduce heat to 375°; bake for 35 minutes or until apples are tender. Meanwhile, in a saucepan over low heat, melt caramels with milk, stirring frequently. Remove foil from pie. Pour caramel mixture over apples. Sprinkle with topping; return to the oven for 5 minutes. Serve warm. **Yield:** 6-8 servings.

REFRIGERATOR COOKIES

Dottie Gray, Bartlett, Tennessee

During the holidays, I usually keep at least two rolls of this cookie dough in my freezer in case I need something special in a hurry.

> 1 cup butter *or* margarine, softened
> 1 cup sugar
> 2 tablespoons milk
> 1 teaspoon vanilla extract
> 2-1/2 cups all-purpose flour
> 3/4 cup chopped red and green candied cherries
> 1/2 cup finely chopped pecans

In a mixing bowl, cream butter and sugar until fluffy. Add milk and vanilla; mix well. Add flour. Fold in the cherries and pecans. Shape dough into two 8-in. x 2-in. rolls; wrap in waxed paper and freeze. To bake, unwrap and let stand at room temperature for about 10 minutes. Cut into 1/4-in. slices. Place 2 in. apart on ungreased baking sheets. Bake at 375° for 10-12 minutes or until lightly browned. Cool on wire racks. **Yield:** about 7 dozen.

completely on a wire rack. Chill several hours or overnight. Top each square with fruit if desired. **Yield:** 20 servings.

RHUBARB RASPBERRY PIE

Lynda Bailey, Sandpoint, Idaho

My family loves rhubarb and raspberries, so I was happy to find this recipe several years ago. We recently moved from the city to the country and are thoroughly enjoying our new life-style.

  1 cup sugar
  1/4 cup quick-cooking tapioca
  4 cups chopped fresh *or* frozen rhubarb
  1 cup fresh *or* frozen raspberries
  2 tablespoons lemon juice
Pastry for double-crust pie (9 inches)

In a large bowl, combine sugar and tapioca. Add the rhubarb, raspberries and lemon juice; mix gently. Let stand for at least 15 minutes or up to 1 hour to soften tapioca; stir gently several times. Line a pie plate with bottom crust. Pour filling into crust. Top with a lattice crust. Bake at 375° for 45-55 minutes or until the crust is golden and filling is bubbly. Serve warm or at room temperature. **Yield:** 6-8 servings.

CHEESECAKE SQUARES

Shirley Forest, Eau Claire, Wisconsin

(Pictured above)

I lived on a dairy farm when I was young, and my mom always had a lot of sour cream to use. She never wasted any, and this cheesecake was one of my family's favorites. It's great topped with blackberry sauce.

  2 packages (8 ounces *each*) cream cheese, softened
  1 cup ricotta cheese
1-1/2 cups sugar
  4 eggs
  1/4 cup butter *or* margarine, melted and cooled
  3 tablespoons cornstarch
  3 tablespoons all-purpose flour
  1 tablespoon vanilla extract
  2 cups (16 ounces) sour cream
Seasonal fresh fruit, optional

In a mixing bowl, beat cream cheese, ricotta and sugar until smooth. Add the eggs, one at a time, mixing well after each addition. Add butter, cornstarch, flour and vanilla; beat until smooth. Fold in sour cream. Pour into a greased 13-in. x 9-in. x 2-in. baking pan. Bake, uncovered, at 325° for 1 hour. Do not open oven door. Turn oven off. Let cheesecake stand in closed oven for 2 hours. Cool

NO-EGG APPLESAUCE CAKE

Cathryn Hennings, Osceola, Nebraska

When I first saw this recipe, I thought there was a mistake—it doesn't contain even one egg! Applesauce gives this cake its tender moist texture.

✓ This tasty dish uses less sugar, salt or fat.

  1/2 cup low-fat margarine (40% corn oil), softened
  1 cup sugar
  2 cups all-purpose flour
  2 teaspoons baking soda
1-1/2 teaspoons ground cinnamon
  1/2 teaspoon ground cloves
1-1/2 cups unsweetened applesauce
  1/2 cup raisins

In a mixing bowl, cream margarine and sugar until fluffy. Combine flour, baking soda, cinnamon and cloves; add alternately to creamed mixture with applesauce. Beat on low until well blended. Stir in raisins. Pour into a 9-in. square baking pan that has been coated with nonstick cooking spray. Bake at 350° for 35-40 minutes or until a wooden pick inserted near the center comes out clean. Cool on a wire rack. **Yield:** 12 servings.

Nutritional Analysis: One serving equals 247 calories, 83 mg sodium, 0 cholesterol, 43 gm carbohydrate, 3 gm protein, 8 gm fat.

MAPLE BISCUIT DESSERT

Leslie Malter, Waterbury, Vermont

These biscuits have been made by the women in my family for a long time. We use the maple syrup we boil each sugaring season from the trees on our land.

    2 cups all-purpose flour
    1 tablespoon baking powder
1/2 teaspoon salt
1/4 cup shortening
3/4 cup milk
1-1/2 cups maple syrup

In a bowl, combine flour, baking powder and salt; cut in shortening until mixture resembles coarse crumbs. Add milk; stir just until moistened. Turn onto a lightly floured surface; roll to 1/2-in. thickness. Cut with a 2-in. biscuit cutter. Pour syrup into an 11-in. x 7-in. x 2-in. baking dish. Place biscuits on top of syrup. Bake at 450° for 12-15 minutes or until biscuits are golden brown. **Yield:** 10-12 servings.

GHOSTLY CUSTARDS

Suzanne Strocsher, Bothell, Washington

Here's a tasteful way to get into the "spirit" at Halloween! Our young daughter is always eager to help make these desserts.

    1 can (16 ounces) solid-pack pumpkin
    1 can (12 ounces) evaporated milk
1/3 cup sugar
    2 tablespoons honey
    1 teaspoon ground cinnamon
3/4 teaspoon ground allspice
    2 eggs
    2 cups frozen whipped topping, thawed
Mini chocolate chips

In a mixing bowl, combine the first seven ingredients; beat on low until smooth. Place eight ungreased 4-oz. custard cups in two 8-in. square baking pans. Fill each cup with 1/2 cup of pumpkin mixture. Pour hot water around cups into the pans to a depth of 1 in. Bake at 325° for 40-50 minutes or until a knife inserted near the center comes out clean. Remove from pans to cool on wire racks. Before serving, top each with dollops of whipped topping in the shape of a ghost; add chocolate chips for eyes. **Yield:** 8 servings.

CHOCOLATE TRUFFLE COOKIES

Sharon Miller, Thousand Oaks, California

(Pictured below)

I experimented with a chocolate cookie recipe until I was satisfied with the results. I entered these cookies at our county fair and won a blue ribbon. If you love chocolate, I'm sure you'll like them.

1-1/4 cups butter or margarine, softened
2-1/4 cups confectioners' sugar
1/3 cup baking cocoa
1/4 cup sour cream
    1 tablespoon vanilla extract
2-1/4 cups all-purpose flour
    2 cups (12 ounces) semisweet chocolate chips
1/4 cup chocolate sprinkles

In a mixing bowl, cream butter, sugar and cocoa until light and fluffy. Beat in sour cream and vanilla. Add flour; mix well. Stir in chocolate chips. Refrigerate for 1 hour. Roll into 1-in. balls; dip in chocolate sprinkles. Place, sprinkled side up, 2 in. apart on ungreased baking sheets. Bake at 325° for 10 minutes or until set. Cool 5 minutes before removing to a wire rack to cool completely. **Yield:** about 5-1/2 dozen.

CHOCOLATE SHEET CAKE

Dianne Medwid, Dauphin, Manitoba

(Pictured on page 110)

The biggest compliment I've ever gotten on this cake might have come when I baked it for my son's 11th birthday. The children all asked for seconds!

    2 cups sugar
    2 cups all-purpose flour
    1 teaspoon baking soda
    1/2 teaspoon salt
    1/2 cup butter *or* margarine
    1/4 cup baking cocoa
    1 cup water
    2 eggs
    1/2 cup buttermilk
    1 teaspoon vanilla extract
ICING:
    1/2 cup butter *or* margarine
    1/4 cup baking cocoa
    1/3 cup milk
    2 cups confectioners' sugar
    1 teaspoon vanilla extract
    1 cup chopped walnuts

In a mixing bowl, combine the first four ingredients; set aside. In a small saucepan, bring butter, cocoa and water to a boil. Add to dry ingredients and mix well. In a small mixing bowl, beat eggs. Add buttermilk and vanilla; mix well. Stir into cocoa mixture. Pour into a greased 15-in. x 10-in. x 1-in. baking pan. Bake at 375° for 20-22 minutes or until a wooden pick inserted near the center comes out clean. Meanwhile, in a saucepan, bring butter, cocoa and milk to a boil, stirring constantly. Remove from the heat; add sugar and vanilla. Mix well. Spread over hot cake; immediately sprinkle with nuts. Cool completely on a wire rack. **Yield:** 16-20 servings.

BUTTERMILK BANANA CAKE

Arlene Grenz, Linton, North Dakota

(Pictured on page 110)

When I was a girl, this was my family's favorite Sunday cake. Since I'm "nuts" about nuts, I added the pecans. Our youngsters love it, too.

    3/4 cup butter *or* margarine, softened
    1 cup sugar
    1/2 cup packed brown sugar
    2 eggs
    1 cup mashed ripe banana

    1 teaspoon vanilla extract
    2 cups cake flour
    1 teaspoon baking powder
    1 teaspoon baking soda
    1/2 teaspoon salt
    1/2 cup buttermilk
FILLING/FROSTING:
    1/2 cup half-and-half cream
    1/2 cup sugar
    2 tablespoons butter *or* margarine
    2 tablespoons all-purpose flour
    1/4 teaspoon salt
    1 teaspoon vanilla extract
    1/2 cup chopped pecans
    2 cups whipping cream
    1/4 cup confectioners' sugar

In a mixing bowl, cream butter and sugars until fluffy. Add eggs; beat for 2 minutes. Add banana and vanilla; beat for 2 minutes. Combine the flour, baking powder, baking soda and salt; add to creamed mixture alternately with buttermilk. Pour into two greased and floured 9-in. round cake pans. Bake at 375° for 25-30 minutes or until a wooden pick inserted near the center comes out clean. Cool in pans 10 minutes; remove to wire racks and cool completely. For filling, combine half-and-half, sugar, butter, flour and salt in a saucepan. Bring to a boil; cook and stir for 2 minutes. Remove from the heat; stir in vanilla and pecans. Cool. Spread between cake layers. For frosting, beat whipping cream until soft peaks form. Gradually beat in the confectioners' sugar; beat until stiff peaks form. Spread over top and sides of cake. Store in the refrigerator. **Yield:** 12-16 servings.

LEMON MERINGUE CAKE

Debra Blair, Glenwood, Minnesota

(Pictured on page 111)

My husband likes lemon meringue pie, so I figured this would appeal to him. It's his favorite birthday cake.

    1/4 cup butter *or* margarine, softened
    1/2 cup sugar
    1 egg plus 2 egg yolks
    1 cup all-purpose flour
    1 teaspoon baking powder
    1/3 cup milk
    1/2 teaspoon vanilla extract
FILLING:
    2 egg yolks
    1 cup water
    3/4 cup sugar
    1/3 cup all-purpose flour

1/2 teaspoon grated lemon peel
1/4 cup fresh lemon juice
1 tablespoon butter *or* margarine
MERINGUE:
4 egg whites, room temperature
1/2 teaspoon cream of tartar
1/2 cup sugar

In a mixing bowl, cream butter and sugar. Add egg and yolks; mix well. Combine flour and baking powder; add to creamed mixture alternately with milk. Mix well. Add vanilla. Pour into a greased and floured 9-in. round cake pan. Bake at 350° for 25-30 minutes or until a wooden pick inserted near the center comes out clean. Cool in pan 10 minutes; remove to a wire rack and cool completely. In a heavy saucepan, combine egg yolks, water, sugar, flour and peel; bring to a gentle boil over medium heat, stirring constantly. Cook and stir for 2-3 minutes or until thickened. Stir in lemon juice and butter. Place cake on a baking sheet; spoon filling on top of cake up to 1/2 in. from edge. Beat egg whites until foamy. Add cream of tartar; beat on high for 1 minute. Add sugar, 1 tablespoon at a time, beating well after each addition. Beat until stiff peaks form, about 3 minutes. Carefully spread over filling, sealing to edges of cake. Bake at 350° for 12-15 minutes or until lightly browned. **Yield:** 6-8 servings.

CARAMEL APPLE CAKE

Paulette Reyenga, Brantford, Ontario

(Pictured on page 111)

A wonderful harvest of apples that we picked up at a local orchard one year inspired me to adjust a recipe I'd seen and come up with this moist cake.

1/2 cup chopped walnuts
1/3 cup packed brown sugar
1 cup flaked coconut
2-1/2 cups all-purpose flour
1-1/2 cups sugar
1-1/2 teaspoons baking soda
1 teaspoon salt
1/2 teaspoon baking powder
1/4 teaspoon ground cinnamon
2 eggs
1/2 cup evaporated milk
1/3 cup water
2 cups finely shredded peeled apples
CARAMEL TOPPING:
1/3 cup packed brown sugar
1/4 cup evaporated milk
2 tablespoons butter *or* margarine

Combine walnuts, brown sugar and coconut; set aside. In a mixing bowl, combine the next six ingredients. In a small bowl, combine eggs, milk, water and apples; add to flour mixture. Mix well. Pour into a greased 13-in. x 9-in. x 2-in. baking pan. Sprinkle with nut mixture. Bake at 325° for 45-50 minutes or until a wooden pick inserted near the center comes out clean. Meanwhile, in a heavy saucepan, combine the topping ingredients; cook over medium heat, stirring constantly, until the sugar is dissolved and the mixture has thickened slightly, about 8 minutes. Poke holes with a fork in top of the hot cake; immediately spoon topping over cake. Cool completely on a wire rack. **Yield:** 12-15 servings.

SUNFLOWER POTLUCK CAKE

Lola Wiemer, Clarklake, Michigan

(Pictured on page 111)

I wish I knew who to thank for the idea for my cake. I first saw it on the dessert table at a picnic. Later, for something different, I did my own variation.

3/4 cup butter *or* margarine, softened
1-2/3 cups sugar
3 eggs
1 teaspoon vanilla extract
2 cups all-purpose flour
2/3 cup baking cocoa
1-1/4 teaspoons baking soda
1 teaspoon salt
1/4 teaspoon baking powder
1-1/3 cups water
1 cup prepared chocolate frosting, *divided*
1 cup (6 ounces) semisweet chocolate chips
22 cream-filled sponge cakes
1 teaspoon milk
2 craft decorating bees, optional

In a mixing bowl, cream butter and sugar. Add eggs, one at a time, beating well after each addition. Add vanilla. Combine dry ingredients; add to the creamed mixture alternately with water. Pour into two greased and floured 9-in. round cake pans. Bake at 350° for 25-30 minutes or until a wooden pick inserted near the center comes out clean. Cool in pans for 10 minutes; remove to wire racks and cool completely. Freeze one layer for future use. Set aside 1 tablespoon frosting. Frost top and sides of remaining cake. Place cake in the center of a large round tray (about 18 in.). Arrange chocolate chips on top of cake. Place sponge cakes around cake. Mix reserved frosting with milk; drizzle over sponge cakes. Decorate with bees if desired. **Yield:** 22 servings.

CHOCOLATE CHIFFON CAKE

Dorothy Haag, Mt. Horeb, Wisconsin

(Pictured on page 110)

There were 11 of us to cook for when I was young. This cake was always a good way of using up any cracked eggs from the laying hens my mother kept.

    2/3 cup baking cocoa
    3/4 cup hot water
1-1/2 cups cake flour
1-3/4 cups sugar
    1 teaspoon baking soda
    1 teaspoon salt
    1/2 cup vegetable oil
    7 eggs, *separated*
    1 teaspoon vanilla extract
    1/2 teaspoon cream of tartar
Confectioners' sugar

In a small bowl, stir cocoa and water until smooth; cool. In a large bowl, combine flour, sugar, baking soda and salt. Add oil, egg yolks, vanilla and cocoa mixture; stir until smooth. In a mixing bowl, beat the egg whites until foamy. Add cream of tartar; beat until stiff peaks form. Gradually fold in egg yolk mixture. Pour into an ungreased 10-in. tube pan. Bake on lowest rack at 325° for 60-65 minutes or until the top springs back when lightly touched and cracks feel dry. Immediately invert pan on a bottle; cool completely. Loosen sides of cake from pan and remove. Dust with confectioners' sugar. **Yield:** 12-16 servings.

PUMPKIN CAKE WITH CARAMEL SAUCE

Roberta Peck, Fort Hill, Pennsylvania

(Pictured on page 110)

This recipe resulted when I added my favorite key ingredient—pumpkin—to an old recipe for spice cake that I had. Everyone who's tried it has enjoyed it.

    2 cups all-purpose flour
    2 cups sugar
    2 teaspoons baking soda
    2 teaspoons ground cinnamon
    1 teaspoon ground nutmeg
    1/2 teaspoon salt
    4 eggs
    1 can (16 ounces) solid-pack pumpkin
    1 cup vegetable oil
CARAMEL SAUCE:
1-1/2 cups packed brown sugar
    3 tablespoons all-purpose flour
Pinch salt

1-1/4 cups water
    2 tablespoons butter *or* margarine
    1/2 teaspoon vanilla extract

In a mixing bowl, combine the first six ingredients. In another bowl, beat eggs, pumpkin and oil until smooth; add to the dry ingredients. Mix until well blended, about 1 minute. Pour into a greased 13-in. x 9-in. x 2-in. baking pan. Bake at 350° for 35-40 minutes or until a wooden pick inserted near the center comes out clean. Cool on a wire rack. For sauce, combine brown sugar, flour and salt in a saucepan. Stir in water and butter; bring to a boil over medium heat. Boil for 3 minutes, stirring constantly. Remove from the heat; stir in vanilla. Cut cake into squares and serve with warm sauce. **Yield:** 12-15 servings.

MOCHA CUPCAKES

Lorna Smith, New Hazelton, British Columbia

(Pictured on page 111)

This recipe is one that I have called on over the years for numerous occasions—birthdays, PTA meetings, for serving to company, etc.

    1 cup boiling water
    1 cup mayonnaise*
    1 teaspoon vanilla extract
    2 cups all-purpose flour
    1 cup sugar
    1/2 cup baking cocoa
    2 teaspoons baking soda
MOCHA FROSTING:
    3/4 cup confectioners' sugar
    1/4 cup baking cocoa
    1/2 to 1 teaspoon instant coffee granules
Pinch salt
1-1/2 cups whipping cream

In a mixing bowl, combine water, mayonnaise and vanilla. Combine flour, sugar, cocoa and baking soda; add to the mayonnaise mixture and beat until well mixed. Fill greased or paper-lined muffin cups two-thirds full. Bake at 350° for 20-25 minutes or until a wooden pick inserted near the center comes out clean. Cool in tins 10 minutes; remove to wire racks and cool completely. For frosting, combine sugar, cocoa, coffee and salt in a mixing bowl. Stir in cream; cover and chill with beaters for 30 minutes. Beat frosting until stiff peaks form. Frost the cupcakes. **Yield:** about 1-1/2 dozen. **To make a cake:** Prepare batter and bake as directed for cupcakes, except use two greased 8-in. round cake pans. Frost between layers and sides and top of cake. Serves 12. **Editor's Note:** Do not substitute light or low-fat mayonnaise for regular mayonnaise.

Tried-and-True Tips for Top Cakes

• What could be easier? I bake my lemon pound cake ahead and freeze it for last-minute get-togethers and family gatherings. To serve, I just thaw it and top with fresh fruit, ice cream or a dessert sauce. *—Barbara Wellons Charlotte, Tennessee*

• With my scratch recipe for angel food cake, I often add part of a package of my favorite Jell-O flavor to the flour before it goes into the egg whites. It lends nice flavor and a pretty color.
—Mrs. Mervin Eash Burr Oak, Michigan

• When I'm in a hurry, I like to dust my cinnamon apple cake with confectioners' sugar instead of frosting it. For an even prettier look, I place a doily over the cake before sifting sugar over it to produce a lacy effect.
—C.B. LaMay Capitan, New Mexico

• To split a cake in half horizontally, use dental floss or heavy-duty white thread rather than a knife. Simply cut a 2-foot piece of floss or thread...then pull, using a sawing motion, through the center of the cake.
—Helen Morris Newberry, South Carolina

• Before baking a cake, run a knife through the batter to remove air pockets, then drop the pan on the table.

Instead of greasing a cake pan, line the bottom with parchment paper cut to the exact pan measurements. You'll find your cake bakes more evenly, reducing the dome effect in the middle ...plus it's easy to remove from the pan, and there's less cleanup.
—Tammy Stafford, Laotto, Indiana

• To tint coconut for topping a cake, combine a few drops of food coloring with a few drops of water. Add a couple of tablespoons of shredded coconut and toss with a fork until coated.
—Clara Graber Freeman, South Dakota

• Whenever I make layer cakes, I weigh each layer to make sure that I have the same amount of batter in each pan. That way, my layers always end up the same size. *—Pauline Williams Dallas Center, Iowa*

• For instant banana frosting, try this: Empty a container of prepared white frosting into a small mixing bowl and beat in a pureed banana.
—Debra Lee Culp Fort Worth, Texas

• Before you bake a cake, preheat your oven for at least 10 minutes to ensure best results. Afterward, don't frost the cake until it's cooled to room temperature (unless the recipe states otherwise). *—Myrna Shearer Chetek, Wisconsin*

• For higher and lighter cakes, I use cake flour and always let eggs warm to room temperature.
—Arlene Bontrager, Haven, Kansas

Quick & Easy Cake Recipes

NO MATTER how crowded a schedule you may face, you can have your cake and eat it, too! With these quick-to-assemble specialties from fellow bakers across the country, you'll be serving up a scrumptious completed cake in around an hour—one fine for family or company!

COFFEE ANGEL FOOD CAKE

Carol Brown, Cyde, Texas

Here's an easy way to dress up a plain angel food cake mix. It tastes especially good after a heavy dinner.

>   2 teaspoons instant coffee granules
> 1-1/4 cups water
>   1 package (16 ounces) one-step angel
>   food cake mix
> FROSTING:
>   1/2 cup butter *or* margarine
> 3-3/4 cups confectioners' sugar
>   1 to 2 tablespoons instant coffee granules
>   1/4 cup milk
>   1/2 cup sliced almonds, toasted

In a mixing bowl, dissolve coffee in water; add cake mix. Mix, bake and cool as directed on package. For frosting, cream butter and sugar in a mixing bowl. Dissolve coffee in milk; add to the creamed mixture and beat until smooth. Frost the top and sides of cake. Garnish with almonds. **Yield:** 12-16 servings.

ROOT BEER FLOAT CAKE

Gail Toepfer, Iron Ridge, Wisconsin

When I came across this fun and festive recipe, I knew I had to give it a try. I hope you try it, too!

>   1 package (18-1/4 ounces) white cake mix
> 1-1/4 cups root beer
>   2 eggs

>   1/4 cup vegetable oil
> FROSTING:
>   1 packet (1.3 ounces) whipped topping
>   mix
>   1/2 cup chilled root beer

In a mixing bowl, combine the first four ingredients. Beat on low speed for 30 seconds; beat on high for 2 minutes. Pour into a greased 13-in. x 9-in. x 2-in. baking pan. Bake at 350° for 35-40 minutes or until a wooden pick inserted near the center comes out clean. Cool completely on a wire rack. In another mixing bowl, beat frosting ingredients until stiff peaks form. Frost cake. Chill. **Yield:** 12-15 servings.

PINEAPPLE BUNDT CAKE

Pat Remour, East Moline, Illinois

This variation of an upside-down pineapple cake couldn't be easier because it starts with a cake mix.

>   1 can (20 ounces) crushed pineapple
>   1/3 cup packed brown sugar
>   3 tablespoons butter *or* margarine, melted
>   8 maraschino cherries
>   8 pecan halves
>   1 package (16 ounces) pound cake mix
>   1 teaspoon grated lemon peel
>   1 teaspoon vanilla extract

Drain pineapple, reserving juice. Combine 1/2 cup pineapple, brown sugar, butter and 3 tablespoons of pineapple juice. Spoon into a greased 10-in. fluted tube pan. Alternate cherries and pecans over the sugar mixture. Prepare cake batter according to package directions, substituting reserved pineapple juice for water. Stir in lemon peel, vanilla and remaining pineapple. Spoon over cherries and pecans. Bake at 325° for 60-70 minutes or until a wooden pick inserted near the center comes out clean. Cool in pan

10 minutes before removing to a wire rack; cool completely. **Yield:** 12-16 servings.

....

BOSTON CREAM CAKE

Michelle Mirich, Youngstown, Ohio

Folks who like Boston Cream Pie will love this cake. It's a cool and creamy treat for the taste buds.

     1 package (9 ounces) yellow cake mix
 1/2 teaspoon lemon extract
     1 package (3.4 ounces) instant vanilla
       pudding mix
     2 cups cold milk
     1 square (1 ounce) semisweet chocolate
     1 tablespoon butter *or* margarine
 1/2 cup confectioners' sugar
     2 to 3 teaspoons hot water

Mix cake according to package directions, adding lemon extract to batter. Pour into a greased and floured 9-in. round cake pan. Bake at 350° for 25 minutes or until a wooden pick inserted near the center comes out clean. Meanwhile, beat pudding mix and milk according to package directions; refrigerate. Cool cake in pan for 10 minutes before removing to a wire rack to cool completely. In a saucepan over low heat, melt chocolate and butter. Stir in sugar until crumbly. Stir in hot water, 1 teaspoon at a time, until smooth. Split cake in half. Spread pudding on bottom layer. Place second layer over pudding. Pour chocolate glaze over top, letting it drizzle down the sides. Chill. **Yield:** 6-8 servings.

....

MANDARIN ORANGE CAKE

Charlene Wahlenmaier, Grants Pass, Oregon

(Pictured at right)

If you want to make cake but are squeezed for time, count on this recipe for a fast solution.

     1 package (18-1/4 ounces) white cake mix
     2 eggs

 1/3 cup unsweetened applesauce
     1 can (11 ounces) mandarin oranges,
       undrained
     1 carton (8 ounces) frozen whipped
       topping, thawed
     1 can (8 ounces) crushed pineapple,
       undrained
     1 package (3.4 ounces) instant vanilla
       pudding mix

In a mixing bowl, combine the cake mix, eggs, applesauce and oranges. Beat on low speed for 30 seconds; beat on medium for 2 minutes. Pour into two greased and floured 9-in. round cake pans. Bake at 325° for 30 minutes or until a wooden pick inserted near the center comes out clean. Cool in pan for 10 minutes; remove to a wire rack to cool completely. In another mixing bowl, beat whipped topping, pineapple and pudding mix. Spread between layers and over top and sides of cake. Chill. **Yield:** 12 servings.

2 kiwifruit, peeled and thinly sliced
1/3 cup fresh blueberries
GLAZE:
  1/4 cup sugar
  1/4 cup orange juice
  1/4 cup water
  2 teaspoons cornstarch

In a mixing bowl, cream butter and sugar; beat in egg and extracts. Combine flour, baking powder, baking soda and salt; add to creamed mixture. Beat well. Cover and chill for 30 minutes. Press dough into a greased 12-in. or 14-in. pizza pan. Bake at 350° for 12-14 minutes or until light golden brown. Cool completely. In a mixing bowl, beat cream cheese and confectioners' sugar until smooth. Add whipped topping; mix well. Spread over crust. Arrange fruit on top. Combine glaze ingredients in a saucepan; bring to a boil, stirring constantly. Boil for 2 minutes or until thickened. Cool to room temperature, about 30 minutes. Brush over fruit. Store in the refrigerator. **Yield:** 12-16 servings.

‧‧‧‧‧‧‧‧‧‧‧‧‧

CARROT SPICE CAKE

Karen Brodeen, Cook, Minnesota

I've found that no one can resist sampling a generous slice of this spice cake. Grated carrots add color, texture and nutrition.

✓ **This tasty dish uses less sugar, salt and fat.**

1-1/4 cups sugar
  3/4 cup light corn syrup
  3/4 cup skim milk
  8 egg whites
  2 cups all-purpose flour
  2 teaspoons baking powder
  2 teaspoons baking soda
  2 teaspoons ground cinnamon
  1/4 teaspoon salt
  2 cups grated carrots
Confectioners' sugar, optional

In a large mixing bowl, beat sugar, corn syrup, milk and egg whites. Combine dry ingredients; add to batter. Beat well. Pat carrots dry with paper towels; stir into the batter. Pour into a 10-in. fluted tube pan that has been coated with nonstick cooking spray and floured. Bake at 350° for 1 hour or until a wooden pick inserted near the center comes out clean. Cool in pan for 10 minutes; invert onto a wire rack. Cool completely. Lightly dust with confectioners' sugar if desired. **Yield:** 16 servings.
Nutritional Analysis: One serving equals 186 calories, 151 mg sodium, 0 cholesterol, 41 gm carbohydrate, 3 gm protein, trace fat.

‧‧‧‧‧‧‧‧‧‧‧‧‧

SUMMER DESSERT PIZZA

Ida Ruth Wenger, Harrisonburg, Virginia

(Pictured above)

My family enjoys this dessert anytime of the year, but it's especially refreshing during the hot months. You can use whatever fruits are in season.

1/4 cup butter *or* margarine, softened
1/2 cup sugar
  1 egg
1/4 teaspoon vanilla extract
1/4 teaspoon lemon extract
1-1/4 cups all-purpose flour
1/4 teaspoon baking powder
1/4 teaspoon baking soda
1/4 teaspoon salt
  4 ounces cream cheese, softened
1/4 cup confectioners' sugar
  1 cup whipped topping
  1 firm banana, sliced
  1 cup sliced fresh strawberries
  1 can (8 ounces) mandarin oranges, drained

HEAVENLY BLUEBERRY TART

Lyin Schramm, Berwick, Maine

Mmm—not only do I bake the berries with the crust, but after it's done, I top it with just-picked fruit.

1 cup all-purpose flour
2 tablespoons sugar
1/8 teaspoon salt
1/2 cup cold butter *or* margarine
1 tablespoon vinegar
FILLING:
2 pints fresh blueberries, **divided**
2/3 cup sugar
2 tablespoons all-purpose flour
1/2 teaspoon ground cinnamon
1/8 teaspoon ground nutmeg

In a bowl, combine flour, sugar and salt; cut in butter until crumbly. Gently mix in vinegar to moisten. Press into the bottom and up the sides of a lightly greased 9-in. tart pan. Place 1 pint of blueberries over crust. Combine sugar, flour, cinnamon and nutmeg; sprinkle over blueberries. Bake at 400° for 55-60 minutes or until crust is browned and filling is bubbly. Remove from the oven; arrange and press remaining berries in a single layer over top. Cool. **Yield:** 6-8 servings.

LIGHT CHOCOLATE CAKE

Celeste Clarke, Wilmot, New Hampshire

Applesauce makes this cake moist and sweet. A dusting of confectioners' sugar over the top is all that's needed.

✓ This tasty dish uses less sugar, salt or fat.

2 cups sugar
1-3/4 cups all-purpose flour
3/4 cup baking cocoa
1-1/2 teaspoons baking soda
1-1/2 teaspoons baking powder
1 teaspoon salt
1/2 cup egg substitute (equivalent to 2 eggs)
1 cup skim milk
1/2 cup unsweetened applesauce
2 teaspoons vanilla extract
1 cup boiling water
Confectioners' sugar, optional

In a large mixing bowl, combine dry ingredients. Beat in egg substitute, milk, applesauce and vanilla. Add water; beat on medium for 2 minutes (batter will be very thin). Pour into a 13-in. x 9-in. x 2-in. baking pan that has been coated with non-stick cooking spray. Bake at 350° for 30 minutes or until a wooden pick inserted near the center comes out clean. Cool. Lightly dust with confec-

tioners' sugar if desired. **Yield:** 20 servings. **Nutritional Analysis:** One serving equals 139 calories, 174 mg sodium, 0 cholesterol, 32 gm carbohydrate, 3 gm protein, 1 gm fat.

ZUCCHINI DESSERT SQUARES

Nancy Morelli, Livonia, Michigan

(Pictured below)

We planted one too many zucchini plants a few summers ago and harvested a lot. I was looking for ways to use them…this delicious dessert is the result.

4 cups all-purpose flour
2 cups sugar
1/2 teaspoon ground cinnamon
1/2 teaspoon salt
1-1/2 cups cold butter *or* margarine
FILLING:
8 to 10 cups cubed seeded peeled zucchini (4 to 5 pounds)
2/3 cup lemon juice
1 cup sugar
1 teaspoon ground cinnamon
1/2 teaspoon ground nutmeg

In a bowl, combine flour, sugar, cinnamon and salt. Cut in butter until crumbly; reserve 3 cups. Pat remaining crumb mixture into the bottom of a greased 13-in. x 9-in. x 2-in. baking pan. Bake at 375° for 12 minutes. Meanwhile, for filling, place zucchini and lemon juice in a saucepan; bring to a boil. Reduce heat; cover and cook for 6-8 minutes or until zucchini is crisp-tender. Stir in sugar, cinnamon and nutmeg; cover and simmer for 5 minutes (mixture will be thin). Spoon over crust; sprinkle with the reserved crumb mixture. Bake at 375° for 40-45 minutes or until golden. **Yield:** 16-20 servings.

Petite Treats Are Big on Pigs!

WHEN National Pig Day—March 1—rolls around, Becky Baldwin of Annville, Pennsylvania celebrates in sweet fashion. She bakes up a batch of these pretty porkers!

"A friend of mine who loves pigs always gives a party on that day," pens Becky. "One year, I came up with the idea of decorating cookies to look like pig faces. They were a big hit!

"I make them for other gatherings, too…and my sons love to take them to school parties."

Becky shares the recipe here so you can also try them. Don't hog the fun, though. Youngsters will have a "swine" time helping you.

CUTE PIG COOKIES

1 cup butter *or* margarine, softened
1-1/2 cups sugar
2 eggs
1 cup (8 ounces) sour cream
1 teaspoon vanilla extract
3 cups all-purpose flour
1 teaspoon baking powder
1/2 teaspoon salt

FROSTING/DECORATING:
1/2 cup butter *or* margarine
4 cups confectioners' sugar
2 teaspoons vanilla extract
6 tablespoons milk

3 to 4 drops red food coloring
Pink sugar wafer cookies
36 large marshmallows, halved
Reese's candy bar sprinkles

In a mixing bowl, cream butter and sugar. Add eggs, sour cream and vanilla; mix well. Combine dry ingredients; add to creamed mixture and mix well. Drop by tablespoonfuls onto ungreased baking sheets. Bake at 375° for 10-12 minutes or until edges are lightly browned. Cool on wire racks. Melt butter. Add sugar, vanilla, milk and food coloring; mix until smooth. Frost the cookies. Cut sugar wafers into triangles; place two on each cookie for ears. With a toothpick, poke two holes in each marshmallow half for nostrils; press light brown candy bar sprinkles into holes. Place noses on the cookies. Add dark brown candy bar sprinkles for eyes. **Yield:** 6 dozen.

CRANBERRY BARS

Betty Noga, Milwaukie, Oregon

I was thrilled to add this recipe to my collection. I keep cranberries in my freezer all year so I can make these bars whenever I get a craving for their tart cranberry flavor.

FILLING:
3/4 cup sugar
1/2 cup water
2 cups fresh *or* frozen cranberries
1/4 cup orange juice
1 tablespoon grated orange peel
1 tablespoon butter *or* margarine
1/2 teaspoon ground cinnamon
1/4 teaspoon salt
1 cup chopped walnuts

CRUST:
2 cups all-purpose flour
1/4 teaspoon salt
1-1/4 cups cold butter *or* margarine
1 cup sugar
3 cups quick-cooking oats

In a saucepan, bring sugar and water to a boil. Add cranberries and cook until they pop, about 4-6 minutes. Add orange juice, peel, butter, cinnamon and salt. Cook 5 minutes more or until mixture thickens. Remove from the heat; stir in walnuts and set aside. In a bowl, combine the flour and salt; cut in butter until crumbly. Add sugar and oats; mix well. Spoon half into an ungreased 13-in. x 9-in. x 2-in. baking pan; pat firmly into pan. Spread filling evenly over crust. Top with remaining crumb mixture; pat lightly. Bake at 400° for 30-35 minutes. Cool. **Yield:** about 2-1/2 dozen.

Raspberry Marshmallow Delight

Gloria Iden, Kimmell, Indiana

(Pictured at right)

This is one of our family's favorite desserts. It has a tangy unique flavor. After a hard day of working on the farm, this fruity treat is most welcome.

1-1/4 cups graham cracker crumbs
  1/4 cup butter *or* margarine, melted
   50 large marshmallows
    1 cup milk
    1 carton (8 ounces) frozen whipped topping, thawed
    2 packages (10 ounces *each*) frozen raspberries in syrup, thawed
1-1/4 cups water, *divided*
  1/2 cup sugar
    2 teaspoons lemon juice
    6 tablespoons cornstarch
Whipped cream and fresh raspberries, optional

Combine crumbs and butter; press into the bottom of a greased 13-in. x 9-in. 2-in. baking pan. Bake at 350° for 10 minutes. Cool. In a large saucepan over medium heat, stir marshmallows and milk until the marshmallows are melted. Cool to room temperature. Fold in whipped topping; spread over crust. In a saucepan, bring raspberries, 1 cup water, sugar and lemon juice to a boil. Combine cornstarch and remaining water; stir into raspberry mixture. Boil for 2 minutes, stirring constantly. Cool to room temperature. Spread over marshmallow layer. Chill until firm, about 4 hours. Garnish with whipped cream and raspberries if desired. **Yield:** 12-16 servings.

Russian Tea Cakes

Valerie Hudson, Mason City, Iowa

I like to present my favorite holiday cookies in a special way. I pile these fresh-baked tea cakes on pretty plates that I buy throughout the year, then wrap them with colored cellophane to give to friends.

    1 cup butter (no substitutes), softened
  1/2 cup confectioners' sugar
    1 teaspoon vanilla extract
2-1/4 cups all-purpose flour
  1/4 teaspoon salt
  3/4 cup finely chopped nuts
Additional confectioners' sugar

In a mixing bowl, cream butter and sugar. Add vanilla. Combine dry ingredients and nuts; gradually add to creamed mixture. Chill for 1-2 hours.

Roll into 1-in. balls. Place 2 in. apart on ungreased baking sheets. Bake at 400° for 10-12 minutes. Cool on wire racks; roll in confectioners' sugar. **Yield:** about 3-1/2 dozen.

Cream Cheese Pound Cake

Mrs. Michael Ewanek, Hastings, Pennsylvania

I sent a friend of mine some of my favorite zucchini recipes and, in return, she mailed me the recipe for this cake. It's absolutely delicious, and I've made it often.

1-1/2 cups butter (no substitutes), room temperature
    1 package (8 ounces) cream cheese, room temperature
2-1/3 cups sugar
    6 eggs, room temperature
    3 cups all-purpose flour
    1 teaspoon vanilla extract

In a large mixing bowl, cream butter and cream cheese. Gradually add sugar, beating until light and fluffy, about 5-7 minutes. Add eggs, one at a time, beating well after each addition. Gradually add flour; beat just until blended. Stir in vanilla. Pour into a greased and floured 10-in. tube pan. Bake at 300° for 1-1/2 hours or until cake tests done. Cool in pan 15 minutes before removing to a wire rack. Cool completely. **Yield:** 12-16 servings.

Pennsylvania Dutch Funny Cake

Diane Ganssle, Bethlehem, Pennsylvania

(Pictured below)

I can still remember my grandma serving this delicious cake on the big wooden table in her farm kitchen. Every time I bake this unusual cake, it takes me back to those special days at Grandma's.

      2 cups sugar, *divided*
  1/2 cup baking cocoa
1-1/2 cups milk, *divided*
      2 unbaked pastry shells (9 inches)
      2 cups all-purpose flour
      2 teaspoons baking powder
  1/4 teaspoon salt
      1 egg
      2 tablespoons shortening
      1 teaspoon vanilla extract
Whipped cream, optional

In a small saucepan, combine 1 cup of sugar and cocoa. Blend in 1/2 cup milk. Cook and stir over medium heat until mixture comes to a boil. Cook and stir until thickened, about 2 minutes. Pour into unbaked pastry shells, tipping to coat the pastry halfway up the sides; set aside. In a mixing bowl, combine flour, baking powder, salt and remaining sugar. Add egg, shortening, vanilla and remaining milk; beat until smooth. Starting at the edge, spoon batter into the pastry shells, completely covering the chocolate. Bake at 350° for 40 minutes or until a wooden pick inserted near the center comes out clean. Serve warm or chilled with whipped cream if desired. **Yield:** 12-16 servings.

Chocolate-Tipped Butter Cookies

Charolette Westfall, Houston, Texas

These wonderfully moist morsels are too tempting to resist. They melt right in your mouth and are simple to fix, too. Rather than sprinkling the chocolate tips with nuts, you can roll them in red and green jimmies for the holidays or leave them plain.

    1 cup butter *or* margarine, softened
1/2 cup confectioners' sugar
    1 teaspoon vanilla extract
    2 cups all-purpose flour
CHOCOLATE COATING:
    1 cup (6 ounces) semisweet chocolate chips
    1 tablespoon shortening
1/2 cup finely chopped pecans

In a mixing bowl, cream butter and sugar. Add vanilla; mix well. Gradually add flour; mix well. Cover and chill for 1 hour. Shape tablespoonfuls of dough into 2-1/2-in. x 1/2-in. sticks. Place 2 in. apart on ungreased baking sheets. Flatten about three-fourths of each stick lengthwise with a fork. Bake at 350° for 14-16 minutes or until set. Cool on baking sheets. Melt chocolate chips and shortening until smooth; dip the round end of each cookie. Sprinkle with nuts. Place on waxed paper until firm. **Yield:** about 3-1/2 dozen.

Citrus Gingerbread

Margaret Pache, Mesa, Arizona

There are lots of orange and pecan trees here in Arizona, so this recipe is representative of our region. I love to cook, and it's one of my favorite desserts.

1/2 cup butter *or* margarine, softened
3/4 cup sugar
    1 egg
    2 cups all-purpose flour
    1 teaspoon baking soda
    1 teaspoon ground cinnamon
1/2 teaspoon ground ginger

1/2 teaspoon salt
3/4 cup buttermilk
3 tablespoons molasses
1 cup chopped sectioned oranges (without membrane)
1/2 cup chopped pecans
Confectioners' sugar and orange peel, optional

In a mixing bowl, cream butter and sugar. Add egg. Combine the flour, baking soda, cinnamon, ginger and salt; add to creamed mixture alternately with buttermilk. Stir in molasses. Fold in oranges and pecans. Pour into a greased 9-in. square baking pan. Bake at 350° for 45-50 minutes or until a wooden pick inserted near the center comes out clean. Cool completely. If desired, dust with confectioners' sugar and garnish with orange peel. **Yield:** 9 servings.

APPLE STRUDEL

Helen Lesh, Forsyth, Missouri

(Pictured at right)

I frequently turn to this recipe during autumn. The aroma of this dessert baking on a cool crisp day is absolutely wonderful.

1 cup cold butter *or* margarine
2 cups all-purpose flour
1 cup (8 ounces) sour cream
1/4 teaspoon salt
FILLING:
2 cups dry bread crumbs
1/4 cup butter *or* margarine, melted
4 medium baking apples, peeled and chopped
2 cups sugar
1 cup golden raisins
1/2 cup chopped pecans
2 teaspoons ground cinnamon
Confectioners' sugar, optional

In a medium bowl, cut butter into flour until mixture resembles coarse crumbs. Add the sour cream and salt; mix well. Shape into a ball; cover and refrigerate overnight. For filling, combine the bread crumbs and butter. Add apples, sugar, raisins, pecans and cinnamon; mix well and set aside. Divide dough into thirds; turn onto a floured board. Roll each into a 15-in. x 12-in. rectangle. Spoon filling evenly onto dough; spread to within 1 in. of edges. Roll up from one long side; pinch seams and ends to seal. Carefully place seam side down on an ungreased baking sheet. Bake at 350° for 55-60 minutes or until light brown. Cool completely on wire racks. Dust with confectioners' sugar if desired. **Yield:** 3 loaves.

PARTY PECAN PIES

Judy Theriot, Pierre Part, Louisiana

Though they're small, these pleasing "pies" are packed with flavor and sized right for a buffet. What's more, they can be stored in the freezer to make party or gift preparations that much easier.

1 cup butter *or* margarine, softened
1 package (8 ounces) cream cheese, softened
2 cups all-purpose flour
FILLING:
2 cups chopped pecans
1-1/2 cups packed brown sugar
2 eggs, beaten
2 tablespoons butter *or* margarine, melted
2 teaspoons vanilla extract

In a mixing bowl, beat butter and cream cheese. Gradually add flour; mix well. Cover and chill for 1 hour. Press tablespoonfuls of dough into the bottom and up the sides of ungreased miniature muffin cups to form shells; set aside. Combine filling ingredients in a mixing bowl; mix well. Spoon about 1 heaping teaspoon into each shell. Bake at 325° for 25-30 minutes or until crust is brown and filling is set. Cool in pans 10 minutes before removing to wire racks. **Yield:** about 4 dozen.

Cake Contains Sweet Surprise

LOOKING FOR a new way to use up potatoes? With this delicious dessert, which stars *sweet potatoes*, it's a piece of cake.

"My mother came up with the recipe many years ago while she was in the middle of making applesauce cake," confides Jean Kimm of Coeur d'Alene, Idaho.

"When the applesauce ran out, she substituted sweet potatoes. Then she added apricots for a 'little more body'. Her creation was a work of art!

"Nowadays, I make this cake often. My husband and our two grown daughters love it. It's a hit at potlucks, too—I always get compliments on the moist texture and spicy flavor."

Why not try Jean's recipe today...and see if anyone can guess the sweet surprise inside?

SWEET POTATO CAKE

1 cup butter *or* margarine
1-1/4 cups packed brown sugar
3/4 cup sugar
4 eggs
1-1/2 cups mashed cooked sweet potatoes (without added butter or milk)
2-1/2 teaspoons vanilla extract
3 cups all-purpose flour
2-1/2 teaspoons baking powder
2 teaspoons pumpkin pie spice
1 teaspoon baking soda
3/4 teaspoon ground ginger
1/4 teaspoon salt
1 cup finely chopped pecans
1 cup finely chopped dried apricots

APRICOT GLAZE:
2 cups confectioners' sugar
1/2 cup apricot nectar
2 teaspoons grated lemon peel
Pinch salt

In a mixing bowl, cream butter and sugars. Beat in eggs, one at a time, mixing well after each. Beat in potatoes and vanilla. Combine flour, baking powder, pumpkin pie spice, baking soda, ginger and salt; stir into the creamed mixture. Add pecans and apricots. Pour into a greased and floured 10-in. fluted tube pan. Bake at 350° for 1 hour or until a wooden pick inserted near the center comes out clean. Cool in pan 15 minutes before removing to a wire rack. Combine glaze ingredients and drizzle over cake while warm. **Yield:** 12 servings.

SNOWMEN COOKIES

Betty Tabb, Mifflintown, Pennsylvania

These soft cookies are especially well-received at holidays enfolded in colored tissue that are then placed in festive containers. It's a pretty way to deliver these delicious snowmen.

1 cup butter *or* margarine, softened
1 package (8 ounces) cream cheese, softened
2 cups sugar
1 egg
1 teaspoon vanilla extract
1/4 teaspoon almond extract
1/4 teaspoon coconut extract
3-1/2 cups all-purpose flour
1 teaspoon baking powder
Miniature semisweet chocolate chips, milk chocolate kisses and green and red M&M's

FROSTING:
1 cup confectioners' sugar
1 to 2 tablespoons milk
1/8 teaspoon coconut extract
Red *and/or* green food coloring

In a mixing bowl, cream butter, cream cheese and sugar. Add egg and extracts; mix well. Combine flour and baking powder; gradually add to creamed mixture and mix well. Cover and chill overnight. Form dough into 90 balls, 30 each 1 in., 3/4 in. and 1/2 in. Position one ball of each size on an ungreased baking sheet to form a snowman. Repeat with remaining balls. Bake at 325° for 18-20 minutes or until lightly browned. Remove from oven; immediately add chocolate chip eyes and M&M buttons. Carefully remove cookies from baking sheets to wire racks. For frosting, combine sugar, milk and extract in a small bowl until smooth. If two colors of frosting are desired, transfer half of the frosting into another bowl. Add food coloring to frosting. Cut a small hole in the bottom corner of a resealable plastic bag; fill with frosting. Pipe around each snowman's neck to form a scarf. Use frosting to attach a chocolate kiss hat to each snowman. **Yield:** about 2-1/2 dozen.

PEPPERMINT ICE CREAM CAKE

Gloria Kaufmann, Orrville, Ohio

(Pictured at right)

This is the kind of dessert that's perfect for any special occasion. What's also nice is the fact that the cake can be made a few days ahead and stored in the freezer until the celebration starts. It always looks fresh and tastes great.

      4 cups crisp rice cereal
      1 milk chocolate candy bar (7 ounces)
      1/2 cup butter *or* margarine
      1/2 gallon peppermint stick ice cream,
          softened
      2 cups whipped topping
Peppermint candy canes *or* crushed
      peppermint candies

Place cereal in a large bowl. Grate or shave 2 tablespoons of chocolate from candy bar; set aside. In a heavy saucepan, melt butter and remaining chocolate. Pour over cereal and stir to coat. Press into the bottom of a greased 10-in. springform pan. Freeze for 30 minutes. Spoon ice cream over crust. Freeze for 15 minutes. Spread with whipped topping; sprinkle with the shaved chocolate. Cover and freeze for several hours or overnight. Top with candy. Remove cake from freezer 5-10 minutes before serving. Remove sides of pan; cut with a sharp knife and serve immediately. **Yield:** 8-10 servings.

POINSETTIA COOKIES

Helen Burch, Jamestown, New York

To add eye-appeal to my basic butter cookies, I cultivated a new way to shape them. Now, they're as pretty to see as they are to eat!

      1 cup butter *or* margarine, softened
      1 cup confectioners' sugar
      1 egg
1-1/2 teaspoons almond extract
      1 teaspoon vanilla extract
2-1/2 cups all-purpose flour
      1 teaspoon salt
Red decorator's sugar
Red and green candied cherries, quartered

In a mixing bowl, cream butter and sugar. Add egg and extracts; mix well. Combine flour and salt; gradually add to creamed mixture. Divide dough in half; wrap in plastic wrap. Chill overnight or until firm. On a lightly floured surface, roll out one portion of dough to a 12-in. x 10-in. rectangle approximately 1/8-in. thick. Cut into 2-in. squares. In each square, make 1-in. slits in each corner. Bring every other corner up into center to form a pinwheel; press lightly. Sprinkle cookies with red sugar and press a candied cherry piece into the center of each. Place 1 in. apart on ungreased baking sheets. Bake at 350° for 8-10 minutes. Cool 1-2 minutes before removing to a wire rack. **Yield:** about 4 dozen.

DOUBLE PEANUT PIE

Vivian Cleeton, Richmond, Virginia

I created this recipe for a national pie contest and won second place for my state. Many peanuts are grown here, and I always look for ways to use local products.

      2 eggs
1/3 cup creamy peanut butter
1/3 cup sugar
1/3 cup light corn syrup
1/3 cup dark corn syrup
1/3 cup butter *or* margarine, melted
      1 teaspoon vanilla extract
      1 cup salted peanuts
      1 unbaked pastry shell (9 inches)
Whipped cream *or* ice cream, optional

In a mixing bowl, beat the eggs; gradually add peanut butter, sugar, corn syrups, butter and vanilla; mix well. Fold in peanuts. Pour into the crust. Bake at 375° for 30-35 minutes or until set. Cool. Serve with whipped cream or ice cream if desired. **Yield:** 6-8 servings.

LONGING TO LIVE in a log cabin? The house plans on these pages put the next best thing at your fingertips. And a kitchen, not a contractor, is all you need to do the construction!

This miniature abode, created by our Test Kitchen staff, consists mostly of ready-made ingredients. It's so easy to put together that kids (or grandkids) will love to "hire on" as part of your building crew.

So, if a real log cabin's not in your immediate future, why not put up this cozy replica? Then dream of log-cabin Christmases to come!

PRETZEL LOG CABIN

ICING:

    8 cups confectioners' sugar
    6 tablespoons meringue
        powder*
    3/4 to 1 cup warm water
Green liquid *or* paste food coloring

In a mixing bowl, beat sugar, meringue powder and 3/4 cup water on low speed until blended. Beat on high for 8-10 minutes or until stiff peaks form, adding additional water, 1 tablespoon at a time, if

needed. Remove 1-1/2 cups of icing to another bowl and tint with green food coloring for decorating and trees. Place a damp paper towel over each bowl of icing and cover tightly until ready to use.
*Editor's Note: Meringue powder is available where cake decorating supplies are sold. Or use your favorite Royal Icing recipe.

LOG CABIN:

    12 double graham crackers
        (5 inches x 2-1/2 inches)
Waxed paper
Pastry bags *or* heavy-duty
    resealable plastic bags
Medium dot (#5, #10) and leaf (#67)
    decorating tips
    1 bag (10 ounces) pecan halves
    18-inch square base—heavy-
    duty cardboard or piece of
    plywood, covered with foil
    wrapping paper or aluminum foil
Spice jars and tall cans *or* bottles
    3 bags (10 ounces *each*) pretzel
    rods (7-1/2 inches long)
Serrated knife and ruler
Assorted creme wafers
    (2-1/2 inches x 1 inch)
Baking cocoa

Cotton balls, optional
Red-hot candies
Golden raisins *or* chocolate chip
    cookies
Spearmint candies
Sugar ice cream cones

To Assemble Roof: Place two graham crackers on waxed paper. Cut a small hole in the bottom corner of pastry or plastic bag; insert #10 dot tip if desired (or pipe directly from bag). Fill bag two-thirds full with white icing and refill as needed.

Pipe or frost one short end of one cracker and butt the other cracker against it, making a 10-in. x 2-1/2-in. rectangle.

Repeat five more times. Set two long rectangles aside for porch roof and floor. Pipe the 10-in. edge of a long rectangle and butt the 10-in. edge of another long rectangle against it, making a 10-in. x 5-in. rectangle for one side of the roof. Repeat for other side of roof.

Working with one side of the roof at a time, frost entire roof with white icing. Press pecan halves end to end in straight lines along short sides (see photo above). There will be about four rows of 14 pecans per row on each side of roof. Repeat for other side. Repeat for porch roof, pressing on two rows of about 14 pecans per row. Allow to dry, uncovered, overnight.

To Assemble Sides of House: With four pretzel rods lying flat on waxed paper, apply a 1/4-in.-wide strip of icing along the top edge of each, beginning 1/2 in. from one end and ending by icing the tip of the other end.

To form the front of the house, center one iced pretzel rod, icing side down, 7 in. from the front of the foil-covered 18-in.-square base. Add a second pretzel

rod, again icing side down, at right angles to the first, placing it so the iced end is 1/2 in. from the un-iced end of the first rod. Repeat with a third and fourth rod, so that these first four rods form a square base with a 1/2-in. end extending at each corner.

Add a second row, allowing the 1/2-in. un-iced ends to extend in the opposite direction (see photo below). Prop sides upright with spice jars for 2-3 minutes until icing hardens, then remove jars. Repeat process until each side is nine pretzel rods high.

For Side Peaks: Place seven pretzel rods side by side on waxed paper. Using a serrated knife, cut the ends of the rods at an angle to form a triangle with longest one measuring 7 in. and shortest one measuring 1-1/2 in.

Frost the top of the longest rod; butt the next longest pretzel against it. Repeat with remaining cut pretzels. Frost bottom of triangle and adhere to top edge of one side of house (see photo below). Prop with tall cans or jars. Add a small triangle of icing at top of triangle. Repeat process for opposite side. Allow to dry completely.

To Attach Roof: Working with one side of the house at a time, squeeze icing on opposite slanted edges of the front of the house. Carefully place roof piece on the slant high enough so the roof's peak is even with the points on both sides. The bottom edge of roof will overhang the side by about 3/4 in.

Repeat with the other side of the roof (there will be a slight gap at top center). Pipe icing along center peak. Press about 10 pecan halves end to end into icing.

For Porch Floor: Cut off the extending end of bottom pretzel at front of house.

Spread bottom of porch floor crackers with icing and pipe icing along one long edge. Add porch with icing side down, butting it against front edge of house.

For Door: Using two yellow creme wafers, pipe icing on long edge of one wafer; butt against the edge of the other wafer.

For Windows: Cut yellow creme wafers into four 1-1/4-in. pieces. Pipe icing on long edge of one wafer; butt against one other wafer. Repeat for a second window. Spread icing on backs of windows and door and position on house according to Fig. 1.

For Chimney: Using full width of chocolate wafers, cut wafers to length with Patterns A through F at right. Assemble chimney layer as follows: Pipe icing on short edge of piece A. Butt against short edge of piece B. Repeat to put together pieces C, D and E. Pipe icing on one long edge of A/B; butt against C/D/E, aligning bottom edges. Repeat with the second layer of chocolate wafers; ice back of one set and press two layers together for a double thickness. Brush icing with cocoa to cover white seams. Spread icing on back of chimney; position on side of house as in Fig. 1. For chimney top (F), ice wafer pieces together for a double thickness. Pipe icing along slanted edge; position on roof above piece E of chimney. If desired, pull apart a cotton ball to form smoke. Attach with a small dab of icing.

For Garlands and Wreaths: Insert leaf tip into another decorating bag; fill with green icing. Pipe garlands on base of windows. Pipe garland or a wreath on the door and chimney. Decorate with red-hots.

To Assemble Porch: Cut four pretzel rods to 4-1/2 in. for posts. Pipe a dab of white icing on one end of each post. Position evenly 1/2 in. from front edge, on the porch floor. Allow to dry completely.

Pipe icing along one long side of porch roof. Pipe a dab of icing on tops of the posts. Carefully place porch roof over posts, pressing frosted side of porch roof against side of house where slanted side of house roof ends.

To Decorate: Insert #5 dot tip into another decorating bag; fill with white icing. Pipe along entire edge of roof, then pipe white icicles on same edge. Use remaining white icing for snow on base.

Make path with raisins or broken chocolate chip cookies. Adhere spearmint candies with green icing for bushes. Using a leaf tip, starting at the point, pipe green icing on upside-down ice cream cones for trees. Let dry completely.

Display throughout the Christmas season! (**Note:** If stored properly, your log cabin should last for future holidays, although it may require some minor touch-ups.)

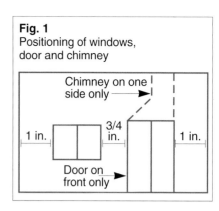

Fig. 1
Positioning of windows, door and chimney

Chimney on one side only

1 in.   3/4 in.   1 in.

Door on front only

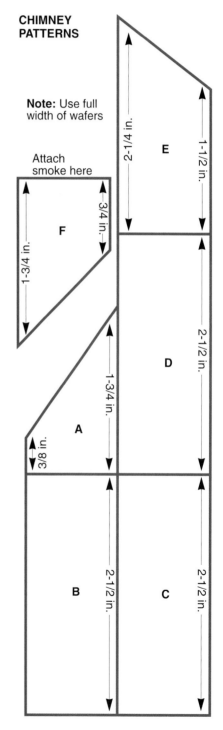

CHIMNEY PATTERNS

Note: Use full width of wafers

Attach smoke here

E — 1-1/2 in.
2-1/4 in.

F
1-3/4 in.
3/4 in.

D — 2-1/2 in.
1-3/4 in.

A
3/8 in.

B — 2-1/2 in.
C — 2-1/2 in.

FRENCH CHRISTMAS COOKIES

Judy Wilder, Mankato, Minnesota

These moist treats will have everyone reaching for more. In fact, the batches I make ahead for my family and store in the freezer seem to mysteriously disappear each year—even though the chocolate topping I put on before serving hasn't been added yet!

    1 cup packed brown sugar
    1/2 cup butter *or* margarine, softened
2-3/4 cups graham cracker crumbs
    2 cups finely chopped walnuts
    2 cups (12 ounces) milk chocolate chips
    1 cup milk
TOPPING:
1-1/4 cups (8 ounces) milk chocolate chips,
    melted

In a mixing bowl, cream sugar and butter. Add crumbs, walnuts, chips and milk; mix well. Fill miniature paper baking cups three-fourths full. Place 1 in. apart on baking sheets. Bake at 375° for 10-12 minutes. Cool on wire racks. Top each cookie with 1/4 teaspoon melted chocolate. Store in the refrigerator. **Yield:** 9-1/2 dozen.

CHOCOLATE CHERRY CAKE

Flo Burtnett, Gage, Oklahoma

Here's a sweet treat to enhance your buffet—a lusciously versatile layer cake. I change the design on top to match the many occasions I serve it.

    1 package (18-1/4 ounces) chocolate cake
    mix
    3/4 teaspoon ground cinnamon
    2 cartons (8 ounces *each*) cherry yogurt
    3 eggs
    1/4 cup milk
    1 teaspoon vanilla extract
    1 carton (8 ounces) frozen whipped
    topping, thawed, *divided*
    1 can (21 ounces) cherry pie filling,
    divided

In a large bowl, combine cake mix, cinnamon, yogurt, eggs, milk and vanilla. Beat on low speed for 30 seconds; beat on medium until smooth, about 3 minutes. Pour into two greased and floured 9-in. round baking pans. Bake at 350° for 30-35 minutes or until a wooden pick inserted near the center comes out clean. Cool in pans 15 minutes before removing to a wire rack; cool completely. Place one cake layer on a serving platter. Spread about 1 cup whipped topping in a circle 1-1/2-in. wide around outer top edge of cake. Spoon 1 cup of cherry pie

BLACKBERRY COBBLER

Tina Hankins, Laconia, New Hampshire

(Pictured above)

Blackberries abound in fields and alongside country roads in late summer around here. It's fun to pick them, especially when we know this dessert will be the result.

    1/4 cup butter *or* margarine, softened
    1/2 cup sugar
    1 cup all-purpose flour
    2 teaspoons baking powder
    1/2 cup milk
    2 cups fresh *or* frozen blackberries
    3/4 cup raspberry *or* apple juice
Ice cream *or* whipped cream, optional

In a mixing bowl, cream butter and sugar. Combine flour and baking powder; add to creamed mixture alternately with milk. Stir just until moistened. Pour into a greased 1-1/2-qt. baking pan. Sprinkle with blackberries. Pour juice over all. Bake at 350° for 45-50 minutes or until golden brown. Serve warm; top with ice cream or cream if desired. **Yield:** 6-8 servings.

filling in the center. Top with second cake layer. Spoon remaining pie filling into desired shape in the center. Pipe or spread remaining whipped topping on top of cake and around bottom of cake. Chill at least 1 hour before serving. Store in the refrigerator. **Yield:** 12 servings.

RICE PUDDING CAKE

Nancy Horsburgh, Everett, Ontario

The secret ingredient in this delicious cake is rice. It tastes a lot like rice pudding, only in a different form.

    1/2 cup raisins
Boiling water
    1 cup uncooked long grain rice
Water
    1 quart milk
    3/4 cup butter *or* margarine, softened
    1 cup sugar
    5 eggs, *separated*
    2 tablespoons grated orange peel
    2 tablespoons graham cracker crumbs
Confectioners' sugar

In a small bowl, cover raisins with boiling water. Let stand for 5 minutes; drain and set aside. In a large saucepan, cover rice with water; bring to a boil. Drain the liquid; add milk to rice. Bring to a boil. Reduce heat; cover and simmer for 15-20 minutes or until rice is tender. In a mixing bowl, cream butter and sugar. Add egg yolks; beat well. Add rice mixture, raisins and orange peel. Beat the egg whites until stiff; fold into the batter. Spoon into a greased 10-in. tube pan. Sprinkle with crumbs. Bake at 350° for 55-60 minutes or until set. Cool in pan for 20 minutes. Loosen sides and center with a knife. Carefully invert onto a serving plate. Dust with confectioners' sugar. Serve warm or chilled. **Yield:** 12-16 servings.

POPPY SEED CHIFFON CAKE

Irene Hirsch, Tustin, California

(Pictured at right)

This cake is quite easy to make, and everyone who tries it tells me how good it tastes. The lemon frosting really accents the flavor of the cake.

2-1/2 cups all-purpose flour
    1 cup sugar
    1 tablespoon baking powder
    1/2 teaspoon salt
    3/4 cup water

    1/2 cup vegetable oil
    5 egg yolks
    1 teaspoon lemon extract
    1 teaspoon grated lemon peel
    1 can (12-1/2 ounces) poppy seed filling
    7 egg whites, room temperature
    1/2 teaspoon cream of tartar
LEMON BUTTER FROSTING:
    6 tablespoons butter *or* margarine, softened
    4 cups confectioners' sugar
    3 to 5 tablespoons milk
    1 tablespoon lemon juice
    1 teaspoon lemon extract

In a mixing bowl, combine flour, sugar, baking powder and salt. Add water, oil, egg yolks, lemon extract, lemon peel and filling; beat until smooth. In another bowl, beat egg whites and cream of tartar until stiff peaks form. Fold into batter; pour into an ungreased 10-in. tube pan. Bake at 350° for 55-60 minutes or until cake springs back when lightly touched. Invert pan on a bottle; cool completely. Remove cake from pan. For frosting, cream butter and sugar in a mixing bowl. Add milk, lemon juice and extract; beat until smooth. Frost cake. **Yield:** 12-16 servings.

ONE TASTE and you'll want to stock up on a variety of these homemade butters, jams, relishes, sauces and more!

SPREADS FOR BREADS. Top to bottom: Breakfast Scones (p. 77), Raspberry Butter (p. 129) and Very Berry Spread (p. 129).

Condiments & Canned Goods

RASPBERRY BUTTER

Helen Lamb, Seymour, Missouri

(Pictured at left)

This sweet butter tastes great with a variety of fresh-from-the-oven goodies. I think it's a nice change from plain butter.

- 1/2 cup butter (no substitutes), softened
- 1/3 cup fresh *or* frozen unsweetened raspberries
- 2 tablespoons confectioners' sugar
- Dash lemon juice

In a small mixing bowl, beat all ingredients until well blended and smooth. Store in a covered container in the refrigerator; bring to room temperature before serving. **Yield:** about 1/2 cup.

BASIL SPAGHETTI SAUCE

Marlane Jones, Allentown, Pennsylvania

My homemade sauce is packed with fresh tomatoes and assorted seasonings. Folks who sample it never seem to miss the meat.

✓ This tasty dish uses less sugar, salt and fat. Recipe includes *Diabetic Exchanges*.

- 1 cup chopped onion
- 8 garlic cloves, minced
- 1/4 cup vegetable oil
- 8 cups coarsely chopped peeled tomatoes (about 5 pounds)
- 1/3 cup minced fresh basil *or* 2 tablespoons dried basil
- 1/4 cup minced fresh parsley
- 1-1/2 teaspoons salt
- 1/2 teaspoon pepper
- 1/2 teaspoon sugar

In a large saucepan or Dutch oven over medium heat, saute onion and garlic in oil until tender. Add tomatoes, basil, parsley, salt, pepper and sugar; bring to a boil. Reduce heat; cover and simmer for 1-1/2 hours. **Yield:** about 8 servings. **Diabetic Exchanges:** One 1-cup serving equals 1-1/2 fat, 1 starch; also, 128 calories, 154 mg sodium, 0 cholesterol, 15 gm carbohydrate, 3 gm protein, 7 gm fat.

VERY BERRY SPREAD

Irene Hagel, Choiceland, Saskatchewan

(Pictured at left)

Two kinds of berries make this jam deliciously different. I always keep some on hand.

- 5 cups fresh *or* frozen raspberries
- 3 cups fresh *or* frozen blueberries
- 1 tablespoon lemon juice
- 1 tablespoon grated lemon peel
- 1 package (1-3/4 ounces) powdered fruit pectin
- 6 cups sugar

In a large kettle, combine the berries, lemon juice, peel and pectin. Bring to a full rolling boil over high heat, stirring constantly. Stir in sugar; return to a full rolling boil. Boil for 1 minute, stirring constantly. Remove from the heat; skim off any foam. Pour hot into hot jars, leaving 1/4-in. headspace. Adjust caps. Process for 10 minutes in a boiling-water bath. **Yield:** about 8 half-pints.

ZESTY TOMATOES

Cathy Hardin, Santa Monica, California

I love having pints of these spicy tomatoes in the freezer to use in place of canned stewed tomatoes with green chilies in my favorite recipes. Besides, home-grown is always much better than store-bought.

- 12 medium tomatoes
- 3 green peppers, chopped
- 2 large onions, chopped
- 1 cup water
- 3 garlic cloves, minced
- 2 to 4 jalapeno peppers, seeded and chopped
- 1-1/2 teaspoons salt

Scald, peel and chop the tomatoes; place in a kettle. Add remaining ingredients. Cook, uncovered, over medium heat for 45 minutes, stirring often. Cool slightly; pack into freezer containers. **Yield:** 5 pints.

OLD-FASHIONED BLUEBERRY JAM

Kay Laney, North Liberty, Indiana

Longtime honey lovers will love the flavor combination in this recipe. It stirs up delicious memories.

5 cups fresh *or* frozen blueberries
1/4 cup water
3 cups sugar
1 cup clover honey

In a large kettle, bring blueberries and water to a boil; mash and stir for 5 minutes. Add sugar and honey; boil gently, uncovered, over medium heat for 30 minutes, stirring frequently. To test for doneness: Remove from heat; spoon about 1 tablespoon of hot jam onto a chilled plate and set plate in freezer until the jam has cooled to room temperature, about 1-2 minutes. When the cooled jam holds its shape when mounded with a spoon, the jam has reached its desired thickness. If necessary, return to heat and repeat test after additional cooking. Skim foam; pour hot into hot jars, leaving 1/4 in. headspace. Adjust caps. Process for 10 minutes in a boiling-water bath. **Yield:** 4 half-pints. **Editor's Note:** This recipe does not require packaged pectin.

HOMEMADE PIZZA SAUCE

Cheryl Kravik, Spanaway, Washington

(Pictured above)

For years, I had trouble finding a pizza my family liked. So I started making my own. The evening I served it to company and they asked for my recipe, I thought, "I finally got it right!"

1 can (29 ounces) tomato sauce
1 can (12 ounces) tomato paste
1 tablespoon Italian seasoning
1 tablespoon dried oregano
1 to 2 teaspoons fennel seed, crushed
1 teaspoon onion powder
1 teaspoon garlic powder
1/2 teaspoon salt

In a saucepan over medium heat, combine tomato sauce and paste. Add remaining ingredients; mix well. Bring to a boil, stirring constantly. Reduce heat; cover and simmer for 1 hour, stirring occasionally. Cool. Pour into freezer containers, leaving 1/2-in. headspace. Freeze for up to 12 months. **Yield:** about 4 cups. **Editor's Note:** Use the sauce with crust and toppings of your choice to make a pizza; 1-1/3 cups of sauce will cover a crust in a 15-in. x 10-in. x 1-in. pan.

RASPBERRY LEMON MARMALADE

Cindy Lou Hickey, Kingston, Massachusetts

I like to be creative with my cooking. This recipe is a result of combining two family favorites. It's great on toast and biscuits or as a glaze on cheesecake.

4 medium lemons
1-1/4 cups water
1/8 teaspoon baking soda
1 cinnamon stick
3 cups crushed fresh *or* frozen raspberries (about 4 pints)
7 cups sugar
1 pouch (3 ounces) liquid fruit pectin

Grate peel from lemons and place in a medium saucepan. Trim white pith from lemons and discard. Cut lemons in half and remove the seeds. Chop pulp; set aside. Add water, baking soda and cinnamon to saucepan; bring to a boil. Reduce heat; cover and simmer for 20 minutes. Add lemon pulp; return to a boil. Reduce heat; simmer, uncovered, for 10 minutes. Remove cinnamon. In a large kettle, combine the raspberries, sugar and lemon mixture; bring to a full rolling boil, stirring constantly. Boil for 2 minutes. Quickly stir in pectin; return to a full rolling boil. Boil for 1 minute, stirring constantly. Remove from the heat; skim off any foam. Pour hot into hot jars, leaving 1/4-in. headspace. Adjust caps. Process for 10 minutes in a boiling-water bath. **Yield:** 8 half-pints.

FRESH SALSA

Sharon Lucas, Raymore, Missouri

The addition of olives makes this salsa a little different from other varieties. You can seed the jalapeno peppers if desired. But if your family likes salsa with some "heat", leave them in.

✓ This tasty dish uses less sugar, salt and fat. Recipe includes *Diabetic Exchanges*.

    8 medium tomatoes, chopped
  3/4 cup sliced green onions
  1/3 cup finely chopped fresh cilantro *or*
        parsley
  1/3 cup chopped onion
    2 small jalapeno peppers, finely chopped
        (seeded if desired)
    1 can (2-1/4 ounces) sliced ripe olives,
        drained
3-1/2 teaspoons fresh lime juice
    1 tablespoon cider vinegar
    1 tablespoon vegetable oil
    1 to 2 teaspoons chili powder
    1 to 2 teaspoons ground cumin
    1 teaspoon garlic powder
    1 teaspoon dried oregano
  1/4 teaspoon salt

Combine all ingredients in a large bowl. Cover and refrigerate overnight. **Yield:** 8 cups. **Diabetic Exchanges:** One 1/4-cup serving equals a free food; also, 16 calories, 31 mg sodium, 0 cholesterol, 2 gm carbohydrate, trace protein, 1 gm fat.

ZESTY HOMEMADE HORSERADISH SAUCE

Sandra Ashcraft, Pueblo, Colorado

This recipe from my mother-in-law can be used in many of your favorite recipes. If you enjoy the "punch" of fresh horseradish, give it a try!

  1/2 cup half-and-half cream
  1/4 cup vinegar
    1 tablespoon brown sugar
    2 teaspoons prepared mustard
    1 teaspoon salt
  1/4 teaspoon pepper
    1 cup chopped peeled horseradish root
        (about 6 ounces)

The Best of Country Cooking 1998

Place all ingredients in a blender container; process until fine. Transfer to a saucepan. Cook and stir over low until heated through; do not boil. Store in refrigerator 1-2 months. **Yield:** 1-1/3 cups.

PEAR HONEY

Bill Stewart, Perry, Iowa

(Pictured below)

My grandpa worked on a 120-acre pear orchard many years ago, and he would bring home damaged fruit. This recipe was a favorite way to use the pears.

  12 to 14 medium ripe pears, peeled and cored
    8 cups sugar
    1 can (20 ounces) crushed pineapple,
        undrained
    3 tablespoons lemon juice

Puree the pears in a food processor or blender; pour into a large kettle or Dutch oven. Add remaining ingredients; bring to a boil. Reduce heat; cook and stir, uncovered, for 50-60 minutes or until thickened. Remove from the heat. Pour hot into hot jars, leaving 1/4-in. headspace. Adjust caps. Process for 20 minutes in a boiling-water bath. **Yield:** 12 half-pints.

LEMON BUTTER SPREAD

Gloria Costes, West Hills, California

(Pictured below)

My grandmother, who was a great cook, brought this recipe with her from England. I use it as a spread on toast, for filling in a cake or on top of ice cream.

- 1 cup butter (no substitutes)
- 2 cups sugar
- 3 eggs, lightly beaten
- 1/2 cup lemon juice
- 1 tablespoon grated lemon peel

In the top of a double boiler over boiling water, melt butter. Stir in sugar, eggs, lemon juice and peel. Cook over simmering water for 1 hour or until thickened, stirring occasionally. Pour into containers. Store in the refrigerator. Use over angel food or pound cake or spread on toast or muffins. **Yield:** 3 cups.

FRESH TOMATO RELISH

Lela Baskins, Windsor, Missouri

My two grown sons actually eat this as a salad, but that's a bit too hot for me! The recipe came from my mother-in-law, and I haven't varied it over the years. I usually make a batch as soon as the first tomatoes of the season are ready. It will keep for months in the freezer.

- 2 cups vinegar
- 1/2 cup sugar
- 2 quarts chopped tomatoes (about 11 large)
- 1/2 cup chopped onion
- 1 medium green pepper, diced
- 1 celery rib, diced
- 1/4 cup prepared horseradish
- 2 tablespoons salt
- 1 tablespoon mustard seed
- 1-1/2 teaspoons pepper
- 1/2 teaspoon ground cinnamon
- 1/2 teaspoon ground cloves

In a saucepan, bring vinegar and sugar to a boil. Remove from the heat; cool completely. In a large bowl, combine remaining ingredients; add vinegar mixture and mix well. Spoon into storage containers, allowing 1/2-in. headspace. Refrigerate up to 2 weeks or freeze up to 12 months. Serve with a slotted spoon. **Yield:** about 6 pints.

FRUITY CHILI SAUCE

Kathy Kalyta, Lakefield, Ontario

Not long ago, I served this with a crown pork roast to a group. Everyone loved it and asked for the recipe, which I got from my sister and her mother-in-law.

- 20 medium tomatoes, chopped
- 6 medium onions, chopped
- 5 medium ripe peaches, peeled and chopped
- 5 medium ripe pears, chopped
- 1 medium green pepper, chopped
- 1 medium sweet red pepper, chopped
- 4 cups sugar
- 1 cup vinegar
- 2 tablespoons salt
- 1/4 cup mixed pickling spices

In a large kettle, combine the first nine ingredients; bring to a boil. Reduce heat to simmer. Tie pickling spices in a double thickness of cheesecloth; add to the tomato mixture. Simmer, uncovered, for 1-1/2 hours or until volume is reduced by half, stirring frequently. Discard the spice bag.

Store in the refrigerator for up to 2 months or ladle hot into hot jars, leaving 1/4-in. headspace. Adjust caps. Process for 15 minutes in a boiling-water bath. Serve over cooked pork, chicken or turkey. **Yield:** about 8 pints.

SPICY TOMATO JUICE

Kathleen Gill, Butte, Montana

(Pictured at right)

You can drink this juice plain or use it in most any recipe like chili that calls for vegetable juice as an ingredient.

    13 pounds ripe tomatoes (about 40 medium)
     2 celery ribs, coarsely chopped
     3 medium onions, coarsely chopped
     1 medium green pepper, coarsely chopped
    1-1/2 cups chopped fresh parsley
    1/2 cup sugar
     1 tablespoon Worcestershire sauce
     4 teaspoons salt
    1/4 teaspoon hot pepper sauce
    1/4 teaspoon cayenne pepper
    1/4 teaspoon pepper

Quarter tomatoes; place in a 6-qt. kettle. Add the celery, onions, green pepper and parsley. Simmer, uncovered, until vegetables are tender, about 45 minutes, stirring occasionally. Cool slightly; put through a sieve or food mill. Return to kettle. Add remaining ingredients; mix well. Bring to a boil. Remove from the heat; cool. Pour into freezer containers, leaving 1/2-in. headspace. Freeze for up to 12 months. **Yield:** about 5 quarts.

SPICED PEACH BUTTER

Marie Basinger, Connellsville, Pennsylvania

My husband especially enjoys this spicy-sweet butter on toast for breakfast. It also makes a great housewarming or hostess gift.

    18 medium ripe peaches, peeled and sliced
       or 4-1/2 pounds frozen sliced peaches
    1/3 cup water
     4 cups sugar
     1 teaspoon ground ginger
     1 teaspoon ground nutmeg

In a large kettle, cook peaches in water until tender. Press through a sieve or process in a food processor. Measure 8 cups pulp; return to kettle. Add sugar, ginger and nutmeg. Cook and stir over medium heat until thickened, about 30 minutes. Immediately ladle into hot jars, leaving 1/4-in. headspace. Adjust caps. Process for 10 minutes in a boiling-water bath. **Yield:** 4 pints.

GREEN TOMATO JAM

Norma Henderson, Hampton, New Brunswick

As the tomato season draws near and you have a bumper crop of green tomatoes on your vine, reach for this one-of-a-kind jam! Everyone is pleased with its great taste.

    2-1/2 cups pureed green tomatoes (about 3
          medium)
       2 cups sugar
       1 package (3 ounces) raspberry gelatin

In a large saucepan, bring tomatoes and sugar to a boil. Reduce heat; simmer, uncovered, for 20 minutes. Remove from the heat; stir in gelatin until dissolved. Skim off any foam. Pour into jars or freezer containers, leaving 1/2-in. headspace. Cool before covering with lids. Refrigerate or freeze. **Yield:** about 3 cups.

Put Up with Summer...Enjoy It All Winter

TENDING TOWARD more tomatoes than you can tabulate each summer? Close to capacity for cucumbers?

When your garden harvest is so prolific that your family can't possibly eat it all, try "putting up"!

Come winter, those jewel-toned jars of summer bounty will taste better than ever. Plus, they make great gifts—who *doesn't* appreciate a jar of homegrown preserves?

Don't worry if you're feeling a little "green" when it comes to canning. Even if you've never taken the plunge, all you need to know is on these pages. We contacted the experts who make Ball brand and Kerr brand home canning products and asked them to share the basics on the boiling-water method.

What's more, whether you're a beginner *or* a seasoned canner, you're sure to enjoy the flavorful recipes they've served up here as well.

BOILING-WATER METHOD FOR CANNING TOMATOES

1. Begin by reading the recipe through so you have all the ingredients and equipment ready and waiting. Take special note of the jar size, canning method and processing time. Changes of any sort shouldn't be made—everything's been thought through very carefully for you.

2. Check canning jars for any nicks, cracks or uneven rims. The canning lids should be free of scratches, and the sealing compound even and complete.

Check bands for proper fit.

3. Wash jars and two-piece caps in hot soapy water. Rinse well. Dry bands; set aside. Heat jars and lids in a saucepot of simmering water (180°F), making sure they don't come to a boil. Leave the jars and lids in hot water until ready to use and remove one at a time as needed.

4. Fill boiling-water canner half-full with hot water. Elevate rack in canner. Put canner lid in place. Heat water just to a simmer (180°F), keeping hot until processing.

5. Select fresh ripe unblemished tomatoes (2-1/2 to 3-1/2 pounds per quart jar). Wash and drain enough tomatoes for one canner load at a time.

6. Place tomatoes in wire basket and lower into a large saucepot of boiling water. Blanch tomatoes for 30 to 60 seconds or until the skins start to crack. Lift from boiling water and dip immediately into cold water.

7. Slip off skins. Trim away any green areas; core. Leave tomatoes whole or cut into halves or quarters. Place in a large saucepot filled with enough water to cover. Boil gently 5 minutes.

8. With a jar lifter, remove canning jar from hot water and set on a towel. Add 2 tablespoons bottled lemon juice or 1/2 teaspoon citric acid to each quart jar. Add 1 tablespoon bottled lemon juice or 1/4 teaspoon citric acid to each pint jar.

9. Gently pack hot tomatoes into hot jars, leaving 1/2-inch headspace. If desired, add 1 teaspoon salt per quart jar or 1/2 teaspoon salt per pint jar.

134 Condiments & Canned Goods

10. Run a nonmetallic spatula between tomatoes and jar; press tomatoes gently to release trapped air bubbles. Repeat 2 to 3 times around jar.

11. Wipe rim and threads of jar with a clean, damp cloth. With tongs or lid wand, remove lid from hot water. Place lid on jar rim with sealing compound next to glass. Screw band down evenly and firmly, just until resistance is met.

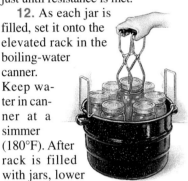

12. As each jar is filled, set it onto the elevated rack in the boiling-water canner. Keep water in canner at a simmer (180°F). After rack is filled with jars, lower rack into canner. Water level must cover the two-piece caps by 1 to 2 inches. Add more boiling water, if necessary.

13. Put lid on canner. Bring water to a boil. Start counting processing time after the water comes to a rolling boil. Process quarts 45 minutes, pints 40 minutes, at a gentle steady boil. For altitudes over 1,000 feet above sea level, refer to the Altitude Chart below.

ALTITUDE CHART BOILING-WATER CANNER

Altitude (Feet)	Increase Processing Time
1,001 - 3,000	5 minutes
3,001 - 6,000	10 minutes
6,001 - 8,000	15 minutes
8,001 -10,000	20 minutes

14. When processing time is over, turn off heat and remove canner lid. Remove jars from canner and set them upright, 1 to 2 inches apart, on a towel to cool. Bands should not be retightened. Let jars cool 12 to 24 hours.

15. After jars have cooled, check lids for a seal by pressing on the center of each lid. If the center is pulled down and does not flex, remove the band and try to lift the lid off. If the lid does not flex and can't be lifted off, the lid has a good vacuum seal. Wipe off lid and jar surface with a clean, damp cloth. Label. Store jars in a cool, dry, dark place. Enjoy!

Apply these basics of the boiling-water method to all recipes on this page. Also prepare home canning jars and lids according to manufacturer's instructions for all recipes you see here.

CHILI SAUCE

4 quarts peeled, cored, chopped tomatoes (about 24 large)
2 cups chopped onions
2 cups chopped sweet red peppers (about 4 medium)
1 hot red pepper, finely chopped
1 cup sugar
3 tablespoons salt
3 tablespoons mixed pickling spices
1 tablespoon celery seed
1 tablespoon mustard seed
2-1/2 cups vinegar (5% acidity)

Combine tomatoes, onions, peppers, sugar and salt; simmer for 45 minutes. Tie pickling spices, celery seed and mustard seed in a cheesecloth bag; add to tomato mixture. Cook until very thick, about 45 minutes, stirring frequently. Add vinegar to tomato mixture; cook to desired thickness. Remove spice bag. Carefully ladle hot sauce into hot jars, leaving 1/4-in. headspace. Adjust caps. Process for 15 minutes in a boiling-water canner. **Yield:** about 6 pints. **Editor's Note:** When cutting or seeding hot peppers, wear rubber gloves to prevent hands from being burned.

PICKLED PEPPERS

4 quarts long red, green *or* yellow peppers (Hungarian, Banana, etc.)
1-1/2 cups canning salt
4 quarts water
10 cups vinegar (5% acidity)
2 cups water
1/4 cup sugar
2 cloves garlic

Cut 2 small slits in each pepper. Dissolve salt in 4 quarts water. Pour over peppers; let stand 12 to 18 hours in a cool place. Drain; rinse and drain thoroughly. Combine remaining ingredients in a medium saucepot; simmer for 15 minutes. Remove garlic. Pack peppers into hot jars, leaving 1/4-in. headspace. Carefully ladle hot liquid over peppers, leaving 1/4-in. headspace. Remove air bubbles with a nonmetallic utensil. Adjust caps. Process 10 minutes in a boiling-water canner. **Yield:** about 8 pints. **Editor's Note:** When cutting or seeding hot peppers, wear rubber gloves to prevent hands from being burned.

CRANBERRY-APPLE RELISH

1 pound apples (about 6 small)
4 cups cranberries, coarsely chopped
2-1/2 cups packed brown sugar
1 cup water
1/2 cup chopped walnuts
1/2 teaspoon cinnamon

Peel, core and chop apples. Combine apples, cranberries, brown sugar and water in a large saucepot. Simmer over medium heat for 15 minutes, stirring frequently. Stir in walnuts and cinnamon; cook for 5 minutes. Carefully ladle hot relish into hot jars, leaving 1/4-in. headspace. Adjust caps. Process for 15 minutes in a boiling-water canner. **Yield:** about 5 half-pints.

ZUCCHINI PICKLES

2 pounds fresh, firm zucchini, cut into 1/4-inch slices
2 small onions, sliced
1/4 cup canning salt
3 cups vinegar (5% acidity)
2 cups sugar
2 teaspoons mustard seed
1 teaspoon celery seed
1 teaspoon turmeric

Combine zucchini and onions in a large bowl; sprinkle with salt and cover with cold water. Let stand for 2 hours; drain thoroughly. Combine remaining ingredients; bring to a boil. Pour over zucchini and onions; let stand for 2 hours. Bring mixture to a boil; reduce heat and simmer for 5 minutes. Carefully pack hot mixture into hot jars, leaving 1/4-in. headspace. Remove air bubbles with a nonmetallic utensil. Adjust caps. Process for 15 minutes in a boiling-water canner. **Yield:** about 4 half-pints.

QUICK AND EASY STRAWBERRY JAM

2 quarts strawberries, washed and stemmed
1 package powdered pectin
6-3/4 cups sugar

Crush strawberries and measure 4-1/2 cups berries into a large saucepot. Stir in pectin and bring to a rolling boil over high heat, stirring frequently. Add sugar and return to a rolling boil. Boil hard for 1 minute, stirring constantly. Remove from heat and skim foam, if necessary. Carefully ladle hot jam into hot jars, leaving 1/4-in. headspace. Adjust caps. Process for 10 minutes in a boiling-water canner. **Yield:** about 7 half-pints.

Down-Under Dinner's A Quick Delight

ALTHOUGH their two sons are both grown with homes of their own, Kathryn Awe of International Falls, Minnesota reports life for her and husband Ralph hasn't hit a much slower speed.

She notes, "Ralph's a seventh-grade teacher, while I'm the office manager for a local marina. Plus, we love to entertain."

So, whether it's rushing to rustle up supper at the end of the day or making sure she has time to spend with guests instead of in the kitchen, Kathryn calls often on this "Meal in Minutes" that can be prepared in under 30 minutes.

"Back 16 years ago," Kathryn explains, "while Ralph was participating in an educational exchange program, our family lived in Australia. On a regular basis, people there invited us over to eat. When we returned to the U.S., I had many new friends—and this new fast-to-fix meal as well.

"The salmon chowder could not be much simpler. Sometimes, I'll make the cucumbers a bit ahead to give the flavors a chance to blend.

"I'll put the no-fuss dessert together while the after-dinner coffee is perking."

Why not serve your "mates" Kathryn's dinner from down under? It's a meal that's guaranteed to make for a "g'day" at your place!

PANTRY-SHELF SALMON CHOWDER

My family enjoys homemade soup, but I don't always have the time to make it from scratch. This simple recipe calls for ingredients I can keep on hand, so I can serve steaming bowls of chowder in a hurry.

  1 small onion, thinly sliced
  1 tablespoon butter *or* margarine
  1 can (10-3/4 ounces) condensed cream of
    celery soup, undiluted
1-1/3 cups milk
  1 can (7-1/2 ounces) salmon, drained, skin
    and bones removed
  1 can (15 ounces) cream-style corn
  1 tablespoon minced fresh parsley

In a large saucepan, saute onion in butter until tender. Stir in remaining ingredients; heat through. **Yield:** 4 servings.

DILLED CUCUMBERS

I especially appreciate this recipe in summer when I have a bumper crop of cucumbers. Everyone likes this cool and crunchy side dish.

  1 large cucumber, thinly sliced
1/2 teaspoon salt
1/8 teaspoon pepper
  2 teaspoons chopped fresh dill *or* 1
    teaspoon dill weed
1/2 cup sour cream

Place cucumber slices in a medium bowl; sprinkle with salt and pepper. Stir in dill and sour cream. Chill until ready to serve. **Yield:** 4 servings.

PEACH MELBA DESSERT

This dessert is a nice change from traditional strawberry shortcake. It's a pretty addition to any table.

4 individual round sponge cakes *or*
  shortcakes
4 canned peach halves in syrup
4 scoops vanilla *or* peach ice cream
2 tablespoons raspberry jam
1 tablespoon chopped nuts

Place cakes on dessert plates. Drain the peaches, reserving 2 tablespoons syrup; spoon 1-1/2 teaspoons syrup over each cake. Place peach halves, hollow side up, on cakes. Put a scoop of ice cream in each peach. Heat jam; drizzle over ice cream. Sprinkle with nuts. Serve immediately. **Yield:** 4 servings.

Create a Stir With Squash Supper

A PART-TIME JOB has made it more important than ever for Joyce Hunsberger, Quakertown, Pennsylvania, to pare minutes from preparing meals.

"A few days a week," Joyce relates, "I work from early morning to evening, 30 miles from our country home. My husband, William, and I get in after 6 p.m. When we do, we're hungry for something quick, easy and good.

"The spaghetti squash dish came off the top of my head, while I found the basic recipe for the muffins in one of my many cookbooks. The dessert is an old standby I've had for years.

"For a change of pace, you can substitute ground beef or turkey for the Italian sausage in the squash dish. For chili lovers, season it with some cumin and chili powder—or both.

"Meat lovers might like having little pieces of chopped ham added to the muffins...or you could vary the shape and make a loaf of corn bread.

"With the dessert, you can substitute apple pie filling for apples. It's a bit thicker and sweeter. Plus, you can top the apples with cinnamon—or even use brown sugar in place of maple syrup, thicken it with cornstarch and use it as a pie filling."

Joyce and William have two grown daughters. When she's not cooking—"one of my favorite creative outlets"—Joyce can be found hunting antiques, watching birds, gardening or playing the piano. She's also a choir member and substitute Sunday school teacher.

▪▪▪▪▪▪▪▪▪▪▪▪

SPAGHETTI SQUASH SUPPER

This recipe is a deliciously different way to get your family to eat vegetables. It's a favorite summer meal at our house.

> 1 medium spaghetti squash (3 to 3-1/2 pounds)
> 1/2 cup water
> 1 pound bulk Italian sausage
> 1 medium onion, chopped
> 1 medium green pepper, chopped
> 1 small zucchini, diced
> 1 garlic clove, minced
> 1 can (15-1/2 ounces) great northern beans, rinsed and drained

> 1 can (14-1/2 ounces) Italian stewed tomatoes
> 1 teaspoon Italian seasoning
> 1/4 teaspoon seasoned salt
> Shredded Parmesan cheese

Halve squash lengthwise and discard seeds. Pierce skin with a fork or knife; place, cut side down, in a microwave-safe dish. Add the water; cover and microwave on high for 10-15 minutes or until squash is tender. Let stand for 5 minutes. Meanwhile, in a skillet, brown sausage; drain. Add onion, green pepper, zucchini and garlic. Cook and stir, uncovered, for 10 minutes or until the vegetables are crisp-tender; drain. Add beans, tomatoes, Italian seasoning and salt. Cover and simmer for 10 minutes. Using a fork, scoop out the spaghetti squash strands; place in a serving dish. Top with sausage mixture. Sprinkle with Parmesan cheese. **Yield:** 6 servings.

▪▪▪▪▪▪▪▪▪▪▪▪

CHEESY CORN MUFFINS

When the aroma of these muffins fills the house, my family's eager to be called to the dinner table for the first mouth-watering taste.

> 1/4 cup chopped onion
> 1 tablespoon butter *or* margarine
> 2 packages (8-1/2 ounces *each*) corn muffin mix
> 1/2 cup sour cream
> 1/2 cup shredded cheddar cheese

In a small skillet, saute onion in butter until tender; set aside. Prepare muffin mixes according to package directions; fold in the onion. Fill greased or paper-lined muffin cups two-thirds full. Combine sour cream and cheese; drop by rounded teaspoonfuls onto each muffin. Bake at 400° for 15-20 minutes or until muffins test done. Cool in pan for 5 minutes before removing to a wire rack. **Yield:** 1 dozen.

▪▪▪▪▪▪▪▪▪▪▪▪

SAUTEED APPLES A LA MODE

These sweet apples are so tasty we've been known to forgo the ice cream and eat them by themselves!

> 4 large baking apples, sliced
> 1/3 cup water
> 1/3 cup maple syrup
> Dash salt
> Vanilla ice cream

In a skillet, combine apples, water, syrup and salt; bring to a boil. Reduce heat; cover and simmer for 5-7 minutes or until apples are tender. Serve warm over ice cream. **Yield:** 6 servings.

Enjoy Dinner Without Delay

WHEN the meal she's making must be both fast *and* good, Sue McLaughlin of Onawa, Iowa most often turns to this one that can be ready to serve in less than half an hour.

"I'm a part-time nurse," she notes. "Husband Bob is a teacher. And we're the parents of three—all under 10. Plus, we like spending as much time in the outdoors as we can.

"My 'Meal in Minutes' is so quick to fix that I can get the kids started playing a game and serve it up before they even realize that they're hungry!

"The pizza is a great change of pace. It's soft… easy to chew…and just plain fun to eat—the kids feel like they are each getting a personal pizza of their own.

"Comments that I've heard on my salad include 'refreshing', 'eye-catching' and 'full of texture and taste'. It's a hit with folks who like Chinese food.

"As for the dessert, it's actually best to start with the bars when preparing the meal so everything has time to cool and set. The bars are excellent 'keepers', too. Bob really prefers them 'hot' out of the freezer!"

Variations? "With the pizza," says Sue, "I sometimes substitute spaghetti sauce for the pizza sauce. For a garden pizza, cover it with your favorite vegetables in place of the ground beef.

"With the dessert, you can eliminate the peanut butter and butterscotch chips if you like and go totally chocolate."

However *you* decide to make Sue's speedy meal, enjoy it—without delay.

FRENCH BREAD PIZZA

Why reach for a frozen pizza when you can make this easy-to-prepare homemade version? It appeals to kids of all ages.

  1/2 pound ground beef
  1 can (16 ounces) pizza sauce
  1 jar (8 ounces) sliced mushrooms, drained
  1 loaf (1 pound) French bread
  2 cups (8 ounces) shredded mozzarella cheese

In a medium skillet, brown beef; drain. Stir in pizza sauce and mushrooms; set aside. Cut bread in half lengthwise, then into eight pieces. Spread meat sauce on bread; place on a greased baking sheet. Sprinkle with mozzarella. Bake, uncovered, at 400° for 10 minutes or until cheese is melted and bubbly. **Yield:** 6-8 servings.

CRUNCHY LETTUCE SALAD

There are several variations to this Oriental-style salad. But this is the one most folks prefer. Toasted almonds, chow mein noodles and sesame seeds contribute to this salad's "crunch".

  1/3 cup sliced almonds
  1/4 cup chow mein noodles
  2 teaspoons sesame seeds
  1/2 cup vegetable oil
  1/4 cup sugar
  2 tablespoons white wine vinegar
  1/2 teaspoon salt
  1/4 teaspoon pepper
  8 cups torn iceberg *or* romaine lettuce
  4 green onions with tops, diced
  5 bacon strips, cooked and crumbled

In a baking pan, combine almonds, chow mein noodles and sesame seeds. Bake, uncovered, at 350° for 8-10 minutes or until lightly toasted; set aside. In a jar with tight-fitting lid, combine oil, sugar, vinegar, salt and pepper; shake well. In a large bowl, toss lettuce, onions and bacon. Just before serving, add almond mixture and dressing; toss. **Yield:** 6-8 servings.

CHOCOLATE PEANUT BUTTER TREATS

This twist on Rice Krispie Treats is chock-full of creamy peanut butter and sweet chocolate. No one can eat just one!

  1/4 cup butter *or* margarine
  1 package (10 ounces) marshmallows
  3/4 cup creamy peanut butter
  5 cups crisp rice cereal
  1 cup (6 ounces) butterscotch chips
  1 cup (6 ounces) semisweet chocolate chips

In a large saucepan or microwave-safe bowl, melt butter and marshmallows. Remove from the heat; stir in peanut butter. Gradually add cereal; mix until well coated. Spread and press into a greased 13-in. x 9-in. x 2-in. pan; set aside. In a microwave-safe bowl or the top of a double boiler over simmering water, melt the chips. Spread over cereal mixture. Cover and freeze for 15-20 minutes or until chocolate is set. **Yield:** 12-16 servings.

Timeless And Tasty Treats

TIME FLIES. Just ask Barb Marshall of Pickerington, Ohio—a wife, mother of four, and at-home seamstress and writer for Christian publications.

"Often," she reports, "I will look at the clock in the morning and then dive into one project or another. The next time I check the clock, it's 'magically' moved ahead 7 hours. The kids will be home from school at any minute, and they're bound to be hungry!"

At times like that, Barb counts on this quick-to-fix "Meal in Minutes".

"It's as easy as 1-2-3," she assures. "First, I stir up the muffins and start them baking. Next, I put on the noodles, broccoli and ham—then, while they cook, I put together the pear salad.

"Finally, I drain the noodle casserole water, add the other ingredients and pull the muffins out of the oven... and dinner's on the table in under 30 minutes."

One other advantage of this meal, Barb notes, is its second-time-around appeal. "My husband, Ronald, works long hours as a truck parts manager," she says. "Frequently, he won't arrive home until past 7 p.m. But the casserole is always still tasty after it's been warmed up in the microwave.

"There's one more good thing about this fast-to-fix meal," Barb adds. "The kids love it—and it's a great way to get them to eat vegetables. They've been known to have second and even third helpings!"

CREAMY NOODLE CASSEROLE

With noodles, broccoli and ham in a creamy cheese sauce, this dish is sure to please everyone in your family. It's become a standby in our house even when I do have time to cook!

    1 package (12 ounces) egg noodles
    1 package (16 ounces) frozen cut broccoli
    3 cups cubed fully cooked ham (1/2-inch pieces)
    1 cup (4 ounces) shredded mozzarella cheese
    1 cup (4 ounces) shredded Parmesan cheese
    1/3 cup butter *or* margarine
    1/2 cup half-and-half cream
    1/4 teaspoon *each* garlic powder, salt and pepper

In a 5-qt. Dutch oven, cook noodles in boiling salted water for 5 minutes. Add the broccoli and ham; cook 5-10 minutes longer or until noodles are tender. Drain; return to pan. Add remaining ingredients. Cook over low heat, stirring constantly, until butter is melted and mixture is heated through. **Yield:** 8 servings.

YANKEE CORN MUFFINS

These traditional corn muffins are perfect alongside the creamy casserole, but they really complement any meal. Topped with a little butter, fresh-from-the-oven treats like these never last too long around our house.

    1 cup all-purpose flour
    3/4 cup yellow cornmeal
    3 tablespoons sugar
    2-1/2 teaspoons baking powder
    1 teaspoon salt
    1 egg
    1 cup milk
    1/4 cup vegetable oil

In a medium bowl, combine flour, cornmeal, sugar, baking powder and salt. In a small bowl, beat egg, milk and oil; stir into the dry ingredients just until moistened. Fill greased or paper-lined muffin cups two-thirds full. Bake at 400° for 16-18 minutes. **Yield:** 8 muffins.

PRETTY PEAR SALAD

Sweetened cream cheese is a simple and satisfying way to dress up canned pears. Plus, they look so pretty on the table. For a different twist, you can use canned peaches in place of the pears.

    2 cans (one 16 ounces, one 29 ounces) pear halves
    1 package (8 ounces) cream cheese, softened
    1 tablespoon sugar
    1/2 cup seedless grapes, halved

Drain the pear halves, reserving 1 tablespoon of syrup. In a small bowl, beat the cream cheese, sugar and reserved syrup until smooth. Fill pear halves; top with grapes. **Yield:** 8 servings.

Recipes For Rushed Days

HOW'S THIS for a "recipe" for rushing? Take a husband who works a late shift...add a mom with an outside job...and toss in two teenage girls!

Those are the ingredients each day in the busy life Sheryl Christian, her husband, Randal, and their daughters, lead in the outskirts of Watertown, Wisconsin.

Smiles Sheryl, "The magic words for me when it comes to cooking are 'quick' and 'easy'!"

She adds, "Even though everyone's always coming and going, we feel it's important for all of us to sit down and have a meal together at least once a day. It allows us the chance to share what's been happening and to plan things as a family."

With that in mind, the whole year long for both lunch and supper, Sheryl relies on this "Meal in Minutes" standby.

"Actually, I do things backward," she admits. "I start with the tarts and chill them. Next, I get the water cooking for the salad noodles, do my chopping—since I use green pepper and onion in both the salad and sandwiches, I save time by doing that all at once—and toss the salad together.

"Last, I stack the sandwiches before cooking them and the sauce.

"There is a funny family story involving that sauce, by the way," Sheryl notes. "Years ago, when our older girl was little, she dipped her sandwich into the broth, took a bite and piped up, 'Mom, I *like* these coffee sandwiches.' We've kept that 'handle' for them ever since!"

PHILLY STEAK SANDWICHES

These steak sandwiches are hearty enough to serve for dinner as well as lunch. The beef broth used for "dunking" adds an extra-special touch.

    1/2 pound fresh mushrooms, sliced
      2 medium onions, thinly sliced
      1 medium green pepper, sliced
      2 tablespoons butter *or* margarine
      1 pound thinly sliced cooked roast beef
      6 hoagie rolls, split
      6 slices (8 ounces) mozzarella cheese
      4 beef bouillon cubes
      2 cups water

In a skillet, saute mushrooms, onions and green pepper in butter until tender. Divide beef among rolls. Top with vegetables and cheese; replace roll tops. Place on an ungreased baking sheet; cover with foil. Bake at 350° for 15 minutes or until heated through. In a small saucepan, heat bouillon and water until cubes are dissolved; serve as a dipping sauce. **Yield:** 6 servings. **Editor's Note:** Sandwiches may be heated in the microwave on high for 1 minute instead of baking.

SWEET-AND-SOUR SALAD

Here's a tasty twist to pasta salad that my family really enjoys. The sweet-and-sour dressing is irresistible.

      8 ounces elbow macaroni *or* mostaccioli
      1 medium green *or* sweet red pepper, coarsely chopped
    1/2 medium cucumber, sliced
      1 small onion, coarsely chopped
      1 cup cider vinegar
    3/4 cup sugar
      1 tablespoon dried parsley flakes
  1-1/2 teaspoons salt
      1 teaspoon garlic powder
    1/4 teaspoon pepper

Cook pasta according to package directions; drain and rinse with cold water. Place in a bowl; add pepper, cucumber and onion. In a jar with tight-fitting lid, combine remaining ingredients; shake until sugar is dissolved. Pour over salad; toss. Chill. **Yield:** 6 servings.

PEANUT BUTTER TARTS

This big batch of tarts doesn't last long around our house. But I don't mind...it's so simple to whip up more in a matter of minutes.

      1 carton (8 ounces) frozen whipped topping, thawed
  10 to 12 individual graham cracker tart shells
      1 cup cold milk
    2/3 cup creamy peanut butter
      1 package (3.4 ounces) instant vanilla pudding mix
      2 tablespoons jelly

Spoon a tablespoonful of whipped topping into the bottom of each tart shell; set aside. In a mixing bowl, beat milk and peanut butter until well mixed. Add pudding mix; beat for 1 minute. Fold in remaining whipped topping. Spoon about 1/2 cup filling into each shell. Chill. Just before serving, top each with 1/2 teaspoon jelly. Leftovers may be frozen. **Yield:** 10-12 servings.

Turkey Salad With A Twist

WITH four of six children still at home...a husband, Calvin, who teaches night classes...a full schedule of church involvement...and her own at-home craft business on the family hobby farm 20 miles outside of Twin Falls, Idaho, Jane Payne faces a real challenge each week.

"Our calendar has very few blank spots," she admits. "Even so, eating together is very important for us."

The solution? "Meals in Minutes" that go from start to serving in a half hour or less—like this one Jane terms her "pressed-for-time standby".

The turkey salad, she notes, is nicely versatile. "Sometimes," Jane relates, "I serve it plain by the scoop. At other times, I spoon it into pastry puffs or mini-hamburger buns.

"The breadsticks are great on days I don't have time to make bread. Another time-saving plus: They come out of the oven already buttery and ready to eat. They go well, too, with spaghetti, lasagna or any soup or entree needing a bit of bread.

"The fudge sauce is an all-purpose topping... it's so good I've even given it as a special fresh-from-the-kitchen Christmas present to friends!"

Over the years, Jane's worked out her meal timing this way: "I make the breadsticks first. Next, I mix the salad and slide it into the oven, where I've already started the breadsticks.

"I make the fudge sauce last. That way, it can warm while we're eating...it's just the right temperature when it's time for dessert...and we can enjoy its chocolaty aroma all through dinner!"

HOT TURKEY SALAD

When you're looking for a cold salad to serve, turn here! Just combine the ingredients—eliminating the crushed potato chips—and serve chilled instead. Whether you serve it hot or cold, it's delicious.

  4 cups cubed cooked turkey *or* chicken
  2 cups diced celery
  1 cup slivered almonds, toasted
  1 teaspoon salt
1/2 teaspoon dried thyme
1/4 teaspoon pepper
1-1/2 cups mayonnaise
  1 cup shredded cheddar cheese
  1 cup crushed potato chips

In a greased 2-qt. baking dish, combine the first eight ingredients. Top with potato chips. Bake, uncovered, at 450° for 15 minutes or until heated through. **Yield:** 4-6 servings.

BUTTERED BREADSTICKS

After sampling these homemade breadsticks, you'll never rely on store-bought varieties again. They always bake up buttery and golden brown.

1-1/2 cups all-purpose flour, *divided*
  2 teaspoons baking powder
  2 teaspoons sugar
  1 teaspoon salt
2/3 cup milk
1/4 cup butter *or* margarine, melted

In a medium bowl, combine 1-1/3 cups flour, baking powder, sugar and salt. Gradually add milk; stir in the remaining flour to form a soft dough. Turn onto a lightly floured board; knead gently for 1-2 minutes. Roll into a 1/4-in.-thick rectangle. Cut in half widthwise, then cut each lengthwise into six strips. Brush one side with butter. Place, butter side down, on a greased baking sheet; butter other side and fold each strip nearly in half. Bake at 450° for 10-12 minutes or until golden brown. **Yield:** 1 dozen.

HEAVENLY FUDGE SAUCE

In addition to topping fresh fruit and angel food cake, this sweet sauce is tasty over vanilla ice cream. It's easy to double the recipe when you want to make some to give as gifts.

  1 ounce (1 square) unsweetened chocolate
1/4 cup butter *or* margarine
1-1/2 cups confectioners' sugar
1/4 teaspoon salt
1/3 cup evaporated milk
Sliced bananas, orange sections *or* cubed angel food cake

In a small saucepan over very low heat, melt chocolate and butter. Whisk in sugar and salt alternately with milk; bring just to a boil over medium-low heat, stirring constantly. Serve warm over bananas, oranges or cake. **Yield:** 4-6 servings (1 cup).

Our Most Memorable Meals

Savor the flavors of yesteryear with these complete meals made up of old-fashioned dishes from individual cooks we combined in our test kitchen.

Tempt Your Taste Buds With Trout

YOUR FAMILY will fall hook-line-and-sinker for this meal that starts with Pan-Fried Trout, which is shared by Felicia Cummings from Raymond, Maine.

"One summer when my husband and I were enjoying our first 'getaway' in years, we found ourselves stranded in our cabin cruiser with a dead battery," recalls Felicia. "When hunger set in, my husband rigged up a fishing line, and soon there were two trout sizzling on the portable grill. We eventually made it home all right…and kept the recipe we devised."

The origin of Creamed Sweet Peas dates to the garden of Jean Patten's mom in the 1940's. "Her garden provided us with many delicious vegetables, but sweet peas were the best," submits Jean from Pineville, Louisiana. "She would pick them fresh, shell them and fix the best creamed sweet peas *ever* on her huge wood stove."

Every time Millie Feather prepares Caraway Rye Bread at home in Baroda, Michigan, she gets nostalgic for her childhood. "It was probably 45 years ago when the thrashers came to dinner at our house and Mother served this bread," Millie recollects. "My parents were emigrants from Czechoslovakia and couldn't speak English very well. The thrashers hardly talked anyway—they were too busy enjoying Mother's delicious food, including thick slices of her Caraway Rye Bread!"

Lemon Bars, from Etta Soucy, Mesa, Arizona, have a wonderful tangy flavor and are a hit with any meal. Offers Etta, "This dessert is from my mother's file. I've been serving these bars for many years. For variety of color and shape, they're a nice addition to a platter of cookies."

PAN-FRIED TROUT

    4 lake trout fillets (about 8 ounces *each*)
1/2 cup grated Parmesan cheese
1/2 cup bacon-flavored crackers, crushed
1/2 cup cornmeal
1/4 to 1/2 teaspoon garlic salt
Pinch pepper
    2 eggs
1/2 cup milk
1/2 cup vegetable oil
Lemon wedges *and/or* snipped fresh chives *or* parsley, optional

Rinse fish in cold water; pat dry. In a shallow bowl, combine the cheese, cracker crumbs, cornmeal, garlic salt and pepper. In another bowl, beat eggs and milk. Dip fish in the egg mixture, then gently roll in the crumb mixture. In a skillet, fry fish in oil for 5-7 minutes or until it flakes easily with a fork, turning once. If desired, garnish with lemon, chives and/or parsley. **Yield:** 4 servings.

CREAMED SWEET PEAS

    1 tablespoon all-purpose flour
1/4 cup sugar
2/3 cup milk
    2 cups fresh sweet peas *or* 1 package (10 ounces) frozen peas, thawed
1/4 teaspoon pepper

In a medium saucepan, combine flour, sugar and milk; mix well. Add peas and pepper; bring to a boil. Reduce heat; simmer for 10-12 minutes or until peas are heated through and sauce has thickened. **Yield:** 4 servings.

CARAWAY RYE BREAD

    2 packages (1/4 ounce *each*) active dry yeast
    2 cups warm water (110° to 115°), *divided*
1/4 cup packed brown sugar

1 tablespoon caraway seed
1 tablespoon vegetable oil
2 teaspoons salt
2-1/2 cups rye flour
2-3/4 to 3-1/4 cups all-purpose flour, *divided*

In a large mixing bowl, dissolve yeast in 1/2 cup warm water. Add brown sugar, caraway, oil, salt and remaining water; mix well. Stir in rye flour and 1 cup all-purpose flour; beat until smooth. Add enough remaining all-purpose flour to form a soft dough. Turn onto a floured board; knead until smooth and elastic, about 6-8 minutes. Place in a greased bowl, turning once to grease top. Cover and let rise in a warm place until doubled, about 1 hour. Punch dough down; divide in half. Shape each half into a ball; place in two greased 8-in. round cake pans. Flatten balls to a 6-in. diameter. Cover and let rise until nearly doubled, about 30 minutes. Bake at 375° for 25-30 minutes or until golden brown. **Yield:** 2 loaves.

LEMON BARS

1 cup all-purpose flour
1/2 cup butter *or* margarine, softened
1/4 cup confectioners' sugar
FILLING:
2 eggs
1 cup sugar
2 tablespoons all-purpose flour
1/2 teaspoon baking powder
2 tablespoons lemon juice
1 teaspoon grated lemon peel
Additional confectioners' sugar

Combine the first three ingredients; pat into an ungreased 8-in. square baking pan. Bake at 350° for 20 minutes. Meanwhile, beat eggs in a mixing bowl. Add sugar, flour, baking powder, lemon juice and peel; beat until frothy. Pour over the crust. Bake at 350° for 25 minutes or until light golden brown. Cool. Dust with confectioners' sugar. **Yield:** 9 servings.

Finger-Lickin'- Good Favorites

WHEN SUMMER rolls around, gather family and friends to sample these delicious down-home foods.

Oven-Barbecued Spareribs are at the heart of special meals at LaVerna Mjones' home in Moorhead, Minnesota. "All our married children live nearby, so we have family get-togethers often," remarks LaVerna. "Whenever I prepare these ribs, I need a large quantity—most everyone asks for seconds."

As a child, Marjorie Thompson would be met at the door by the enticing aroma of Old-Fashioned Baked Beans when she went to her grandma's for Sunday dinner. "These savory beans were Grandma's specialty," declares Marjorie from West Sacramento, California. "Just thinking of this dish takes me back in time. Every dish Grandma made was a labor of love."

For Beth Miller in Ocala, Florida, summer wouldn't be the same without her Salad with Creamy Dressing. "When our children were growing up, our vegetable garden was always bountiful. Many of the dishes I prepared came right from the garden," Beth informs. "I still enjoy creating new combinations of vegetables. This salad is especially tasty in the early growing season when all the greens are tender and fresh."

When you want to "surprise" folks, try Zucchini Cobbler from Joanne Fazio of Carbondale, Pennsylvania. "No one ever guesses that the secret ingredient is zucchini. Everyone says it tastes like apples," chuckles Joanne.

"This cobbler is a great dessert to make for a potluck supper or to serve a crowd. It's been requested time and again in my house, and I'm always happy to bake it."

OVEN-BARBECUED SPARERIBS

- 6 pounds pork spareribs
- 3 cups ketchup
- 1-1/2 cups packed brown sugar
- 3/4 cup chopped onion
- 1 teaspoon garlic powder
- 4 to 5 teaspoons liquid smoke, optional

Cut ribs into serving-size pieces; place with bone side down on a rack in a shallow roasting pan. Bake, uncovered, at 350° for 30 minutes. Meanwhile, in a medium saucepan, combine remaining ingredients; simmer, uncovered, for 20 minutes, stirring occasionally. Drain ribs; pour sauce over all. Cover and bake for 30-40 minutes or until tender. Uncover; bake 30 minutes longer, brushing several times with sauce. **Yield:** 6-8 servings.

OLD-FASHIONED BAKED BEANS

- 1 pound dry great northern beans
- 2 quarts water, *divided*
- 1/2 teaspoon salt
- 1 medium onion, chopped
- 2 tablespoons prepared mustard
- 2 tablespoons brown sugar
- 2 tablespoons dark molasses
- 1/2 pound sliced bacon, cooked and crumbled

Place beans and 1 qt. water in a saucepan; bring to a boil. Boil for 2 minutes. Remove from the heat; cover and let stand for 1 hour. Drain and rinse; return beans to saucepan. Add salt and remaining water; bring to a boil. Reduce heat; cover and simmer for 1 to 1-1/4 hours or until the beans are tender. Drain, reserving 2 cups cooking liquid. In a greased 13-in. x 9-in. x 2-in. baking dish, combine beans, onion, mustard, brown sugar, molasses, bacon and 1 cup of reserved cooking liquid. Cover and bake at 400° for 45 minutes or until the beans have reached desired thickness, stirring occasionally (add additional reserved cooking liquid if needed). **Yield:** 12-16 servings.

SALAD WITH CREAMY DRESSING

- 2/3 cup sour cream
- 2/3 cup mayonnaise *or* salad dressing
- 2/3 cup milk
- 2-1/2 teaspoons sugar
- 1-1/4 teaspoons prepared mustard
- 3/4 teaspoon garlic powder
- 3/4 teaspoon lemon-pepper seasoning
- 1 large head iceberg lettuce, torn
- 2 to 3 cups torn fresh spinach
- 1 small onion, sliced
- 1 large tomato, cut into wedges
- 1 medium green pepper, julienned
- 1 cup seasoned croutons

In a small bowl, combine the first seven ingredients and whisk until smooth. Cover and refriger-

ate for at least 1 hour. In a large salad bowl, combine lettuce, spinach, onion, tomato, green pepper and croutons. Add dressing and toss; serve immediately. **Yield:** 12-16 servings.

ZUCCHINI COBBLER

8 cups chopped seeded peeled zucchini
(about 3 pounds)
2/3 cup lemon juice
1 cup sugar
1 teaspoon ground cinnamon
1/2 teaspoon ground nutmeg
CRUST:
4 cups all-purpose flour
2 cups sugar
1-1/2 cups cold butter *or* margarine
1 teaspoon ground cinnamon

In a large saucepan over medium-low heat, cook and stir zucchini and lemon juice for 15-20 minutes or until zucchini is tender. Add sugar, cinnamon and nutmeg; simmer 1 minute longer. Remove from the heat; set aside. For crust, combine the flour and sugar in a bowl; cut in butter until the mixture resembles coarse crumbs. Stir 1/2 cup into zucchini mixture. Press half of remaining crust mixture into a greased 15-in. x 10-in. x 1-in. baking pan. Spread zucchini over top; crumble remaining crust mixture over zucchini. Sprinkle with cinnamon. Bake at 375° for 35-40 minutes or until golden and bubbly. **Yield:** 16-20 servings.

Mouth-Watering Mealtime Memories

SUNDAY DINNERS were always special when Frances Wilson of Tulsa, Oklahoma was growing up. "We packed up the car and headed to my grandparents' house," she explains. "Grandmother was the best cook anywhere.

"All her meals were delicious, but I especially loved dinners featuring savory Spiced Pot Roast," continues Frances. "The appealing aroma welcomed us into Grandmother's cozy kitchen. This pot roast is wonderful with garden-fresh vegetables on the side and a dessert made with apples."

Dorothy Dick of St. Louis, Missouri comments, "Although my grandmother lived in the city, she always tended a large vegetable garden. Toward the end of summer, we helped her pick the vegetables for a variety of dishes.

"Like most kids, we didn't care much for turnips," admits Dorothy. "But when Grandmother fixed Turnip Souffle, we'd ask for seconds."

Joan Kasura's husband wanted to recapture some of his grandmother's cooking. "Like most women of her generation, his grandmother was a 'no-measure cook'," says this Silver Spring, Maryland cook.

"Grandma's Apples and Rice recipe suffered as it was handed down, so I made an effort to work out the kinks. Finally, my husband pronounced the results as good as he remembered, and we declared it the 'official' recipe."

To round out this memorable meal, serve Baking Powder Biscuits from Catherine Yoder of Bertha, Minnesota. "When I was growing up, Mother made these wonderful biscuits often," shares Catherine.

"Some time ago, I consulted her box of old recipes and was delighted to find this childhood treat. Now these warm and tender biscuits are a special treat for my family, too."

Why not plan a Sunday supper for your family soon?

SPICED POT ROAST

    1/3 cup all-purpose flour
    1 teaspoon salt
    1/4 teaspoon pepper
    1 boneless beef rump *or* chuck roast
       (3 pounds)
    2 tablespoons vegetable oil
1-1/2 cups beef broth
    1/2 cup chutney
    1/2 cup raisins
    1/2 cup chopped onion
1-1/2 teaspoons curry powder
    1/2 teaspoon garlic powder
    1/2 teaspoon ground ginger

Combine flour, salt and pepper; rub over entire roast. In a Dutch oven, brown roast in oil on all sides. Combine remaining ingredients and pour over roast. Cover and bake at 325° for 3 hours or until meat is tender. Thicken gravy if desired. **Yield:** 6-8 servings.

TURNIP SOUFFLE

1-1/2 pounds turnips (about 6 medium),
       peeled and sliced
1-1/2 teaspoons salt, *divided*
    1/2 teaspoon sugar
    1/2 cup butter *or* margarine
    2 tablespoons all-purpose flour
    2/3 cup milk
    4 eggs, *separated*
    3 bacon strips, cooked and crumbled

Place turnips, 1/2 teaspoon of salt and sugar in a saucepan; cover with water. Cover and cook until turnips are tender, about 15-20 minutes; drain well and mash (do not add milk or butter). Set aside. In another saucepan, melt butter; stir in the flour and remaining salt until smooth. Add milk; bring to a boil. Cook and stir for 2 minutes. Beat egg yolks in a small bowl; gradually stir in 1/2 cup hot milk mixture. Return all to pan; cook and stir for 1 minute. Stir in turnips; remove from the heat. Beat egg whites until stiff peaks form; fold into batter. Spoon into a greased 11-in. x 7-in. x 2-in. glass baking dish. Sprinkle with bacon. Bake, uncovered, at 350° for 30 minutes or until golden brown. **Yield:** 6-8 servings.

GRANDMA'S APPLES AND RICE

1-1/4 cups uncooked brown rice
    4 tablespoons butter *or* margarine, *divided*
2-1/2 cups chunky applesauce
    1 cup cubed peeled apples
    1/4 cup packed brown sugar
1-3/4 teaspoons ground cinnamon, *divided*
Dash salt

Cook rice according to package directions. Stir 2

tablespoons butter into hot rice. Add apple-sauce, apples, brown sugar, 1-1/2 teaspoons cinnamon and salt. Spoon into a greased deep 2-qt. baking dish. Dot with remaining butter; sprinkle with remaining cinnamon. Bake, uncovered, at 350° for 35 minutes or until heated through. Serve warm or cold. **Yield:** 6-8 servings.

BAKING POWDER BISCUITS

2 cups all-purpose flour
2 tablespoons sugar
4 teaspoons baking powder
1/2 teaspoon cream of tartar
1/2 teaspoon salt
1/2 cup shortening
1 egg
2/3 cup milk

In a large bowl, combine flour, sugar, baking powder, cream of tartar and salt. Cut in shortening until mixture resembles coarse crumbs. Beat egg and milk; stir into dry ingredients just until moistened. Turn onto a lightly floured surface; roll to 1/2-in. thickness. Cut with a 2-1/2-in. biscuit cutter; place on an ungreased baking sheet. Bake at 450° for 10-12 minutes or until golden brown. **Yield:** 10 biscuits.

Early-Morning Entertaining Made Easy

NEXT TIME you're planning a breakfast or brunch, turn to these recipes that are loaded with pleasant memories and wonderful flavor.

"Brunch Egg Bake is an easy tasty dish to make for company because it allows you to spend plenty of time with your guests," shares Gloria Rohlfing from York, Pennsylvania.

"I grew up in the heart of Pennsylvania Dutch Country, and food was always the center of attention at our family get-togethers," Gloria adds. "We think brunch is the best meal of the day to gather and enjoy."

Willie Mae Philen's mother-in-law created the recipe for Fruit 'n' Nut Salad using leftover fruit from holiday baking. States this Mexia, Alabama cook, "It tasted so good that it became standard fare every time we had ham or turkey. It's a perfect side dish for those entrees. For color and a touch of sweetness, I sometimes add miniature marshmallows."

Although Marilyn Kutzli, from Preston, Iowa, mostly enjoyed her mom's Parsley Potatoes at Sunday dinner with pork chops, asparagus and rhubarb pie, they complement meals around the clock. "There were no refrigerators or freezers when I grew up, so we were eager to taste those first fresh vegetables from the garden," shares Marilyn. "We were especially fond of these potatoes."

From Phoenix Arizona, Muriel Doherty provides a new twist to Old-Fashioned Carrot Cake. "The frosting is a pleasant departure from the usual cream cheese frosting that tops most carrot cakes," explains Muriel. "My family thinks this is the best carrot cake ever...it doesn't last very long around our house!"

BRUNCH EGG BAKE

    3 cups (12 ounces) shredded cheddar
      cheese
    3 cups (12 ounces) shredded mozzarella
      cheese
    1 jar (4-1/2 ounces) sliced mushrooms,
      drained
  1/3 cup sliced green onions
  1/2 cup chopped sweet red pepper
    2 tablespoons butter *or* margarine
    2 cups diced fully cooked ham
    8 eggs
1-3/4 cups milk
  1/2 cup all-purpose flour
    2 tablespoons minced fresh parsley
  1/2 teaspoon dried basil
  1/2 teaspoon salt
  1/4 teaspoon pepper

Combine cheeses; place 3 cups in an ungreased 13-in. x 9-in. x 2-in. baking dish and set aside. In a medium skillet, saute mushrooms, onions and red pepper in butter until tender; drain. Place over cheese; top with ham. Sprinkle with remaining cheese. In a bowl, beat eggs. Add milk, flour, parsley, basil, salt and pepper; mix well. Slowly pour over the cheese. Bake at 350° for 35-40 minutes or until a knife inserted near the center comes out clean. Let stand 10 minutes before cutting. **Yield:** 12 servings.

FRUIT 'N' NUT SALAD

    2 medium apples, chopped
    2 medium oranges, sectioned and cut into
      bite-size pieces
    1 cup raisins
    1 jar (10 ounces) maraschino cherries,
      drained and chopped
1-1/2 cups chopped pecans
    1 cup mayonnaise
  1/2 cup sugar
    1 tablespoon lemon juice
    2 medium firm bananas, sliced

In a large bowl, combine the apples, oranges, raisins, cherries and pecans. Combine mayonnaise, sugar and lemon juice; mix well. Add to fruit mixture and stir to coat. Chill. Just before serving, stir in bananas. **Yield:** 12-16 servings.

PARSLEY POTATOES

    4 pounds small red potatoes
  1/2 cup butter *or* margarine
  1/2 cup minced fresh parsley

Cook potatoes in boiling salted water for 20-30 minutes or until tender; drain. Cool for 5 minutes. Remove skins. In a large skillet over medium heat, cook and stir the potatoes in butter until lightly browned, about 20 minutes. Stir in parsley. **Yield:** 12 servings.

OLD-FASHIONED CARROT CAKE

4 eggs
2 cups sugar
3 cups finely shredded carrots
1 package (8 ounces) cream cheese, softened
1-1/2 cups vegetable oil
2 cups all-purpose flour
2 teaspoons baking soda
2 teaspoons ground cinnamon
1 teaspoon salt
1 can (8 ounces) crushed pineapple, drained
1 cup chopped walnuts

FLUFFY FROSTING:
1/4 cup all-purpose flour
3/4 cup milk
3/4 cup butter *or* margarine, softened
3/4 cup sugar
1/2 teaspoon salt
1 teaspoon vanilla extract
2 cups confectioners' sugar

Additional chopped walnuts

Beat eggs and sugar. Add carrots, cream cheese and oil; beat until smooth. Add dry ingredients; mix well. Stir in pineapple and nuts. Pour into a greased 13-in. x 9-in. x 2-in. baking pan. Bake at 350° for 55-60 minutes or until cake tests done. Cool. In a heavy saucepan, cook and stir flour and milk over medium-low heat until a thick paste forms, about 10 minutes. Chill for 30 minutes. Cream butter, sugar and salt. Gradually add chilled flour mixture; beat until fluffy, about 5 minutes. Add vanilla and sugar; beat well. Frost cake. Sprinkle with nuts. **Yield:** 12-16 servings.

Chase Away Those Winter Chills

WELCOME family and friends in from the cold with country-style dishes that warm body and soul.

"When I was married some 45 years ago, my mother gave me the recipe for Barbecued Pot Roast," shares Emma Nye of New Oxford, Pennsylvania. "I always prepared this recipe when we had company because it never failed and tasted so good!

"Through the years, it became one of my family's favorite meals, and now I still often fix it for my husband and myself so we can enjoy the leftovers," admits Emma.

Fresh-from-the-oven bread is a nice touch to any meal. The recipe for Poppy Seed Cheese Bread from Elaine Mundt, Detroit, Michigan, goes well with pot roast, a salad luncheon or casserole dinner. "I especially like to serve it with spaghetti and pasta dishes," shares Elaine. "The cheese topping is its crowning glory!"

Dorothy Pritchett, from Wills Point, Texas, assures that Tomato Crouton Casserole is a perfect accompaniment to most any entree because it's so attractive and quick to fix. "I've enjoyed making this dish for so many years that I don't recall where I got the recipe," she states.

In Reston, Virginia, Tracy Betzler's friends rave about her Sour Cream Drops. "My mother is an excellent baker, and this is her recipe," credits Tracy. "Whether Mom makes these cookies or I do, they disappear quickly. My young children enjoy all kinds of cookies, but these are their most requested."

BARBECUED POT ROAST

     2 teaspoons salt
 1/4 teaspoon pepper
     1 beef chuck roast (3 pounds)
     3 tablespoons vegetable oil
     1 can (8 ounces) tomato sauce
     1 cup water
     3 medium onions, sliced
     2 garlic cloves, minced
 1/4 cup lemon juice
 1/4 cup ketchup
     2 tablespoons brown sugar
     1 tablespoon Worcestershire sauce
 1/2 teaspoon ground mustard

Combine salt and pepper; rub over roast. Heat oil in a Dutch oven; brown roast on all sides. Add the tomato sauce, water, onions and garlic. Cover and simmer for 30 minutes. Combine remaining ingredients; pour over meat. Cover and simmer for 3-4 hours or until the meat is tender. **Yield:** 6 servings.

POPPY SEED CHEESE BREAD

     1 package (1/4 ounce) active dry yeast
     2 teaspoons sugar
 1/4 cup warm water (110° to 115°)
 3/4 cup warm milk (110° to 115°)
     2 tablespoons shortening
     1 teaspoon salt
2-1/4 to 2-1/2 cups all-purpose flour
TOPPING:
     1 egg
     5 tablespoons milk
     1 teaspoon minced onion
     2 cups (8 ounces) shredded sharp cheddar cheese
Poppy seeds

In a mixing bowl, dissolve the yeast and sugar in water. Combine milk, shortening and salt; stir into yeast mixture. Add enough flour to make a soft dough. Turn onto a floured board; knead until smooth and elastic, about 3 minutes. Place in a greased bowl, turning once to grease top. Cover and let rise in a warm place until doubled, about 1-1/2 hours. Punch the dough down; press into a greased 13-in. x 9-in. x 2-in. baking pan. Cover and let rise in a warm place until nearly doubled, about 45 minutes. Combine egg, milk, onion and cheese; spread over top of dough. Sprinkle with poppy seeds. Bake at 425° for 15-20 minutes. Cut into squares; serve warm. **Yield:** 12-15 servings.

TOMATO CROUTON CASSEROLE

     1 can (28 ounces) diced tomatoes, undrained
     2 cups seasoned stuffing croutons, *divided*
     1 small onion, chopped
     1 tablespoon sugar
 1/4 teaspoon dried oregano
 1/4 teaspoon salt
 1/8 teaspoon pepper
     3 tablespoons butter *or* margarine

In a greased 2-qt. casserole, mix tomatoes and 1 cup croutons. Stir in onion, sugar, oregano, salt

and pepper. Dot with butter; sprinkle with remaining croutons. Bake, uncovered, at 375° for 30-35 minutes. **Yield:** 6 servings.

SOUR CREAM DROPS

    1/4 cup shortening
    3/4 cup sugar
      1 egg
    1/2 cup sour cream
    1/2 teaspoon vanilla extract
  1-1/3 cups all-purpose flour
    1/4 teaspoon baking soda
    1/4 teaspoon baking powder
    1/4 teaspoon salt

BURNT SUGAR FROSTING:
    2 tablespoons butter *or* margarine
    1/2 cup confectioners' sugar
    1/4 teaspoon vanilla extract
      3 to 4 teaspoons hot water

In a mixing bowl, cream shortening, sugar and egg. Add sour cream and vanilla. Combine dry ingredients; add to the creamed mixture. Chill for at least 1 hour. Drop by tablespoonfuls 2 in. apart onto greased baking sheets. Bake at 425° for 7-8 minutes or until lightly browned. Remove to wire racks to cool. For frosting, melt butter in a small saucepan until golden brown; stir in the sugar, vanilla and enough water to achieve a spreading consistency. Frost cooled cookies. **Yield:** about 2-1/2 dozen.

Homemade For the Holidays

IMPRESSIVE easy-to-prepare recipes are the key to successful holiday dining. That's why country cooks depend on tried-and-true recipes.

Explains Margaret Pache of Mesa, Arizona, "The wonderful orange juice-based sauce in my Lamb Chops with Prunes is simple to prepare, and its hint of spices really complements the lamb."

Mary Ann Evans' Blue-Ribbon Herb Rolls won an award nearly 25 years ago at a county fair near her Tarpon Springs, Florida home. "They're still a favorite here," Mary Ann shares.

Even those who aren't fond of spinach will find Spinach Cheese Bake very tasty. Merriam, Kansas cook Elaine Hoehn, who shares the recipe, attests, "The spinach flavor is mellowed by the cheese and eggs. I discovered this delicious recipe at a church luncheon, and it's a classic."

For a festive finale, reach for Chocolate Yum-Yum Cake from Dorothy Colli of West Hartford, Connecticut. "My grandmother first made this cake, and my mother made it often when I was a little girl. Now *I'm* still baking it. What better testimony to a great recipe!" declares Dorothy.

LAMB CHOPS WITH PRUNES

    8 loin lamb chops (1 inch thick)
    1 tablespoon vegetable oil
Salt and pepper to taste
    3/4 cup orange juice, *divided*
    2 tablespoons maple syrup
    1/2 teaspoon ground ginger
    1/4 teaspoon ground allspice
    8 ounces pitted prunes
1-1/2 teaspoons cornstarch

In a medium skillet, brown chops in oil on both sides; sprinkle with salt and pepper. Drain; return chops to skillet. Set aside 1 tablespoon of orange juice; pour remaining juice into skillet. Add syrup, ginger and allspice; cover and cook over medium-low heat for 15 minutes, turning chops once. Add prunes. Cover and simmer until chops are tender. Remove the chops to a serving platter and keep warm. Combine cornstarch and reserved orange juice; add to skillet. Bring to a boil over medium heat; cook and stir for 2 minutes. Spoon over lamb. **Yield:** 4 servings.

BLUE-RIBBON HERB ROLLS

✓ This tasty dish uses less sugar, salt and fat. Recipe includes *Diabetic Exchanges*.

    2 packages (1/4 ounce *each*) active dry
      yeast
2-3/4 cups warm water (110° to 115°),
      divided
    1 egg, beaten
    1/3 cup vegetable oil
    1/4 cup honey *or* molasses
    1 tablespoon salt
    2 teaspoons dill weed
    2 teaspoons dried thyme
    2 teaspoons dried basil
    1 teaspoon onion powder
    4 cups whole wheat flour
    4 to 4-1/2 cups all-purpose flour

In a mixing bowl, dissolve yeast in 1/2 cup warm water. Add next nine ingredients and remaining water; beat until smooth. Gradually add enough all-purpose flour to form a soft dough. Turn onto a floured board; knead until smooth and elastic, 6-8 minutes. Place in a greased bowl; turn once to grease top. Cover and let rise in a warm place until doubled, about 1 hour. Punch dough down. Shape into 1-in. balls. Place three balls each in greased muffin cups. Cover and let rise until doubled, 20-25 minutes. Bake at 375° for 12-15 minutes or until tops are golden brown. Remove from pan to a wire rack. **Yield:** 4 dozen. **Diabetic Exchanges:** One roll equals 1 starch; also, 94 calories, 136 mg sodium, 4 mg cholesterol, 17 gm carbohydrate, 3 gm protein, 2 gm fat.

SPINACH CHEESE BAKE

    3 tablespoons butter *or* margarine
    3 tablespoons all-purpose flour
1-1/2 cups milk
    2 cups (8 ounces) shredded process
      American cheese
    1 package (10 ounces) frozen chopped
      spinach, thawed and drained
1-1/2 cups soft bread crumbs
    3 eggs, lightly beaten
    1/2 teaspoon garlic salt
    1/4 teaspoon dried oregano
    1/4 teaspoon pepper

In a medium saucepan over low heat, melt butter; blend in flour until smooth. Cook and stir for 1-2 minutes. Gradually stir in milk; bring to a boil. Cook and stir for 2 minutes. Remove from the

heat; stir in cheese until melted. Add spinach, bread crumbs, eggs and seasonings; mix well. Spoon into an ungreased 1-1/2-qt. baking dish. Bake, uncovered, at 350° for 45-50 minutes or until lightly browned. **Yield:** 6-8 servings.

CHOCOLATE YUM-YUM CAKE

     1/2 **cup butter** *or* **margarine**
       2 **squares (1 ounce** *each***) unsweetened baking chocolate**
       1 **cup sugar**
     1/2 **cup raisins**
 1-1/2 **cups water**
     1/2 **teaspoon ground cinnamon**
     1/4 **teaspoon ground cloves**
Pinch salt
 1-1/2 **teaspoons vanilla extract**

 1-3/4 **cups all-purpose flour**
       1 **teaspoon baking soda**
ICING:
     1/2 **cup confectioners' sugar**
     1/4 **teaspoon vanilla extract**
       1 **to 2 teaspoons milk**

In a large saucepan over low heat, melt butter and chocolate, stirring constantly. Add sugar, raisins, water, cinnamon and cloves; bring to a boil. Boil for 5 minutes, stirring occasionally. Remove from the heat; pour into a mixing bowl and cool for 15 minutes. Add salt and vanilla. Combine flour and baking soda; add to chocolate mixture and mix well. Pour into a greased and floured 8-cup fluted tube pan. Bake at 350° for 45 minutes or until a wooden pick inserted near the center comes out clean. Cool in pan for 10 minutes before removing to a wire rack to cool. Combine icing ingredients; spoon over cooled cake. **Yield:** 8-10 servings.

Cooking for Two

These pared-down pleasing recipes prove that smaller servings don't require sacrificing full flavor.

HONEY BAKED CHICKEN

Helen Whelan, Jarrettsville, Maryland

I buy some meats in quantity and freeze extras for future menus. My husband especially loves this chicken recipe, which I scaled down to fit our life-style today. The honey and mustard sauce gives it a unique flavor.

    2 chicken breast halves (bone-in)
    2 tablespoons butter *or* margarine
    1/2 cup honey
    1/2 teaspoon salt
    1 tablespoon prepared mustard

Place the chicken in a greased or foil-lined 9-in. square baking pan. Bake, uncovered, at 325° for 30 minutes. Meanwhile, in a small saucepan, combine remaining ingredients; cook and stir over low heat until well blended and heated through. Pour over chicken. Bake, uncovered, 30-35 minutes longer or until chicken juices run clear. Baste before serving. **Yield:** 2 servings.

ASPARAGUS WITH BLUE CHEESE SAUCE

Leona Luecking, West Burlington, Iowa

My sister introduced me to this recipe several years ago because she knows I love blue cheese. This dish is a simple way to dress up asparagus, giving it a tangy taste altogether different from the usual cheese sauce.

    1/2 pound fresh asparagus spears
    2 ounces cream cheese, softened
    3 tablespoons evaporated milk *or*
      half-and-half cream
    1/8 teaspoon salt
    1 to 2 tablespoons crumbled blue cheese

In a small saucepan, cook the asparagus in a small amount of water until crisp-tender. Meanwhile, in another saucepan, whisk cream cheese, milk and salt over low heat until smooth. Stir in blue cheese and heat through. Drain asparagus and top with sauce. **Yield:** 2 servings.

SESAME RICE

Norma Poole, Auburndale, Florida

This side dish is compatible with any meat entree you serve. The secret of its tasty flavor is the chicken broth. The recipe's been a favorite with us for a long time.

    1 tablespoon sesame seeds
    1 tablespoon butter *or* margarine
    1/2 cup uncooked long grain rice
    1/2 cup chopped celery
    1/4 cup chopped onion
    1 chicken bouillon cube
    1/4 teaspoon salt
  1-1/4 cups hot water

In a medium skillet, saute the sesame seeds in butter for 2-3 minutes or until golden. Add rice, celery and onion; saute until the rice is browned. Spoon into an ungreased 1-1/2-qt. baking dish. Dissolve bouillon and salt in water; pour over the rice mixture. Cover and bake at 325° for 50-60 minutes or until rice is tender. **Yield:** 2 servings.

PEACHY DESSERT SAUCE

Helene Belanger, Denver, Colorado

We love this pretty peach sauce over ice cream and also served on angel food cake. It's delicious. I've always clipped recipes that catch my eye, and this one proved to be a real winner.

    1 teaspoon cornstarch
    1/4 cup water
    2 tablespoons apricot jam *or* preserves
    1/2 teaspoon lemon juice
  1-1/2 teaspoons sugar
    3/4 cup sliced fresh *or* canned peaches
Vanilla ice cream

In a small saucepan, mix the cornstarch and water. Add the jam, lemon juice and sugar; bring to a boil. Cook and stir for 1-2 minutes; reduce heat. Add peaches and heat through. Serve warm over ice cream. **Yield:** 3/4 cup.

STUFFED PEPPERS FOR TWO

Elaine Carpenter, Horseshoe Bay, Texas

My husband likes stuffed peppers, but my old recipe made too much. I devised this recipe to accommodate just the two of us. It helps to use a small-size casserole so the peppers won't tip over while baking. For color, I serve steamed carrots with the peppers, rounding out the meal perfectly!

    2 medium green peppers
  1/2 pound ground beef
    1 can (8 ounces) tomato sauce, *divided*
  1/4 cup uncooked instant rice
    3 tablespoons shredded cheddar cheese, *divided*
    1 tablespoon chopped onion
  1/2 teaspoon Worcestershire sauce
  1/2 teaspoon salt
  1/4 teaspoon pepper
    1 egg, beaten

Cut tops off of the peppers and discard; remove seeds. Blanch peppers in boiling water for 5 minutes. Drain and rinse in cold water; set aside. In a bowl, combine beef, 1/4 cup of tomato sauce, rice, 2 tablespoons of cheese, onion, Worcestershire sauce, salt, pepper and egg; mix well. Stuff the peppers; place in an ungreased 1-1/2-qt. baking dish. Pour the remaining tomato sauce over peppers. Cover and bake at 350° for 45-60 minutes or until meat is no longer pink and peppers are tender. Sprinkle with remaining cheese; return to the oven for 5 minutes or until cheese is melted. **Yield:** 2 servings.

FRUITY COLESLAW

Margaret Wampler, Butler, Pennsylvania

I received this recipe from a friend a long time ago, and it's been a family favorite ever since. The tartness of the slaw and the sweetness of the fruit give it a unique flavor. We like it best served with ham or pork chops, but it really pairs nicely with a variety of meaty main courses.

    1 can (8 ounces) pineapple chunks
    2 cups shredded cabbage
  3/4 cup mandarin oranges
    1 carrot, thinly sliced
    1 tablespoon finely chopped onion
    1 tablespoon vegetable oil
1-1/2 teaspoons cider vinegar
    1 teaspoon sugar
  1/8 teaspoon salt
  1/8 teaspoon pepper

Drain pineapple, reserving 1 tablespoon juice. In a bowl, combine pineapple, cabbage, oranges and carrot; mix well. Combine onion, oil, vinegar, sugar, salt, pepper and reserved pineapple juice; stir into cabbage mixture. Cover and refrigerate until ready to serve. **Yield:** 2 servings.

SKILLET SQUASH AND POTATOES

Bonnie Milner, DeRidder, Louisiana

My niece suggested I try cooking squash and potatoes together. I found that potatoes really do enhance the flavor of squash. I made up this recipe, and it turned out to be a keeper—a great side dish for any entree and a complement to other vegetables as well.

    1 small potato, peeled and thinly sliced
  1/4 cup chopped onion
    1 tablespoon vegetable oil
    1 small yellow summer squash, sliced
  1/4 teaspoon salt
  1/8 teaspoon pepper
Dash paprika

In a covered skillet over medium-low heat, cook the potato and onion in oil for 12 minutes. Add squash; cook, uncovered, for 8-10 minutes or until the vegetables are tender, stirring occasionally. Season with salt, pepper and paprika. **Yield:** 2 servings.

COCONUT MACAROONS

Penny Ann Habeck, Shawano, Wisconsin

These cookies earned me a first-place ribbon at the county fair. They remain my husband's favorite whenever I make them to give away, he always asks me where his batch is! I especially like the fact that the recipe makes a small enough batch for the two of us to nibble on.

1-1/3 cups flaked coconut
  1/3 cup sugar
    2 tablespoons all-purpose flour
  1/8 teaspoon salt
    2 egg whites
  1/2 teaspoon vanilla extract

In a small bowl, combine the coconut, sugar, flour and salt. Stir in egg whites and vanilla; mix well. Drop by rounded teaspoonfuls onto greased baking sheets. Bake at 325° for 18-20 minutes or until golden brown. Cool on a wire rack. **Yield:** about 1-1/2 dozen.

GRILLED TURKEY SANDWICHES

Dollypearle Martin, Douglastown, New Brunswick

These special grilled sandwiches are great for lunch or supper. Time spent in the kitchen is kept to a minimum when this entree is on the menu.

- 4 teaspoons cream cheese, softened
- 4 slices whole wheat *or* white bread
- 2 slices (1 ounce *each*) cheddar, Swiss *or* provolone cheese
- 4 thin slices cooked turkey
- 6 to 12 fresh spinach leaves
- 1 tablespoon butter *or* margarine, softened

Spread the cream cheese on two slices of bread. Layer cheese, turkey and spinach over cream cheese; top with remaining bread. Spread butter on top and bottom of sandwiches. Cook on both sides on a hot griddle or skillet until the bread is browned and cheese is melted. Serve immediately. **Yield:** 2 servings.

GRANDMA'S TOMATO SOUP

Gerri Sysun, Narragansett, Rhode Island

This recipe is my grandmother's. Originally Gram even made the tomato juice in it from scratch!

- 2 tablespoons butter *or* margarine
- 1 tablespoon all-purpose flour
- 2 cups tomato juice
- 1/2 cup water
- 2 tablespoons sugar
- 1/8 teaspoon salt
- 3/4 cup cooked wide egg noodles

In a saucepan over medium heat, melt the butter. Add flour; stir to form a smooth paste. Gradually add tomato juice and water, stirring constantly; bring to a boil. Cook and stir for 2 minutes or until thickened. Add sugar and salt. Stir in egg noodles and heat through. **Yield:** 2 servings.

SLAW FOR TWO

Sylvia Fora, Kennett, Missouri

Tasty and colorful, this salad is a welcome addition to any meal.

- 1 cup shredded cabbage
- 1/4 cup shredded carrot
- 1/4 cup chopped celery
- 1/4 cup chopped green pepper
- 2 tablespoons vegetable oil
- 2 tablespoons mayonnaise
- 1 teaspoon prepared mustard
- 1/4 teaspoon hot pepper sauce
- Salt to taste

In a medium bowl, combine the cabbage, carrot, celery and green pepper. In another bowl, combine oil, mayonnaise, mustard, hot pepper sauce and salt; pour over vegetables and toss. Cover and chill for several hours. Stir before serving. **Yield:** 2 servings.

QUICK AMBROSIA

Eleanor Lock, Escondido, California

After I'd raised my family, it wasn't easy to scale down my cooking habits, so I ventured into recipes— like this one— that didn't take a lot of time to prepare.

- 1/4 cup flaked coconut, toasted
- 2 tablespoons confectioners' sugar
- 1 orange, peeled and sectioned
- 1 firm banana, sliced
- 1/4 cup orange juice
- Maraschino cherries, optional

Combine the coconut and confectioners' sugar. Place orange sections and banana slices in two small bowls; pour orange juice over all. Sprinkle with coconut mixture. Chill or serve. Garnish with cherries if desired. **Yield:** 2 servings.

CREAMED SPINACH OMELET

Jo Ann Van Kesteren, Onancock, Virginia

(Not pictured)

Spinach adds a plateful of beautiful color and flavor that sparks interest and appetites alike.

- 3 cups loosely packed sliced fresh spinach
- 2 tablespoons butter *or* margarine, *divided*
- 2 tablespoons all-purpose flour
- 6 to 8 tablespoons milk, *divided*
- Pinch salt
- 4 eggs
- Salt and pepper to taste

In a skillet, saute the spinach in 1 tablespoon butter for 1 minute, stirring constantly. In a small bowl, stir flour, 5-7 tablespoons milk and salt until smooth. Add to spinach; cook and stir until thickened, about 1 minute. Set aside and keep warm. In another bowl, whisk eggs, salt, pepper and remaining milk. In another skillet over medium heat, cook egg mixture in remaining butter. As the eggs set, lift edges, letting uncooked portion flow underneath. When eggs are set, spread spinach mixture over half of the omelet. Fold omelet in half and transfer to a warm platter. **Yield:** 2 servings.

Pepper Steak

Mrs. Henry Sepanski, Altlanta, New York

I came across this recipe more than 40 years ago as a newlywed. I still make it for my husband and me in pared-down quantity.

✓ This tasty dish uses less sugar, salt and fat. Recipe includes *Diabetic Exchanges.*

- 1/2 pound round steak (3/4 inch thick), trimmed
- 1 tablespoon vegetable oil
- 1/4 cup chopped onion
- 1 garlic clove, minced
- 1 beef bouillon cube
- 3/4 cup boiling water
- 1/8 teaspoon pepper
- 1 can (14-1/2 ounces) stewed tomatoes
- 1 medium green pepper, cut into rings
- 1/4 cup cold water
- 2 tablespoons cornstarch
- 2 tablespoons soy sauce
- Hot cooked noodles, optional

Cut meat into 2-in. x 1-in. strips; brown in a skillet in oil for 10 minutes. Add onion and garlic; cook for 3-4 minutes. Dissolve bouillon in boiling water; pour into skillet. Sprinkle meat with pepper. Cover and simmer for 35-40 minutes or until meat is tender. Add tomatoes and green pepper; cover and simmer for 10 minutes. Combine cold water, cornstarch and soy sauce; stir into broth. Bring to a boil; cook and stir for 2 minutes. Serve over noodles if desired. **Yield:** 2 servings. **Diabetic Exchanges:** One serving (prepared with low-sodium bouillon and tomatoes and light soy sauce and served without noodles) equals 3 lean meat, 2 vegetable, 1 starch; also, 355 calories, 233 mg sodium, 82 mg cholesterol, 25 gm carbohydrate, 32 gm protein, 14 gm fat.

Corn Fritters

Auton Miller, Piney Flats, Tennessee

These corn fritters were Mom's special treat. She served them as a bread or a vegetable.

- 1/3 cup all-purpose flour
- 1/8 teaspoon salt
- 1/4 teaspoon baking powder
- 1/4 teaspoon paprika
- 1 egg, *separated*
- 3/4 cup frozen corn, thawed
- Vegetable oil for deep-fat frying

In a bowl, combine the flour, salt, baking powder and paprika. In another bowl, beat egg yolk; stir in corn. Add to flour mixture and mix well. Beat egg white until soft peaks form; fold into flour mixture. In a deep-fat fryer, heat oil to 375°. Drop batter by heaping tablespoonfuls into oil; fry for 3-4 minutes or until golden brown. Drain on paper towels. **Yield:** 2-4 servings.

Onion Barley Casserole

Elaine Kremenak, Grants Pass, Oregon

I always felt I was giving my family the best when I prepared this healthy dish. They loved the nutty flavor and chewy texture of the barley.

- 1/2 cup medium barley
- 1 tablespoon vegetable oil
- 1-1/2 cups water
- 1 teaspoon beef bouillon granules
- 1/4 teaspoon salt
- 1/2 cup sliced green onions
- 1 can (4 ounces) whole button mushrooms, drained

In an ovenproof skillet, saute barley in oil until golden brown. Stir in water, bouillon and salt; bring to a boil. Remove from the heat; add onions and mushrooms. Cover and bake at 350° for 40-50 minutes or until barley is tender. **Yield:** 2-4 servings.

Spiced Baked Apples

Lorraine Chausse, Cornwall, Ontario

I love being able to cook with fresh produce from gardens and groves. The spices and touch of orange make the flavor of these apples just perfect!

- 3 tablespoons raisins
- 2 tablespoons chopped walnuts
- 1/4 teaspoon grated orange peel
- 1/4 cup packed brown sugar
- 1/4 cup water
- 1 tablespoon butter *or* margarine
- 1/4 teaspoon ground cinnamon
- 1/4 teaspoon ground nutmeg
- 2 large baking apples

Combine the raisins, nuts and orange peel; set aside. In a saucepan, bring brown sugar, water, butter, cinnamon and nutmeg to a boil. Reduce heat; simmer, uncovered, for 2 minutes, stirring occasionally. Core apples and place in an ungreased 1-1/2-qt. baking dish; fill with raisin mixture. Pour sugar mixture over and around apples. Bake, uncovered, at 350° for 30-35 minutes or until apples are tender. Let stand 15 minutes before serving. **Yield:** 2 servings.

MARINATED TURKEY FOR TWO

Rachel Wellborne, Jacksonville, North Carolina

For years, I've been exchanging recipes by correspondence with friends. A dear friend in North Carolina shared this one. What's best about this recipe is that you can enjoy wonderful turkey flavor without preparing a whole bird.

>   2   turkey breast tenderloins (about 1 pound)
> 1-1/2 cups pineapple juice
>   1/3 cup sugar
>   3/4 teaspoon salt
>   1/8 teaspoon pepper
>   1/8 teaspoon ground ginger
> **Dash ground cloves**
> **Dash garlic powder**

Place the turkey in a shallow glass dish. Combine remaining ingredients; mix well. Set aside 1/3 cup; cover and refrigerate. Pour the remaining marinade over turkey. Cover and refrigerate 4 hours or overnight. Drain and discard marinade. Place turkey in an ungreased 11-in. x 7-in. x 2-in. baking dish. Pour reserved marinade over turkey. Cover and bake at 350° for 30 minutes. Uncover and bake 20-30 minutes longer or until no longer pink, basting twice. Slice and serve immediately. **Yield:** 2 servings.

TWICE-BAKED POTATOES

Leonora Wilkie, Bellbrook, Ohio

I came up with my dish when looking for a different way to use leftover baked potatoes. I wanted to do something besides simply frying them or making potato salad, so I found a recipe and added some of my own ingredients. This is the tasty result.

>   2   medium baking potatoes (1 to 1-1/2 pounds)
>   1/3 cup sour cream
>   3   tablespoons milk
>   2   teaspoons grated Parmesan cheese
>   1/8 teaspoon salt
>   2   bacon strips, cooked and crumbled
>   4   teaspoons shredded cheddar cheese
>   1   to 2 tablespoons chopped tomato, optional

Bake potatoes at 425° for 40-45 minutes or until tender. Allow to cool to the touch. In a bowl, combine sour cream, milk, Parmesan cheese and salt. Cut a thin slice off the top of potatoes; carefully scoop out the pulp, leaving a thin shell. Mash pulp with sour cream mixture; stuff shells.

Sprinkle with bacon and cheddar cheese. Bake at 325° for 20 minutes or until heated through. Top with tomato if desired. **Yield:** 2 servings.

POPOVERS

Emma Magielda, Amsterdam, New York

A popular restaurant was noted for the giant popovers it served with its meals. I decided to do the same for special birthdays and other occasions. These popovers soon became family favorites, and they've been one of my specialties for 40 years.

>   1/2 cup milk, room temperature
>   1   egg, room temperature
>   1/2 cup all-purpose flour
>   1/4 teaspoon salt

In a bowl, beat all ingredients just until smooth. Pour into four greased muffin cups. Fill the remaining muffin cups two-thirds full with water. Bake at 450° for 15 minutes. Reduce heat to 350° (do not open door). Bake 20 minutes longer or until deep golden brown (do not underbake). **Yield:** 2 servings.

SWISS CHERRY DESSERT

Laura Mae Peterson, Salem, Oregon

My beloved Swiss mother-in-law gave me this recipe years ago. It's quick and easy to prepare and, as she was so frugal, easy on the pocketbook! I've served this delicious dessert to groups, but it's best served like this.

>   4   tablespoons butter *or* margarine, ***divided***
>   2   to 3 slices day-old bread, cut into 1-inch cubes
>   1   can (15 ounces) dark sweet *or* Bing pitted cherries
> 2-1/2 teaspoons cornstarch
> 1-1/2 teaspoons sugar
>   1/2 teaspoon vanilla extract
>   1/4 teaspoon almond extract
> **Whipped cream and fresh mint, optional**

In a medium skillet, melt 2 tablespoons butter. Add bread cubes; cook and stir until browned. Remove from the heat; set aside. Drain syrup from cherries into a medium saucepan. Add cornstarch, sugar, extracts and remaining butter; bring to a boil. Boil and stir for 2 minutes. Remove from the heat; cool slightly. Stir in cherries. Divide bread cubes among two serving dishes; top with the cherry mixture. Garnish with whipped cream and mint if desired. **Yield:** 2 servings.

INDIVIDUAL MEAT LOAVES

Kim McMurl, Fargo, North Dakota

Pork gives this meat loaf a moist tasty flavor.

- 1 egg
- 3 tablespoons milk
- 1/2 teaspoon Worcestershire sauce
- 1/2 teaspoon onion salt
- 1/4 teaspoon pepper
- 1/4 cup cracker crumbs
- 1/2 pound uncooked ground pork
- 1/3 cup packed brown sugar
- 1/4 cup ketchup
- 3 tablespoons vinegar
- 1/2 teaspoon prepared mustard

In a medium bowl, beat egg; add milk, Worcestershire sauce, onion salt, pepper and crumbs. Add pork and mix well. Shape into two 5-in. x 2-1/2-in. loaves; place in a small baking pan. Combine remaining ingredients; pour over loaves. Bake, uncovered, at 325° for 1 hour or until no longer pink. **Yield: 2 servings.**

BROCCOLI-POTATO PANCAKES

Patty Kile, Greentown, Pennsylvania

I came up with this recipe by combining two others.

- 1 cup fresh *or* frozen finely chopped broccoli
- 1 cup boiling water
- 3 eggs
- 2 green onions, sliced
- 2 tablespoons all-purpose flour
- 1/2 teaspoon salt
- 1/8 teaspoon pepper
- 1 large baking potato, peeled

Vegetable oil

In a bowl, combine the broccoli and boiling water. Let stand for 5 minutes; drain thoroughly. In another bowl, beat eggs. Add onions, flour, salt and pepper; mix well. Add broccoli. Just before cooking, finely shred potato; add to broccoli mixture. In a large skillet, heat about 1/4 in. of oil over medium-high heat. Pour batter by 1/2 cupfuls into skillet. Fry over medium heat for 3-4 minutes on each side or until lightly browned. **Yield: 2 servings.**

MACARONI AND CHEESE FOR TWO

Betty Allen, East Point, Georgia

Mother rarely used cookbooks, so when asked for this recipe, she only estimated. The results were wonderful!

- 1-1/2 cups cooked elbow macaroni
- 1 cup (4 ounces) shredded sharp cheddar cheese
- 1/2 cup milk
- 1 egg, lightly beaten
- 1/2 teaspoon salt
- 1 tablespoon butter *or* margarine

In a medium bowl, combine the macaroni, cheese, milk, egg and salt; mix well. Pour into a greased 1-qt. shallow baking dish; dot with butter. Bake, uncovered, at 350° for 30-35 minutes or until a knife inserted in the center comes out clean. **Yield: 2 servings.**

PEANUT BUTTER PARFAITS

Mildred Sherrer, Bay City, Texas

This dessert makes an elegant finish to any meal.

- 1/2 cup packed light brown sugar
- 3 tablespoons milk
- 2 tablespoons light corn syrup
- 2 teaspoons butter *or* margarine
- 2 tablespoons creamy peanut butter

Vanilla ice cream
- 1/4 cup peanuts

In a saucepan, combine the brown sugar, milk, corn syrup and butter. Cook and stir over medium heat until sugar is dissolved and mixture is smooth, about 4 minutes. Remove from the heat; stir in peanut butter until smooth. Cool to room temperature. Spoon half into two parfait glasses; top with ice cream. Repeat layers. Sprinkle with peanuts. **Yield: 2 servings.**

BLUE CHEESE SPINACH SALAD

Myra Innes, Auburn, Kansas

(Not pictured)

Perk up spinach with bacon, cheese and a dressing.

- 3 tablespoons olive *or* vegetable oil
- 4 teaspoons lemon juice
- 1/4 teaspoon salt
- 1/8 teaspoon pepper
- 2 cups torn fresh spinach
- 1/4 cup thinly sliced red onion
- 1/2 cup sliced fresh mushrooms
- 2 bacon strips, cooked and crumbled
- 1/4 cup crumbled blue cheese

Combine the first four ingredients; mix well and set aside. In a medium salad bowl, toss spinach, onion and mushrooms. Just before serving, pour dressing over salad and toss well. Sprinkle with bacon and blue cheese. **Yield: 2 servings.**

Savory Braised Beef

Eva Knight, Nashua, New Hampshire

Both my husband and I enjoy this delicious dish—with meat, potatoes and vegetables, it's a meal in itself.

✓ This tasty dish uses less sugar, salt and fat. Recipe includes *Diabetic Exchanges.*

- 1/2 pound boneless beef chuck roast
- 3/4 cup water
- 1 small apple, thinly sliced
- 1 small onion, thinly sliced
- 1/4 teaspoon salt, optional
- 1/4 teaspoon pepper
- 4 small new potatoes, halved
- 2 cabbage wedges (about 2 inches thick)
- 1 can (14-1/2 ounces) stewed tomatoes
- 1-1/2 teaspoons cornstarch
- 1-1/2 teaspoons water

Trim fat from meat and cut into 1-in. cubes; brown in a skillet coated with nonstick cooking spray. Add water, apple, onion, salt if desired and pepper. Cover and simmer for 1-1/4 hours. Add potatoes and cabbage; cover and simmer for 35 minutes or until vegetables are tender. Stir in tomatoes; cover and simmer for 10 minutes. Blend cornstarch and water; stir into skillet. Bring to a boil; cook and stir for 2 minutes. **Yield:** 2 servings. **Diabetic Exchanges:** One serving (prepared without salt) equals 3 lean meat, 2 starch, 2 vegetable, 1/2 fruit; also, 401 calories, 560 mg sodium, 101 mg cholesterol, 46 gm carbohydrate, 38 gm protein, 13 gm fat.

Festive Tossed Salad

Ruby Williams, Bogalusa, Louisiana

I still do a lot of cooking, even though the numbers have changed. I owe my discovery of this salad to my sister-in-law, a Louisiana native and a fabulous cook. It's always been a hit with everyone.

- 2 tablespoons vegetable oil
- 1 tablespoon lemon juice
- 1 tablespoon honey
- 1/4 teaspoon sugar
- 1/4 teaspoon garlic powder
- Dash salt
- 2 to 3 cups torn salad greens
- 1 celery rib, sliced
- 1 medium carrot, shredded
- 2 green onions, sliced
- 1/2 cup mandarin oranges
- 1 tablespoon sliced almonds, toasted

In a jar with tight-fitting lid, combine the first six ingredients; shake well. In a salad bowl, toss the greens, celery, carrot, onions and oranges. Add dressing and toss to coat; sprinkle with almonds. Serve immediately. **Yield:** 2 servings.

Orange Pan Rolls

Jackie Riley, Holland, Michigan

A hint of orange in the dough makes these rolls refreshingly different. Similar in texture to a biscuit, they bake to a beautiful golden brown. I make them anytime I want something warm from the oven.

- 1 tablespoon sugar
- 1/8 teaspoon ground nutmeg
- 1/2 cup all-purpose flour
- 3/4 teaspoon baking powder
- 1/8 teaspoon cream of tartar
- 1/8 teaspoon salt
- 1/2 teaspoon grated orange peel
- 2 tablespoons shortening
- 3 tablespoons milk
- 1 tablespoon butter *or* margarine, melted

In a small bowl, combine the sugar and nutmeg; set aside. In a medium bowl, combine flour, baking powder, cream of tartar and salt. Add orange peel; cut in shortening until the mixture resembles coarse crumbs. Stir in milk just until moistened. Divide dough into fourths. With floured hands, roll each piece of dough into a ball; dip in butter, then in sugar mixture. Evenly space in a greased 9-in. round baking pan. Bake at 450° for 10-12 minutes or until golden brown. **Yield:** 4 rolls.

Easy Trifle for Two

Betty Kibbe, Albuquerque, New Mexico

Since there are just the two of us in the household now, I need to "keep it small" in my cooking. Vanilla wafers work perfectly in smaller portions.

- 16 vanilla wafers
- 2 tablespoons raspberry preserves
- 1/2 cup prepared vanilla pudding
- 2 tablespoons flaked coconut, toasted
- 1/3 cup prepared tapioca pudding

Spread the flat side of 12 wafers with 1/2 teaspoon raspberry preserves each. Crumble remaining wafers and set aside. Place five wafers each around the edges of two individual 4- to 6-oz. dishes, preserves side facing in. Place one wafer in the bottom of each dish, preserves side up. Spoon vanilla pudding in the center; sprinkle with wafer crumbs and half of the coconut. Top with tapioca pudding and remaining coconut. Cover and refrigerate for at least 3 hours. **Yield:** 2 servings.

SALMON PATTIES

Beverly Willis, Bridgetown, Nova Scotia

These lighter-than-air salmon patties are especially good served with green beans and a tossed salad.

- 1 cup mashed potatoes (with milk and butter)
- 1 can (6 ounces) salmon, drained, skin and bones removed
- 1/4 cup chopped onion
- 3 saltine crackers, crushed
- 1 tablespoon minced fresh parsley
- 1/8 teaspoon salt
- 1/8 teaspoon pepper
- 1 egg, *separated*
- 2 tablespoons vegetable oil

In a medium bowl, combine the potatoes, salmon, onion, cracker crumbs, parsley, salt, pepper and egg yolk; mix well. Beat egg white until stiff peaks form; fold into salmon mixture. Shape into six patties. Heat oil in skillet; fry patties over medium for 3-4 minutes per side or until lightly browned. **Yield:** 2 servings.

VEGETABLE RICE MEDLEY

Auton Miller, Piney Flats, Tennessee

We've been eating this wonderful old-time side dish for as long as I can remember.

- 1/2 cup cooked rice
- 1/4 cup chopped onion
- 2 teaspoons vegetable oil
- 1/2 cup chopped fresh tomato
- 1/4 cup chopped yellow *or* sweet red pepper
- 1/4 cup water
- 1/4 teaspoon salt
- 1/2 cup frozen peas

In a skillet over medium heat, saute the rice and onion in oil until rice is lightly browned. Add tomato, pepper, water and salt; reduce heat. Cover and simmer for 5 minutes. Stir in peas and heat through. **Yield:** 2 servings.

TEXAS CORN CHOWDER

Mildred Sherrer, Bay City, Texas

I cut this family recipe down to serve us "empty-nesters". The jalapeno adds a little zip and color!

- 1/4 cup chopped onion
- 1 tablespoon butter *or* margarine
- 1 tablespoon all-purpose flour
- 1 cup diced peeled potato (1 medium)
- 1 cup water
- 1 chicken bouillon cube
- 1 cup fresh *or* frozen corn
- 1 to 2 teaspoons finely chopped jalapeno *or* green chilies
- 2 cups milk
- 1/4 teaspoon garlic salt
- 1/8 teaspoon pepper
- Dash paprika

In a medium saucepan, saute the onion in butter until tender. Stir in flour. Add the potato, water and bouillon; bring to a boil. Reduce heat; cover and simmer for 7-10 minutes or until potato is tender. Add corn, jalapeno, milk and seasonings. Cover and simmer for 15 minutes. **Yield:** 2 servings.

PECAN SANDIES

Martha Crowe, La Plata, Maryland

Our grandchildren go through these cookies like locusts in a wheat field!

- 1/2 cup butter *or* margarine, softened
- 1/4 cup sugar
- 1 teaspoon vanilla extract
- 1 cup cake flour
- 1/2 cup finely chopped pecans

In a mixing bowl, cream butter and sugar; stir in vanilla. Add flour; mix on low until well blended. Stir in pecans; mix well. Chill for 30 minutes. Roll into 1-in. balls; place on a greased baking sheet. Bake at 350° for 15-18 minutes or until bottom edges are golden brown. Cool on a wire rack. **Yield:** about 1-1/2 dozen.

TOMATO-ARTICHOKE SIDE DISH

Valree Augustine, Pisgah Forest, North Carolina

(Not pictured)

Artichokes, tomatoes and other ingredients blend so nicely that I often take this to potlucks.

- 1 jar (6-1/2 ounces) marinated quartered artichoke hearts
- 1 tablespoon chopped green onions
- 1/4 teaspoon sugar
- 1/8 teaspoon dried basil
- 1/8 teaspoon pepper
- 1/8 teaspoon garlic powder
- 4 Roma tomatoes, quartered

Drain artichokes, reserving 1 tablespoon marinade. In a small skillet, saute onions in reserved marinade until tender. Stir in sugar, basil, pepper and garlic powder. Add tomatoes and artichokes; heat through, stirring gently. **Yield:** 2 servings.

PORK AND CABBAGE SUPPER

Tina Brown, Chino, California

This all-in-one dish makes a meal with great flavor. It's perfect if you're cooking for one or two, but the ingredients can also be multiplied to serve a larger number. My mother-in-law shared this recipe with me years ago. Quick and easy to prepare, it has been one of our family's favorites.

2 pork loin chops (1/2 inch thick)
1 tablespoon vegetable oil
1 can (10-3/4 ounces) condensed cream of mushroom soup, undiluted
1/2 teaspoon garlic powder
1/4 teaspoon salt
1/4 teaspoon pepper
3 cups shredded cabbage

In an ovenproof skillet, brown the chops in oil on both sides; remove and set aside. To drippings, add soup and seasonings; bring to a boil. Return chops to skillet; add cabbage. Cover and bake at 350° for 50-60 minutes or until meat is tender. **Yield:** 2 servings.

WINTER VEGETABLE SOUP

Mavis Diment, Marcus, Iowa

I've enjoyed this soup for years because it tastes good, is simple to make and doesn't leave a lot of leftovers. When there's a chill in the air, a steaming bowl of it is welcome. You can easily adjust the ingredients to suit your family's tastes. Cauliflower, celery and green beans are nice substitutions. Also feel free to add other seasonings.

✓ This tasty dish uses less sugar, salt and fat. Recipe includes *Diabetic Exchanges*.

1/2 cup sliced green onions
1 tablespoon vegetable oil
1 can (14-1/2 ounces) chicken broth
1 small potato, peeled and cubed
1 large carrot, sliced
1/4 teaspoon dried thyme
1 cup broccoli florets
1/4 teaspoon salt, optional
1/8 teaspoon pepper

In a medium saucepan, saute the onions in oil until tender. Add the next four ingredients; bring to a boil. Reduce heat; simmer, uncovered, for 5 minutes. Add the broccoli, salt if desired and pepper; simmer, uncovered, for 7 minutes or until vegetables are tender. **Yield:** 2 servings.
Diabetic Exchanges: One 1-1/3-cup serving (prepared with low-sodium broth and without salt) equals 1-1/2 fat, 1 starch, 1 vegetable; also,

168 calories, 125 mg sodium, 5 mg cholesterol, 19 gm carbohydrate, 5 gm protein, 8 gm fat.

COPPER CARROTS

Billie Scoggins, Long Beach, Mississippi

When I prepare this delicious carrot recipe, I'm reminded of a fabulous church supper our family attended back in 1942. I had never seen so much delicious food before—truly Southern cooking in full flower. These carrots were one of the side dishes served.

3 medium carrots, julienned
2 teaspoons sugar
1/2 teaspoon cornstarch
1/4 teaspoon salt
1/8 teaspoon ground ginger
2 tablespoons orange juice
1 tablespoon butter *or* margarine
Chopped fresh parsley, optional

In a small saucepan, cook the carrots in water until tender; drain. Remove carrots; set aside and keep warm. In the same saucepan, combine sugar, cornstarch, salt and ginger. Gradually stir in orange juice; bring to a boil. Cook and stir for 2 minutes. Add butter. Return carrots to pan; heat through. Sprinkle with parsley if desired. **Yield:** 2 servings.

BREAD PUDDING FOR TWO

Romaine Wetzel, Lancaster, Pennsylvania

This tried-and-true dessert was printed in a cookbook published by a local organization. I have made a few changes, and it has become one of our favorites. I like to eat mine warm with a dollop of whipped cream...but my husband eats his cold with a scoop of ice cream!

1-1/2 cups day-old buttered bread cubes (2 slices)
2 eggs
1 cup milk
1/4 cup sugar
1/4 teaspoon ground cinnamon
1/8 teaspoon ground nutmeg
Dash salt

Divide bread between two greased 8-oz. baking dishes; set aside. In a bowl, beat eggs, milk, sugar, cinnamon, nutmeg and salt. Pour over bread. Bake, uncovered, at 350° for 40-45 minutes or until a knife inserted near the center comes out clean. Cool slightly. Serve warm. **Yield:** 2 servings.

ZUCCHINI FRITTATA

Carol Blumenberg, Lehigh Acres, Florida

This recipe was always one of my family's favorites, and it remains so for my husband and me.

    1/2 cup chopped onion
      1 cup shredded zucchini
      1 teaspoon vegetable oil
      3 eggs, beaten
    1/4 teaspoon salt
      1 cup (4 ounces) shredded Swiss cheese

In an 8-in. ovenproof skillet over medium heat, saute the onion and zucchini in oil for 2-3 minutes. Pour eggs over top; sprinkle with salt. Cook until almost set, 6-7 minutes. Sprinkle with cheese. Bake at 350° for 4-5 minutes or until the cheese is melted. **Yield:** 2 servings.

OVEN-CRISPED POTATOES

Precious Owens, Elizabethtown, Kentucky

I often make this easy potato dish when I invite someone over for lunch. The aroma of it baking whets the appetite.

      2 medium potatoes, peeled and thinly sliced
      3 tablespoons butter *or* margarine, melted
      1 tablespoon finely chopped onion
    1/8 teaspoon pepper

Arrange potatoes in an ungreased 1-1/2-qt. baking dish. Combine butter, onion and pepper; pour over potatoes. Bake, uncovered, at 425° for 1 hour or until potatoes are tender. **Yield:** 2 servings.

SAUSAGE CASSEROLE FOR TWO

Kathryn Curtis, Lakeport, California

I don't know if Mother made up this recipe or if it was handed down to her, but it's scrumptious and can be made in small portions to satisfy two people.

      2 smoked cooked Polish sausages (about 6 ounces)
    1/4 cup sliced fresh mushrooms
    1/4 cup finely chopped onion
      1 tablespoon butter *or* margarine
      2 tablespoons whipping cream
  1-1/2 teaspoons Dijon mustard
    1/8 teaspoon garlic powder
    1/2 cup shredded cheddar cheese
      4 tomato slices

Cut sausages in half lengthwise; place in a greased 1-1/2-qt. baking dish. In a medium saucepan, saute mushrooms and onion in butter until lightly browned. Stir in cream, mustard and garlic powder; bring to a boil. Cook and stir until slightly thickened. Pour over sausages; top with cheese. Bake, uncovered, at 450° for 15-20 minutes or until cheese is melted. Garnish with tomato slices. **Yield:** 2 servings.

CHEESE DANISH

Mary Margaret Merritt, Washington Court House, Ohio

I saw this recipe in our local newspaper and modified it so that it serves two. When company drops by, I simply double the recipe to accommodate my guests.

      1 tube (4 ounces) refrigerated crescent rolls
      1 package (3 ounces) cream cheese, softened
    1/4 cup sugar
    1/4 teaspoon vanilla extract
      1 teaspoon butter *or* margarine, melted
  Cinnamon-sugar, optional

Unroll crescent roll dough and separate into two rectangles; place on an ungreased baking sheet and press the perforations together. In a small mixing bowl, beat cream cheese, sugar and vanilla until smooth. Spread over half of each rectangle; fold over opposite half of rectangle and pinch to seal. Brush with butter; sprinkle with cinnamon-sugar if desired. Bake at 350° for 15-20 minutes or until golden brown. **Yield:** 2 servings.

DUTCH CREAM WAFFLES

Barbara Syme, Peoria, Arizona
(Not pictured)

These waffles were originally made by my grandmother in a waffle iron on a wood-burning stove.

      1 cup all-purpose flour
    1/4 teaspoon salt
      3 eggs, *separated*
      1 cup heavy cream

In a large mixing bowl, combine the flour and salt. In a small mixing bowl, beat egg yolks on low while adding cream. Beat for 1 minute. Add to flour mixture; blend on low speed, then beat on medium-high until smooth. In another small mixing bowl, beat egg whites on high until stiff but not dry. Gently fold into batter. Bake in a preheated waffle iron according to manufacturer's directions. Serve warm. **Yield:** 2-3 servings.

Index

A

APPLES
Apple Strudel, 121
Caramel Apple Cake, 109
Caramel-Crunch Apple Pie, 105
Carrot-Apple Side Dish, 73
Cranberry-Apple Relish, 135
Glazed Apple Tart, 99
Grandma's Apples and Rice, 152
No-Egg Applesauce Cake, 106
Sausage 'n' Sweet Potatoes, 19
Sauteed Apples a la Mode, 139
Spiced Baked Apples, 167

APRICOTS
Apricot Cheese Danish, 87
Cherry Apricot Tea Bread, 82
Sweet Potato Cake, 122

ASPARAGUS
Asparagus Mushroom Salad, 60
Asparagus Tomato Quiche, 28
Asparagus with Blue Cheese Sauce, 161
Creamed Asparagus and Tomato, 75

B

BACON
Beef and Potato Boats, 16
Blue Cheese Spinach Salad, 171
Country-Style Scrambled Eggs, 18
Meaty Three-Bean Chili, 42
Mushroom Bacon Burgers, 13
Old-Fashioned Baked Beans, 150
Potato Delight, 36

BANANAS
Banana Streusel Pie, 100
Buttermilk Banana Cake, 108

BARLEY
Beans and Barley Chili, 53
Beef Barley Soup, 45
Onion Barley Casserole, 167

BEANS
Barbecued Butter Beans, 74
Beans and Barley Chili, 53

Black Bean Sausage Chili, 41
Corn and Bean Chili, 51
Make-Ahead Vegetable Medley, 65
Meaty Three-Bean Chili, 42
Old-Fashioned Baked Beans, 150
Two-Bean Rice Salad, 63
Vegetable Bean Chili, 44

BEEF *(also see Ground Beef)*
Barbecued Pot Roast, 156
Beef Barley Soup, 45
Beef Stew with Potato Dumplings, 8
Chunky Beef Chili, 48
Classic Swiss Steak, 27
Corned Beef and Cabbage, 9
Grilled Steak Pinwheels, 36
Hearty Hash, 18
Herbed Cornish Pasties, 7
Hungarian Goulash Soup, 54
Italian Beef Roll-Ups, 22
Low-Fat Beef Stew, 13
Pepper Steak, 167
Philly Steak Sandwiches, 145
Roast Beef Pasta Salad, 59
Robust Beef Sandwiches, 32
Round Steak Chili, 43
Savory Beef Stew, 38
Savory Braised Beef, 173
Shamrock Stew, 11
Spiced Pot Roast, 152
Steak Potpie, 35

BEETS
Cranberry-Glazed Beets, 68
Spiced Baked Beets, 72

BEVERAGE
Spicy Tomato Juice, 132

BISCUITS & SCONES
Baking Powder Biscuits, 153
Breakfast Scones, 77
Festive Fruited Scones, 82
Raisin Mini-Scones, 87
Sweet Potato Biscuits, 91

BLACKBERRIES
Blackberry Cobbler, 126
Blackberry Muffins, 96

BLUE-RIBBON RECIPES
Breads and Rolls
    Apricot Cheese Danish, 87

Caramel Pecan Rolls, 78
Christmas Bread, 77
Cranberry Eggnog Bread, 78
Finnish Bread, 97
Milk-and-Honey White Bread, 93
Scandinavian Cinnamon Rolls, 96
Three-Day Yeast Rolls, 77
Cakes & Pie
    Carrot Layer Cake, 104
    Cranberry-Orange Pound Cake, 104
    Cream Cheese Pound Cake, 119
    Double Peanut Pie, 123
    Peanut Butter Chocolate Cake, 103
    Pumpkin-Pecan Cake, 103
Chili and Soups
    Black Bean Sausage Chili, 41
    Chili with Tortilla Dumplings, 41
    Hungarian Goulash Soup, 54
    Meaty Three-Bean Chili, 42
    Santa Fe Chicken Chili, 42
    Tomato Dill Soup, 49
Desserts
    Apple Strudel, 121
    Blackberry Cobbler, 126
    Cheesecake Squares, 106
    Festive Fruitcake, 100
    Maple Biscuit Dessert, 107
    Zucchini Dessert Squares, 117
Main Dishes
    Beef Stew with Potato Dumplings, 8
    Chicken Avocado Melt, 16
    Chicken Creole, 20
    Chicken Potato Bake, 8
    Fruity Chili Sauce, 132
    Green Chili Pork Stew, 32
    Grilled Steak Pinwheels, 36
    Herbed Cornish Pasties, 7
    Meat Loaf Potato Surprise, 7
    New England Fish Bake, 23
    Rutabaga Pie, 20
    Shamrock Stew, 11
    Tomato-French Bread Lasagna, 25
    Upper Peninsula Pasties, 16
Salads
    Italian Potato Salad, 61
    Peachy Chicken Salad, 60
Side Dishes
    Root Vegetable Medley, 67
    Zucchini-Garlic Pasta, 71

BLUEBERRIES
Blueberry Spinach Salad, 59
Heavenly Blueberry Tart, 117

Old-Fashioned Blueberry Jam, 130
Very Berry Spread, 129

BREADS (*also see Biscuits & Scones;*
Coffee Cakes; French Toast, Pancakes &
Waffles; Muffins; Rolls & Buns; Yeast
Breads)
A to Z Bread, 81
Autumn Pear Bread, 92
Buttered Breadsticks, 147
Cheese Danish, 179
Chocolate Tea Bread, 88
Corn Fritters, 167
Cranberry Eggnog Bread, 78
Herbed Monkey Bread, 89
Popovers, 169
Pumpkin Bread, 79
Pumpkin Spice Bread, 81
Triple-Chocolate Quick Bread, 83

BROCCOLI
Broccoli Cheese Soup, 55
Broccoli-Hazelnut Bake, 68
Broccoli-Potato Pancakes, 171
Creamy Noodle Casserole, 143
Wild Rice and Ham Casserole, 29

BUTTERS
Lemon Butter Spread, 132
Raspberry Butter, 129
Spiced Peach Butter, 132

C

CABBAGE
Corned Beef and Cabbage, 9
Fruity Coleslaw, 163
Pork and Cabbage Supper, 177
Ruby Slaw, 63
Sausage 'n' Noodle Dinner, 17
Savory Braised Beef, 173
Scalloped Cabbage Casserole, 71
Slaw for Two, 165
Sunday Boiled Dinner, 26

CAKES & CUPCAKES
Boston Cream Cake, 115
Buttermilk Banana Cake, 108
Caramel Apple Cake, 109
Carrot Layer Cake, 104
Carrot Spice Cake, 116
Chocolate Cherry Cake, 126
Chocolate Chiffon Cake, 112
Chocolate Sheet Cake, 108
Chocolate Yum-Yum Cake, 159
Coffee Angel Food Cake, 114
Cranberry-Orange Pound Cake, 104
Cream Cheese Pound Cake, 119
Devil's Food Sheet Cake, 101
Lemon Meringue Cake, 108

Light Chocolate Cake, 117
Mandarin Orange Cake, 115
Mocha Cupcakes, 112
No-Egg Applesauce Cake, 106
Old-Fashioned Carrot Cake, 155
Peanut Butter Chocolate Cake, 103
Pennsylvania Dutch Funny Cake, 120
Pineapple Bundt Cake, 114
Poppy Seed Chiffon Cake, 127
Pumpkin Cake with Caramel Sauce, 112
Pumpkin-Pecan Cake, 103
Rice Pudding Cake, 127
Root Beer Float Cake, 114
Sunflower Potluck Cake, 109
Sweet Potato Cake, 122

CARAMEL
Caramel Apple Cake, 109
Caramel-Crunch Apple Pie, 105
Caramel Pecan Rolls, 78
Pumpkin Cake with Caramel Sauce, 112

CARROTS
Carrot-Apple Side Dish, 73
Carrot Casserole, 74
Carrot Layer Cake, 104
Carrot Spice Cake, 116
Copper Carrots, 177
Country Carrot Soup, 42
Golden Carrot Buns, 92
Old-Fashioned Carrot Cake, 155

CASSEROLES (*also see Lasagna; Meat*
Pies & Potpies)
Main Dishes
   Brunch Egg Bake, 154
   Creamy Noodle Casserole, 143
   Curry Chicken Dinner, 33
   Farm-Style Sausage Bake, 37
   Hot Turkey Salad, 147
   Macaroni and Cheese for Two, 171
   New England Fish Bake, 23
   Penny Casserole, 19
   Sausage 'n' Sweet Potatoes, 19
   Sausage Casserole for Two, 179
   Seafood Rice Casserole, 15
   Wild Rice and Ham Casserole, 29
   Zucchini Pork Chop Supper, 30
Side Dishes
   Broccoli-Hazelnut Bake, 68
   Carrot Casserole, 74
   Chili Cheese Grits, 71
   Creamy Mushroom-Potato Bake, 69
   Grandma's Apples and Rice, 152
   Onion Barley Casserole, 167
   Onion Potato Pie, 73
   Potato Cheese Casserole, 75
   Scalloped Cabbage Casserole, 71
   Sesame Rice, 161
   Spiced Baked Beets, 72
   Spinach Cheese Bake, 158
   Tomato Crouton Casserole, 156

Turnip Souffle, 152

CHEESE
Apricot Cheese Danish, 87
Asparagus with Blue Cheese Sauce, 161
Beef and Cheddar Quiche, 9
Berry Cream Coffee Cake, 88
Blue Cheese Spinach Salad, 171
Broccoli Cheese Soup, 55
Brunch Egg Bake, 154
Cheese Danish, 179
Cheesecake Squares, 106
Cheesy Corn Muffins, 139
Chili Cheese Grits, 71
Cream Cheese Pound Cake, 119
Creamy Noodle Casserole, 143
Green Tomatoes Parmesan, 69
Macaroni and Cheese for Two, 171
Parmesan Potato Soup, 43
Poppy Seed Cheese Bread, 156
Potato Cheese Casserole, 75
Scalloped Cabbage Casserole, 71
Spinach Cheese Bake, 158

CHERRIES
Cherry Almond Braid, 89
Cherry Apricot Tea Bread, 82
Cherry Torte, 101
Chocolate Cherry Cake, 126
Swiss Cherry Dessert, 169
Tart Cherry Salad, 65

CHICKEN
Baked Lemon Chicken, 15
Bayou Chicken Pasta, 35
Chicken Avocado Melt, 16
Chicken Creole, 20
Chicken Pasta Salad, 57
Chicken Potato Bake, 8
Chicken Stew, 24
Chicken with Potato Stuffing, 14
Citrus-Glazed Chicken, 10
Country Fried Chicken, 28
Curry Chicken Dinner, 33
Honey Baked Chicken, 161
Orange-Glazed Chicken with Rice, 26
Peachy Chicken Salad, 60
Santa Fe Chicken Chili, 42
Spicy White Chili, 48

CHILI
All-American Chili, 50
Aloha Chili, 51
Beans and Barley Chili, 53
Black Bean Sausage Chili, 41
Chili for a Crowd, 49
Chili in No Time, 41
Chili with Tortilla Dumplings, 41
Chunky Beef Chili, 48
Corn and Bean Chili, 51
Garden Harvest Chili, 44
Hearty Italian Chili, 48
Margie's Chili, 51

CHILI (continued)
Meaty Three-Bean Chili, 42
Round Steak Chili, 43
Santa Fe Chicken Chili, 42
Sausage Onion Chili, 51
Speedy Chili, 50
Spicy White Chili, 48
Tangy Oven Chili, 45
Vegetable Bean Chili, 44
Wild West Chili, 55
Zesty Colorado Chili, 44

CHOCOLATE
Breads
    Chocolate Chip Coffee Ring, 86
    Chocolate Tea Bread, 88
    Triple-Chocolate Quick Bread, 83
Cakes and Cupcakes
    Boston Cream Cake, 115
    Chocolate Cherry Cake, 126
    Chocolate Chiffon Cake, 112
    Chocolate Sheet Cake, 108
    Chocolate Yum-Yum Cake, 159
    Devil's Food Sheet Cake, 101
    Light Chocolate Cake, 117
    Mocha Cupcakes, 112
    Peanut Butter Chocolate Cake, 103
    Pennsylvania Dutch Funny Cake, 120
    Sunflower Potluck Cake, 109
Cookies and Bars
    Chocolate Peanut Butter Treats, 141
    Chocolate-Tipped Butter Cookies, 120
    Chocolate Truffle Cookies, 107
    French Christmas Cookies, 126
    Snowmen Cookies, 122
Desserts
    Heavenly Fudge Sauce, 147
    Peppermint Ice Cream Cake, 123

CHOWDER
Pantry-Shelf Salmon Chowder, 137
Texas Corn Chowder, 175

COFFEE CAKES
Berry Cream Coffee Cake, 88
Cherry Almond Braid, 89
Chocolate Chip Coffee Ring, 86
Cranberry Coffee Cake, 97
Springtime Coffee Cake, 91

COLESLAW
Fruity Coleslaw, 163
Ruby Slaw, 63
Slaw for Two, 165

COOKIES & BARS
Bars
    Chocolate Peanut Butter Treats, 141
    Cranberry Bars, 118
    Lemon Bars, 149
Cookies
    Chocolate-Tipped Butter Cookies, 120
    Chocolate Truffle Cookies, 107

Coconut Macaroons, 163
Cute Pig Cookies, 118
French Christmas Cookies, 126
Pecan Sandies, 175
Poinsettia Cookies, 123
Refrigerator Cookies, 105
Russian Tea Cakes, 119
Snowmen Cookies, 122
Sour Cream Drops, 157
Sunflower Seed Cookies, 105

COOKING FOR TWO
Breads
    Cheese Danish, 179
    Corn Fritters, 167
    Dutch Cream Waffles, 179
    Orange Pan Rolls, 173
    Popovers, 169
Desserts
    Bread Pudding for Two, 177
    Coconut Macaroons, 163
    Easy Trifle for Two, 173
    Peachy Dessert Sauce, 161
    Peanut Butter Parfaits, 171
    Pecan Sandies, 175
    Quick Ambrosia, 165
    Spiced Baked Apples, 167
    Swiss Cherry Dessert, 169
Main Dishes
    Creamed Spinach Omelet, 165
    Honey Baked Chicken, 161
    Individual Meat Loaves, 171
    Macaroni and Cheese for Two, 171
    Marinated Turkey for Two, 169
    Pepper Steak, 167
    Pork and Cabbage Supper, 177
    Salmon Patties, 175
    Sausage Casserole for Two, 179
    Savory Braised Beef, 173
    Stuffed Peppers for Two, 163
    Zucchini Frittata, 179
Salads
    Blue Cheese Spinach Salad, 171
    Festive Tossed Salad, 173
    Fruity Coleslaw, 163
    Slaw for Two, 165
Side Dishes
    Asparagus with Blue Cheese Sauce, 161
    Broccoli-Potato Pancakes, 171
    Copper Carrots, 177
    Onion Barley Casserole, 167
    Oven-Crisped Potatoes, 179
    Sesame Rice, 161
    Skillet Squash and Potatoes, 163
    Tomato-Artichoke Side Dish, 175
    Twice-Baked Potatoes, 169
    Vegetable Rice Medley, 175
Soups and Sandwiches
    Grandma's Tomato Soup, 165
    Grilled Turkey Sandwiches, 165
    Texas Corn Chowder, 175
    Winter Vegetable Soup, 177

CORN
Cheesy Corn Muffins, 139
Corn and Bean Chili, 51
Corn Fritters, 167
Texas Corn Chowder, 175
Zesty Grilled Corn, 67

CORN BREAD & CORNMEAL
Cheesy Corn Muffins, 139
Hot Tamale Pie, 33
Mexican Chili Pie, 31
Yankee Corn Muffins, 143

CRANBERRIES
Cranberry-Apple Relish, 135
Cranberry Bars, 118
Cranberry Coffee Cake, 97
Cranberry Eggnog Bread, 78
Cranberry-Glazed Beets, 68
Cranberry-Orange Pound Cake, 104

CUCUMBERS
Dilled Cucumbers, 137
Marinated Onion Salad, 64
Tomato Cucumber Salad, 57

D

DESSERTS (also see Cakes & Cupcakes;
Cookies & Bars; Ice Cream; Pies)
Apple Strudel, 121
Blackberry Cobbler, 126
Bread Pudding for Two, 177
Cheesecake Squares, 106
Cherry Torte, 101
Citrus Gingerbread, 120
Easy Trifle for Two, 173
Festive Fruitcake, 100
Ghostly Custards, 107
Glazed Apple Tart, 99
Heavenly Blueberry Tart, 117
Heavenly Fudge Sauce, 147
Maple Biscuit Dessert, 107
Peach Melba Dessert, 137
Peachy Dessert Sauce, 161
Peanut Butter Tarts, 145
Pretzel Log Cabin, 124
Quick Ambrosia, 165
Raspberry Marshmallow Delight, 119
Sauteed Apples a la Mode, 139
Spiced Baked Apples, 167
Summer Dessert Pizza, 116
Swiss Cherry Dessert, 169
Zucchini Cobbler, 151
Zucchini Dessert Squares, 117

✓ **DIABETIC EXCHANGE &
NUTRITIONAL ANALYSIS RECIPES**
(Lower in salt, sugar, fat and cholesterol)
Breads and Rolls
    Blue-Ribbon Herb Rolls, 158

English Muffin Bread, 90
Low-Fat Cinnamon Rolls, 93
Oat-Bran Bread, 96
Raisin Mini-Scones, 87

Cakes
Carrot Spice Cake, 116
Light Chocolate Cake, 117
No-Egg Applesauce Cake, 106

Chili and Soups
Beans and Barley Chili, 53
Garden Harvest Chili, 44
Hungarian Goulash Soup, 54
Vegetable Bean Chili, 44
Winter Vegetable Soup, 177

Main Dishes
Baked Lemon Chicken, 15
Baked Walleye, 10
Chicken Creole, 20
Chicken Stew, 24
Low-Fat Beef Stew, 13
Pepper Steak, 167
Pork and Sweet Potatoes, 29
Potato Delight, 36
Savory Beef Stew, 38
Savory Braised Beef, 173
Seafood Rice Casserole, 15
Shamrock Stew, 11
Taco Skillet Supper, 12

Salads
Sunflower Strawberry Salad, 57
Two-Bean Rice Salad, 63

Sauces
Basil Spaghetti Sauce, 129
Fresh Salsa, 131

Side Dishes
Roasted Root Veggies, 74
Root Vegetable Medley, 67
Spiced Baked Beets, 72

DUMPLINGS
Beef Stew with Potato Dumplings, 8
Chili with Tortilla Dumplings, 41
Shamrock Stew, 11

E

EGGS (also see Quiche)
Brunch Egg Bake, 154
Country-Style Scrambled Eggs, 18
Cranberry Eggnog Bread, 78
Creamed Spinach Omelet, 165
German Pizza, 19
Onion Potato Pie, 73
Turnip Souffle, 152
Zucchini Frittata, 179

F

FISH & SEAFOOD
Baked Walleye, 10

New England Fish Bake, 23
Pan-Fried Trout, 148
Pantry-Shelf Salmon Chowder, 137
Salmon Patties, 175
Seafood Rice Casserole, 15

**FRENCH TOAST,
PANCAKES & WAFFLES**
Country Crunch Pancakes, 92
Dutch Cream Waffles, 179
Overnight French Toast, 79

FRUIT (also see specific kinds)
A to Z Bread, 81
Chicken Avocado Melt, 16
Christmas Bread, 77
Festive Fruitcake, 100
Frozen Fruit Salad, 64
Fruit 'n' Nut Bread, 88
Fruit 'n' Salad, 154
Fruity Chili Sauce, 132
Fruity Coleslaw, 163
German Stollen, 83
Lamb Chops with Prunes, 158
Quick Ambrosia, 165
Raisin Mini-Scones, 87
Summer Dessert Pizza, 116

G

GAME
Wild West Chili, 55

GRILLED & BROILED
Barbecued Spareribs, 38
Grilled Steak Pinwheels, 36
Mushroom Bacon Burgers, 13
Zesty Grilled Corn, 67

GRITS
Chili Cheese Grits, 71

GROUND BEEF
Chili and Soup
All-American Chili, 50
Aloha Chili, 51
Chili for a Crowd, 49
Chili in No Time, 41
Chili with Tortilla Dumplings, 41
Chunky Beef Chili, 48
Corn and Bean Chili, 51
Country Carrot Soup, 42
Hearty Italian Chili, 48
Margie's Chili, 51
Meaty Three-Bean Chili, 42
Sausage Onion Chili, 51
Speedy Chili, 50
Tangy Oven Chili, 45
Wild West Chili, 55
Zesty Colorado Chili, 44

Main Dishes
Beef and Cheddar Quiche, 9
Beef and Potato Boats, 16
Beef 'n' Rice Hot Dish, 30
Hot Tamale Pie, 33
Italian Beef Roll-Ups, 22
French Bread Pizza, 141
Meat Loaf Potato Surprise, 7
Mexican Chili Pie, 31
Rutabaga Pie, 20
Shepherd's Pie, 31
Stuffed Peppers for Two, 163
Tomato-French Bread Lasagna, 25
Upper Peninsula Pasties, 16

Sandwiches
Coney Dogs, 14
Mushroom Bacon Burgers, 13

Stews
Quick Beef Stew, 18
Vegetable Meatball Stew, 22

H

HAM
Brunch Egg Bake, 154
Creamy Noodle Casserole, 143
German Pizza, 19
Ham Slice with Peaches, 9
Hearty Rice Salad, 58
Potato Delight, 36
Sunday Boiled Dinner, 26
Wild Rice and Ham Casserole, 29

HONEY
Honey Baked Chicken, 161
Milk-and-Honey White Bread, 93
Pear Honey, 131

I

ICE CREAM
Ice Cream Peaches, 103
Peach Melba Dessert, 137
Peanut Butter Parfaits, 171
Peppermint Ice Cream Cake, 123
Sauteed Apples a la Mode, 139
Watermelon Sherbet, 99

J

JAMS & MARMALADE
Green Tomato Jam, 133
Old-Fashioned Blueberry Jam, 130

The Best of Country Cooking 1998

JAMS & MARMALADE (continued)
Quick and Easy Strawberry Jam, 135
Raspberry Lemon Marmalade, 130

L

LAMB
Lamb Chops with Prunes, 158

LASAGNA
Potato Lasagna, 12
Tomato-French Bread Lasagna, 25

LEMON
Baked Lemon Chicken, 15
Citrus-Glazed Chicken, 10
Lemon Bars, 149
Lemon Butter Spread, 132
Lemon Meringue Cake, 108
Lemon Tea Cakes, 79
Poppy Seed Chiffon Cake, 127
Raspberry Lemon Marmalade, 130

M

MEALS IN MINUTES
• Creamy Noodle Casserole/Yankee Corn
  Muffins/Pretty Pear Salad, 143
• French Bread Pizza/Crunchy Lettuce
  Salad/Chocolate Peanut Butter
  Treats, 141
• Hot Turkey Salad/Buttered Breadsticks/
  Heavenly Fudge Sauce, 147
• Pantry-Shelf Salmon Chowder/Dilled
  Cucumbers/Peach Melba Dessert, 137
• Philly Steak Sandwiches/Sweet-and-
  Sour Salad/Peanut Butter Tarts, 145
• Spaghetti Squash Supper/Cheesy Corn
  Muffins/Sauteed Apples a la Mode, 139

MEAT LOAVES & MEATBALLS
Individual Meat Loaves, 171
Meat Loaf Potato Surprise, 7
Vegetable Meatball Stew, 22

MEAT PIES & POTPIES (also see Pizza)
Herbed Cornish Pasties, 7
Mexican Chili Pie, 31
Rutabaga Pie, 20
Shepherd's Pie, 31
Steak Potpie, 35
Upper Peninsula Pasties, 16

MELON
Summertime Melon Soup, 54
Watermelon Sherbet, 99

MEMORABLE MEALS
• Barbecued Pot Roast/Poppy Seed Cheese
  Bread/Tomato Crouton Casserole/Sour
  Cream Drops, 156-157
• Brunch Egg Bake/Fruit 'n' Nut Salad/
  Parsley Potatoes/Old-Fashioned Carrot
  Cake, 154-155
• Lamb Chops with Prunes/Blue-Ribbon
  Herb Rolls/Spinach Cheese Bake/
  Chocolate Yum-Yum Cake, 158-159
• Oven-Barbecued Spareribs/Old-Fashioned
  Baked Beans/Salad with Creamy
  Dressing/Zucchini Cobbler, 150-151
• Pan-Fried Trout/Creamed Sweet Peas/
  Caraway Rye Bread/Lemon Bars, 148-149
• Spiced Pot Roast/Turnip Souffle/
  Grandma's Apples and Rice/Baking
  Powder Biscuits, 152-153

MICROWAVE RECIPE
Speedy Chili, 50

MUFFINS
Blackberry Muffins, 96
Cheesy Corn Muffins, 139
Lemon Tea Cakes, 79
Raspberry Streusel Muffins, 90
Yankee Corn Muffins, 143

MUSHROOMS
Asparagus Mushroom Salad, 60
Blue Cheese Spinach Salad, 171
Creamy Mushroom-Potato Bake, 69
Mushroom Bacon Burgers, 13
Turkey in Mushroom Sauce, 32

N

NUTS (also see Peanut Butter)
Broccoli-Hazelnut Bake, 68
Caramel Pecan Rolls, 78
Cherry Almond Braid, 89
Country Crunch Pancakes, 92
Double Peanut Pie, 123
Fruit 'n' Nut Bread, 88
Fruit 'n' Salad, 154
Overnight French Toast, 79
Party Pecan Pies, 121
Pecan Sandies, 175
Pumpkin-Pecan Cake, 103

O

OATS
Country Crunch Pancakes, 92
Cranberry Bars, 118

Oat-Bran Bread, 96

ONIONS
Fried Onion Rings, 69
Marinated Onion Salad, 64
Onion Barley Casserole, 167
Onion Potato Pie, 73
Onion Rolls, 95
Sausage Onion Chili, 51

ORANGE
Citrus-Glazed Chicken, 10
Citrus Gingerbread, 120
Cranberry-Orange Pound Cake, 104
Mandarin Orange Cake, 115
Mandarin Pork Medallions, 39
Orange-Glazed Chicken with Rice, 26
Orange Pan Rolls, 173
Orange Rice Pilaf, 67
Rosemary Orange Bread, 86

P

PASTA & NOODLES (also see Lasagna)
Bayou Chicken Pasta, 35
Broccoli Cheese Soup, 55
Chicken Pasta Salad, 57
Creamy Noodle Casserole, 143
Grandma's Tomato Soup, 165
Macaroni and Cheese for Two, 171
Mandarin Pork Medallions, 39
Pasta with Sausage and Tomatoes, 39
Picnic Pasta Salad, 60
Roast Beef Pasta Salad, 59
Sausage 'n' Noodle Dinner, 17
Sweet-and-Sour Salad, 145
Three-Pepper Pasta Salad, 58
Turkey in Mushroom Sauce, 32
Zucchini-Garlic Pasta, 71

PEACHES
Barbecued Spareribs, 38
Ham Slice with Peaches, 9
Ice Cream Peaches, 103
Peach Melba Dessert, 137
Peachy Chicken Salad, 60
Peachy Dessert Sauce, 161
Spiced Peach Butter, 132

PEANUT BUTTER
Chocolate Peanut Butter Treats, 141
Double Peanut Pie, 123
Peanut Butter Chocolate Cake, 103
Peanut Butter Parfaits, 171
Peanut Butter Tarts, 145

PEARS
Autumn Pear Bread, 92
Pear Honey, 131
Pretty Pear Salad, 143

PEPPERS
Pepper Steak, 167
Pickled Peppers, 135
Stuffed Peppers for Two, 163
Three-Pepper Pasta Salad, 58

PIES
Banana Streusel Pie, 100
Caramel-Crunch Apple Pie, 105
Creamy Pineapple Pie, 99
Double Peanut Pie, 123
Party Pecan Pies, 121
Rhubarb Raspberry Pie, 106

PINEAPPLE
Aloha Chili, 51
Creamy Pineapple Pie, 99
Pineapple Bundt Cake, 114

PIZZA
French Bread Pizza, 141
German Pizza, 19
Homemade Pizza Sauce, 130

PORK (also see Bacon; Ham; Sausage)
Barbecued Spareribs, 38
Chili Chops, 21
Green Chili Pork Stew, 32
Herbed Pork Roast, 24
Individual Meat Loaves, 171
Mandarin Pork Medallions, 39
Oven-Barbecued Spareribs, 150
Pork and Cabbage Supper, 177
Pork and Sweet Potatoes, 29
Pork Roast, 10
Roasted Pork and Potato Roses, 36
Sunday Boiled Dinner, 26
Upper Peninsula Pasties, 16
Zesty Colorado Chili, 44
Zucchini Pork Chop Supper, 30

POTATOES (also see Sweet Potatoes)
Beef and Potato Boats, 16
Beef Stew with Potato Dumplings, 8
Broccoli-Potato Pancakes, 171
Chicken Potato Bake, 8
Chicken with Potato Stuffing, 14
Country-Style Scrambled Eggs, 18
Creamy Mushroom-Potato Bake, 69
Farm-Style Sausage Bake, 37
German Pizza, 19
Hearty Hash, 18
Hot German Potato Salad, 61
Italian Potato Salad, 61
Meat Loaf Potato Surprise, 7
New England Fish Bake, 23
Onion Potato Pie, 73
Oven-Crisped Potatoes, 179
Parmesan Potato Soup, 43
Parsley Potatoes, 154
Penny Casserole, 19
Potato Cheese Casserole, 75
Potato Delight, 36

Potato Lasagna, 12
Roasted Pork and Potato Roses, 36
Skillet Squash and Potatoes, 163
Twice-Baked Potatoes, 169

PUMPKIN
Ghostly Custards, 107
Pumpkin Bread, 79
Pumpkin Cake with Caramel Sauce, 112
Pumpkin-Pecan Cake, 103
Pumpkin Spice Bread, 81

Q

QUICHE
Asparagus Tomato Quiche, 28
Beef and Cheddar Quiche, 9

R

RASPBERRIES
Berry Cream Coffee Cake, 88
Easy Trifle for Two, 173
Raspberry Butter, 129
Raspberry Lemon Marmalade, 130
Raspberry Marshmallow Delight, 119
Raspberry Streusel Muffins, 90
Rhubarb Raspberry Pie, 106
Very Berry Spread, 129

RELISHES
Cranberry-Apple Relish, 135
Fresh Tomato Relish, 132
Pickled Peppers, 135
Zucchini Pickles, 135

RHUBARB
Rhubarb Raspberry Pie, 106
Springtime Coffee Cake, 91

RICE & WILD RICE
Beef 'n' Rice Hot Dish, 30
Grandma's Apples and Rice, 152
Hearty Rice Salad, 58
Orange-Glazed Chicken with Rice, 26
Orange Rice Pilaf, 67
Rice Pudding Cake, 127
Seafood Rice Casserole, 15
Sesame Rice, 161
Two-Bean Rice Salad, 63
Vegetable Rice Medley, 175
Wild Rice and Ham Casserole, 29

ROLLS & BUNS
Blue-Ribbon Herb Rolls, 158
Caramel Pecan Rolls, 78
French Crescent Rolls, 82
Golden Carrot Buns, 92

Low-Fat Cinnamon Rolls, 93
Onion Rolls, 95
Orange Pan Rolls, 173
Scandinavian Cinnamon Rolls, 96
Soft Herb Breadsticks, 95
Three-Day Yeast Rolls, 77

S

SALADS (also see Coleslaw)
Bean Salad
  Two-Bean Rice Salad, 63
Fruit Salads
  Frozen Fruit Salad, 64
  Fruit 'n' Salad, 154
  Pretty Pear Salad, 143
  Sunflower Strawberry Salad, 57
  Tart Cherry Salad, 65
Lettuce Salads
  Blue Cheese Spinach Salad, 171
  Blueberry Spinach Salad, 59
  Crunchy Lettuce Salad, 141
  Festive Tossed Salad, 173
  Salad with Creamy Dressing, 150
Main-Dish Salads
  Hearty Rice Salad, 58
  Hot Turkey Salad, 147
  Peachy Chicken Salad, 60
Pasta Salads
  Chicken Pasta Salad, 57
  Picnic Pasta Salad, 60
  Roast Beef Pasta Salad, 59
  Sweet-and-Sour Salad, 145
  Three-Pepper Pasta Salad, 58
Potato Salads
  Hot German Potato Salad, 61
  Italian Potato Salad, 61
Vegetable Salads
  Asparagus Mushroom Salad, 60
  Dilled Cucumbers, 137
  Herbed Cherry Tomatoes, 64
  Make-Ahead Vegetable Medley, 65
  Marinated Onion Salad, 64
  Tomato Cucumber Salad, 57
  Zippy Radish Salad, 58

SANDWICHES
Coney Dogs, 14
Grilled Turkey Sandwiches, 165
Mushroom Bacon Burgers, 13
Philly Steak Sandwiches, 145
Robust Beef Sandwiches, 32

SAUCES & GRAVY
Basil Spaghetti Sauce, 129
Chili Sauce, 135
Fresh Salsa, 131
Fruity Chili Sauce, 132
Heavenly Fudge Sauce, 147
Homemade Pizza Sauce, 130
Old-Fashioned Tomato Gravy, 27

SAUCES & GRAVY (continued)
Peachy Dessert Sauce, 161
Zesty Homemade Horseradish Sauce, 131
Zesty Tomatoes, 129

SAUSAGE
Black Bean Sausage Chili, 41
Chicken with Potato Stuffing, 14
Chili for a Crowd, 49
Coney Dogs, 14
Farm-Style Sausage Bake, 37
Hearty Italian Chili, 48
Hot German Potato Salad, 61
Italian Stuffed Tomatoes, 20
Meaty Three-Bean Chili, 42
Pasta with Sausage and Tomatoes, 39
Penny Casserole, 19
Potato Lasagna, 12
Sausage 'n' Noodle Dinner, 17
Sausage 'n' Sweet Potatoes, 19
Sausage Casserole for Two, 179
Sausage Onion Chili, 51
Spaghetti Squash Supper, 139
Zesty Colorado Chili, 44

SKILLETS & STIR-FRIES
Bayou Chicken Pasta, 35
Beef 'n' Rice Hot Dish, 30
Chicken Creole, 20
Citrus-Glazed Chicken, 10
Classic Swiss Steak, 27
Ham Slice with Peaches, 9
Hearty Hash, 18
Hot Tamale Pie, 33
Lamb Chops with Prunes, 158
Mandarin Pork Medallions, 39
Old-Fashioned Tomato Gravy, 27
Pan-Fried Trout, 148
Pasta with Sausage and Tomatoes, 39
Pepper Steak, 167
Potato Delight, 36
Sausage 'n' Noodle Dinner, 17
Skillet Squash and Potatoes, 163
Sunday Boiled Dinner, 26
Taco Skillet Supper, 12
Turkey in Mushroom Sauce, 32

SOUPS (also see Chili; Chowder)
Beef Barley Soup, 45
Broccoli Cheese Soup, 55
Country Carrot Soup, 42
Garden Tomato Soup, 53
Grandma's Tomato Soup, 165
Hungarian Goulash Soup, 54
Parmesan Potato Soup, 43
Summertime Melon Soup, 54
Tomato Dill Soup, 49
Winter Vegetable Soup, 177

SPINACH
Blue Cheese Spinach Salad, 171
Blueberry Spinach Salad, 59
Creamed Spinach Omelet, 165

Potato Lasagna, 12
Spinach Cheese Bake, 158

SPREADS
Pear Honey, 131
Very Berry Spread, 129

SQUASH & ZUCCHINI
Skillet Squash and Potatoes, 163
Spaghetti Squash Supper, 139
Zucchini Cobbler, 151
Zucchini Dessert Squares, 117
Zucchini Frittata, 179
Zucchini-Garlic Pasta, 71
Zucchini Pickles, 135
Zucchini Pork Chop Supper, 30

STEWS
Beef Stew with Potato Dumplings, 8
Chicken Stew, 24
Green Chili Pork Stew, 32
Low-Fat Beef Stew, 13
Quick Beef Stew, 18
Savory Beef Stew, 38
Shamrock Stew, 11
Vegetable Meatball Stew, 22

STRAWBERRIES
Quick and Easy Strawberry Jam, 135
Springtime Coffee Cake, 91
Sunflower Strawberry Salad, 57

SWEET POTATOES
Pork and Sweet Potatoes, 29
Sausage 'n' Sweet Potatoes, 19
Sweet Potato Biscuits, 91
Sweet Potato Cake, 122
Twice-Baked Sweet Potatoes, 72

T

TIPS
Baking best bread, 80
Getting the most from tomatoes, 62
Meat 'n' potato success, 34
Red-hot chili hints, 52
Root vegetable secrets, 70
Tried-and-true cakes, 113

TOMATOES
Asparagus Tomato Quiche, 28
Basil Spaghetti Sauce, 129
Chicken Creole, 20
Chili Sauce, 135
Creamed Asparagus and Tomato, 75
Fresh Salsa, 131
Fresh Tomato Relish, 132
Fruity Chili Sauce, 132
Garden Tomato Soup, 53
Grandma's Tomato Soup, 165
Green Tomato Jam, 133
Green Tomatoes Parmesan, 69

Herbed Cherry Tomatoes, 64
Homemade Pizza Sauce, 130
Italian Stuffed Tomatoes, 20
Old-Fashioned Tomato Gravy, 27
Pasta with Sausage and Tomatoes, 39
Spicy Tomato Juice, 133
Tomato-Artichoke Side Dish, 175
Tomato Crouton Casserole, 156
Tomato Cucumber Salad, 57
Tomato Dill Soup, 49
Tomato-French Bread Lasagna, 25
Zesty Tomatoes, 129

TURKEY
Grilled Turkey Sandwiches, 165
Hot Turkey Salad, 147
Marinated Turkey for Two, 169
Taco Skillet Supper, 12
Turkey in Mushroom Sauce, 32

V

VEGETABLES (also see specific kinds)
A to Z Bread, 81
Creamed Sweet Peas, 148
Garden Harvest Chili, 44
Hungarian Goulash Soup, 54
Make-Ahead Vegetable Medley, 65
Parsnip Saute, 69
Picnic Pasta Salad, 60
Roasted Root Veggies, 74
Root Vegetable Medley, 67
Rutabaga Pie, 20
Sweet-and-Sour Salad, 145
Tomato-Artichoke Side Dish, 175
Turnip Souffle, 152
Vegetable Bean Chili, 44
Vegetable Meatball Stew, 22
Vegetable Rice Medley, 175
Winter Vegetable Soup, 177
Zippy Radish Salad, 58

Y

YEAST BREADS (also see Rolls & Buns)
Apricot Cheese Danish, 87
Caraway Rye Bread, 148
Cherry Apricot Tea Bread, 82
Christmas Bread, 77
English Muffin Bread, 90
Finnish Bread, 97
Fruit 'n' Nut Bread, 88
German Stollen, 83
Italian Snack Bread, 86
Master Bread Dough and Loaf, 95
Milk-and-Honey White Bread, 93
Oat-Bran Bread, 96
Poppy Seed Cheese Bread, 156
Rosemary Orange Bread, 86